5th Workshop on NLP and XML 2006

(NLPXML 2006)

Multi-Dimensional Markup in Natural Language Processing

Trento, Italy
4 April 2006

ISBN: 978-1-61738-487-5

Printed from e-media with permission by:

Curran Associates, Inc.
57 Morehouse Lane
Red Hook, NY 12571

CURRAN ASSOCIATES INC. proceedings.com

Some format issues inherent in the e-media version may also appear in this print version.

Printed by Curran Associates, Inc. (2010)

Association for Computational Linguistics
209 N. Eighth Street
Stroudsburg, Pennsylvania 18360

Phone: 1-570-476-8006
Fax: 1-570-476-0860

acl@aclweb.org

Additional copies of this publication are available from:

Curran Associates, Inc.
57 Morehouse Lane
Red Hook, NY 12571 USA
Phone: 845-758-0400
Fax: 845-758-2634
Email: curran@proceedings.com
Web: www.proceedings.com

INTRODUCTION

We are delighted to introduce the EACL-2006 workshop on Multi-Dimensional Markup in Natural Language Processing. This is the fifth in the NLPXML series of workshops on natural language processing and XML.

The first two NLPXML workshops (at NLPRS-2001 in Tokyo and at COLING-2002 in Taipei) were concerned with XML-based NLP tools and the use of XML in a wide range of NLP tasks. As XML rapidly became fully accepted within the NLP community, the theme of the third and fourth workshops (at EACL-2003 in Budapest and at ACL-2004 in Barcelona) shifted to the new challenges and opportunities of the Semantic Web, with the focus on RDF and OWL rather than XML. The present workshop moves the focus firmly back to XML.

The special theme of this workshop is multi-dimensional markup. Our goal is to bring together researchers from several different fields—natural language processing, corpus linguistics, markup languages, and information retrieval—to discuss theoretical and practical issues related to the integration of different layers of text annotation. One particularly interesting challenge arises from the difficulty of combining annotations resulting from disparate NLP systems in a single hierarchical structure. For downstream applications that rely on a range of linguistic annotations, problems such as crossing boundaries and overlapping elements from different sources make it difficult to query data with multiple layers of annotation. We are particularly pleased to present papers that discuss the problems associated with such integration as well as those that provide solutions within the four fields mentioned.

An unusual and, we believe, a particularly attractive feature of the workshop program is the emphasis on live demonstrations of practical working systems. We have included two separate demo sessions in the program, with a total of 12 system demos. Short descriptions of the demos are included in these proceedings, in addition to the six full workshop papers.

We would like to thank the members of the NLPXML-2006 program committee for their prompt and expert reviews. In more than one case the reviewers' detailed and well-informed comments enabled significant improvements to the papers included in this volume. We also thank the organizers of EACL-2006 for their support.

David Ahn
Erik Tjong Kim Sang
Graham Wilcock
February 2006

WORKSHOP ORGANIZERS:

David Ahn, University of Amsterdam
Erik Tjong Kim Sang, University of Amsterdam
Graham Wilcock, University of Helsinki

PROGRAM COMMITTEE:

David Ahn, University of Amsterdam (co-chair)
Wouter Alink, NFI, The Hague
Paul Buitelaar, DFKI, Saarbruecken
Jean Carletta, University of Edinburgh
Hamish Cunningham, University of Sheffield
Tomaz Erjavec, Jozef Stefan Institute, Ljubljana
Claire Grover, University of Edinburgh
Nancy Ide, Vassar, New York
Amy Isard, University of Edinburgh
Mounia Lalmas, University of London
Maarten Marx, University of Amsterdam
Guenter Neumann, DFKI, Saarbruecken
Laurent Romary, Loria, Nancy
Valentin Tablan, University of Sheffield
Henry Thompson, University of Edinburgh
Erik Tjong Kim Sang, University of Amsterdam
Arjen de Vries, CWI, Amsterdam
Graham Wilcock, University of Helsinki (co-chair)

WORKSHOP WEBSITE:

`http://ilps.science.uva.nl/nlpxml2006/`

WORKSHOP PROGRAM

Tuesday, April 4

09:00-09:05	Welcome
09:05-09:30	*Representing and Querying Multi-dimensional Markup for Question Answering* Wouter Alink, Valentin Jijkoun, David Ahn, Maarten de Rijke, Peter Boncz, and Arjen de Vries
09:30-10:00	*Annotation and Disambiguation of Semantic Types in Biomedical Text: A Cascaded Approach to Named Entity Recognition* Dietrich Rebholz-Schuhmann, Harald Kirsch, Sylvain Gaudan, Miguel Arregui, and Goran Nenadic
10:00-10:30	*Tools to Address the Interdependence between Tokenisation and Standoff Annotation* Claire Grover, Michael Matthews, and Richard Tobin
10:30-11:00	BREAK
11:00-11:30	*Towards an Alternative Implementation of NXT's Query Language via XQuery* Neil Mayo, Jonathan Kilgour, and Jean Carletta
11:30-11:45	DEMO BOOSTERS, 1
11:45-12:30	DEMO SESSION, 1
12:30-14:30	LUNCH
14:30-15:00	*Multi-dimensional Annotation and Alignment in an English-German Translation Corpus* Silvia Hansen-Schirra, Stella Neumann, and Mihaela Vela
15:00-15:15	DEMO BOOSTERS, 2
15:15-16:00	DEMO SESSION, 2
16:00-16:30	BREAK
16:30-17:00	*Querying XML documents with multi-dimensional markup* Peter Siniakov
17:00-18:00	PANEL DISCUSSION AND CLOSING

Table of Contents

The conference, the workshop and the tutorials are sponsored by:

Center for the Evaluation of Language and Communication Technologies

Celct
c/o BIC, Via dei Solteri, 38
38100 Trento, Italy
http://www.celct.it

Xerox Research Centre Europe
6 Chemin de Maupertuis
38240 Meylan, France
http://www.xrce.xerox.com

CELI s.r.l.
Corso Moncalieri, 21
10131 Torino, Italy
http://www.celi.it

Thales
45 rue de Villiers
92526 Neuilly-sur-Seine Cedex, France
http://www.thalesgroup.com

EACL-2006 is supported by

Trentino S.p.a. and Metalsistem Group

FULL PAPERS

Representing and Querying Multi-dimensional Markup for Question Answering

Wouter Alink, Valentin Jijkoun, David Ahn, Maarten de Rijke
ISLA, University of Amsterdam
alink,jijkoun,ahn,mdr@science.uva.nl

Peter Boncz, Arjen de Vries
CWI, Amsterdam, The Netherlands
boncz,arjen@cwi.nl

Abstract

This paper describes our approach to representing and querying multi-dimensional, possibly overlapping text annotations, as used in our question answering (QA) system. We use a system extending XQuery, the W3C-standard XML query language, with new axes that allow one to jump easily between different annotations of the same data. The new axes are formulated in terms of (partial) overlap and containment. All annotations are made using stand-off XML in a single document, which can be efficiently queried using the XQuery extension. The system is scalable to gigabytes of XML annotations. We show examples of the system in QA scenarios.

1 Introduction

Corpus-based question answering is a complex task that draws from information retrieval, information extraction and computational linguistics to pinpoint information users are interested in. The flexibility of natural language means that potential answers to questions may be phrased in different ways—lexical and syntactic variation, ambiguity, polysemy, and anaphoricity all contribute to a gap between questions and answers. Typically, QA systems rely on a range of linguistic analyses, provided by a variety of different tools, to bridge this gap from questions to possible answers.

In our work, we focus on how we can integrate the analyses provided by completely independent linguistic processing components into a uniform QA framework. On the one hand, we would like to be able, as much as possible, to make use of off-the-shelf NLP tools from various sources without having to worry about whether the output of the tools are compatible, either in a strong sense of forming a single hierarchy or even in a weaker sense of simply sharing common tokenization. On the other hand, we would like to be able to issue simple and clear queries that jointly draw upon annotations provided by different tools.

To this end, we store annotated data as stand-off XML and query it using an extension of XQuery with our new StandOff axes, inspired by (Burkowski, 1992). Key to our approach is the use of stand-off annotation at every stage of the annotation process. The source text, or character data, is stored in a Binary Large OBject (BLOB), and all annotations, in a single XML document. To generate and manage the annotations we have adopted XIRAF (Alink, 2005), a framework for integrating annotation tools which has already been successfully used in digital forensic investigations.

Before performing any linguistic analysis, the source documents, which may contain XML metadata, are split into a BLOB and an XML document, and the XML document is used as the initial annotation. Various linguistic analysis tools are run over the data, such as a named-entity tagger, a temporal expression (timex) tagger, and syntactic phrase structure and dependency parsers. The XML document will grow during this analysis phase as new annotations are added by the NLP tools, while the BLOB remains intact. In the end, the result is a fully annotated stand-off document, and this annotated document is the basis for our QA system, which uses XQuery extended with the new axes to access the annotations.

The remainder of the paper is organized as follows. In Section 2 we briefly discuss related work. Section 3 is devoted to the issue of querying multi-dimensional markup. Then we describe how we coordinate the process of text annotation, in Section 4, before describing the application of our multi-dimensional approach to linguistic annotation to question answering in Section 5. We conclude in Section 6.

2 Related Work

XML is a tree structured language and provides very limited capabilities for representing several annotations of the same data simultaneously, even when each of the annotations is tree-like. In particular, in the case of inline markup, multiple annotation trees can be put together in a single XML document only if elements from different annotations do not cross each other's boundaries.

Several proposals have tried to circumvent this problem in various ways. Some approaches are based on splitting overlapping elements into fragments. Some use SGML with the CONCUR feature or even entirely different markup schemes (such as LMNL, the Layered Markup and Annotation Language (Piez, 2004), or GODDAGs, generalized ordered-descendant directed acyclic graphs (Sperberg-McQueen and Huitfeldt, 2000)) that allow arbitrary intersections of elements from different hierarchies. Some approaches use empty XML elements (*milestones*) to mark beginnings and ends of problematic elements. We refer to (DeRose, 2004) for an in-depth overview.

Although many approaches solve the problem of *representing* possibly overlapping annotations, they often do not address the issue of accessing or *querying* the resulting representations. This is a serious disadvantage, since standard query languages, such as XPath and XQuery, and standard query evaluation engines cannot be used with these representations directly.

The approach of (Sperberg-McQueen and Huitfeldt, 2000) uses GODDAGs as a conceptual model of multiple tree-like annotations of the same data. Operationalizing this approach, (Dekhtyar and Iacob, 2005) describes a system that uses multiple inline XML annotations of the same text to build a GODDAG structure, which can be queried using EXPath, an extension of XPath with new axis steps.

Our approach differs from that of Dekhtyar and Iacob in several ways. First of all, we do not use multiple separate documents; instead, all annotation layers are woven into a single XML document. Secondly, we use stand-off rather than inline annotation; each character in the original document is referred to by a unique offset, which means that specific regions in a document can be denoted unambiguously with only a start and an end offset. On the query side, our extended XPath axes are similar to the axes of Dekhtyar and Iacob, but less specific: e.g., we do not distinguish between left-overlapping and right-overlapping character regions.

In the setting of question answering there are a few examples of querying and retrieving semistructured data. Litowski (Litkowksi, 2003; Litkowksi, 2004) has been advocating the use of an XML-based infrastructure for question answering, with XPath-based querying at the back-end, for a number of years. Ogilvie (2004) outlines the possibility of using multi-dimensional markup for question answering, with no system or experimental results yet. Jijkoun et al. (2005) describe initial experiments with XQuesta, a question answering system based on multi-dimensional markup.

3 Querying Multi-dimensional Markup

Our approach to markup is based on stand-off XML. Stand-off XML is already widely used, although it is often not recognized as such. It can be found in many present-day applications, especially where annotations of audio or video are concerned. Furthermore, many existing multi-dimensional-markup languages, such as LMNL, can be translated into stand-off XML.

We split annotated data into two parts: the *BLOB* (Binary Large OBject) and the XML annotations that refer to specific regions of the BLOB. A BLOB may be an arbitrary byte string (e.g., the contents of a hard drive (Alink, 2005)), and the annotations may refer to regions using positions such as byte offsets, word offsets, points in time or frame numbers (e.g., for audio or video applications). In text-based applications, such as described in this paper, we use character offsets. The advantage of such character-based references over word- or token-based ones is that it allows us to reconcile possibly different tokenizations by different text analysis tools (cf. Section 4).

In short, a multi-dimensional document consists of a BLOB and a set of stand-off XML annotations of the BLOB. Our approach to querying such documents extends the common XML query languages XPath and XQuery by defining 4 new axes that allow one to move from one XML tree to another. Until recently, there have been very few

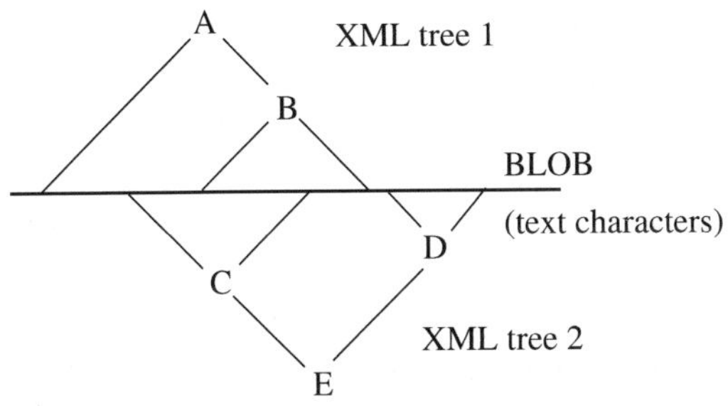

Figure 1: Two annotations of the same data.

approaches to querying stand-off documents. We take the approach of (Alink, 2005), which allows the user to relate different annotations using containment and overlap conditions. This is done using the new StandOff XPath axis steps that we add to the XQuery language. This approach seems to be quite general: in (Alink, 2005) it is shown that many of the query scenarios given in (Iacob et al., 2004) can be easily handled by using these StandOff axis steps.

Let us explain the axis steps by means of an example. Figure 1 shows two annotations of the same character string (BLOB), where the first XML annotation is

```
<A start="10" end="50">
  <B start="30" end="50"/>
</A>
```

and the second is

```
<E start="20" end="60">
  <C start="20" end="40"/>
  <D start="55" end="60">
</E>
```

While each annotation forms a valid XML tree and can be queried using standard XML query languages, together they make up a more complex structure.

StandOff axis steps, inspired by (Burkowski, 1992), allow for querying overlap and containment of regions, but otherwise behave like regular XPath steps, such as `child` (the step between `A` and `B` in Figure 1) or `sibling` (the step between `C` and `D`). The new StandOff axes, denoted with `select-narrow`, `select-wide`, `reject-narrow`, and `reject-wide` select contained, overlapping, non-contained and non-overlapping region elements, respectively, from possibly distinct layers of XML annotation of the data. Table 1 lists some examples for the annotations of our example document.

In XPath, the new axis steps are used in exactly the same way as the standard ones. For example,

Context	Axis	Result nodes
A	select-narrow	B C
A	select-wide	B C E
A	reject-narrow	E D
A	reject-wide	D

Table 1: Example annotations.

the XPath query:

```
//B/select-wide::*
```

returns all nodes that overlap with the span of a `B` node: in our case the nodes `A`, `B`, `C` and `E`. The query:

```
//*[./select-narrow::B]
```

returns nodes that contain the span of `B`: in our case, the nodes `A` and `E`.

In implementing the new steps, one of our design decisions was to put all stand-off annotations in a single document. For this, an XML processor is needed that is capable of handling large amounts of XML. We have decided to use MonetDB/XQuery, an XQuery implementation that consists of the Pathfinder compiler, which translates XQuery statements into a relational algebra, and the relational database MonetDB (Grust, 2002; Boncz, 2002).

The implementation of the new axis steps in MonetDB/XQuery is quite efficient. When the XMark benchmark documents (XMark, 2006) are represented using stand-off notation, querying with the StandOff axis steps is interactive for document size up to 1GB. Even millions of regions are handled efficiently. The reason for the speed of the StandOff axis steps is twofold. First, they are accelerated by keeping a database index on the region attributes, which allows fast merge-algorithms to be used in their evaluation. Such merge-algorithms make a single linear scan through the index to compute each StandOff step. The second technical innovation is "loop-lifting." This is a general principle in MonetDB/XQuery(Boncz et al., 2005) for the efficient execution of XPath steps that occur *nested* in XQuery iterations (i.e., inside `for`-loops). A naive strategy would invoke the StandOff algorithm for each iteration, leading to repeated (potentially many) sequential scans. Loop-lifted versions of the StandOff algorithms, in contrast, handle all iterations together in one sequential scan, keeping the average complexity of the StandOff steps linear.

The StandOff axis steps are part of release 0.10 of the open-source MonetDB/XQuery product, which can be downloaded from `http://www.monetdb.nl/XQuery`.

In addition to the StandOff axis steps, a keyword search function has been added to the XQuery system to allow queries asking for regions containing specific words. This function is called `so-contains($node, $needle)` which will return a boolean specifying whether `$needle` occurs in the given region represented by the element `$node`.

4 Combining Annotations

In our QA application of multi-dimensional markup, we work with corpora of newspaper articles, each of which comes with some basic annotation, such as title, body, keywords, timestamp, topic, etc. We take this initial annotation structure and split it into raw data, which comprises all textual content, and the XML markup. The raw data is the BLOB, and the XML annotations are converted to stand-off format. To each XML element originally containing textual data (now stored in the BLOB), we add a `start` and `end` attribute denoting its position in the BLOB.

We use a separate system, XIRAF, to coordinate the process of automatically annotating the text. XIRAF (Figure 2) combines multiple text processing tools, each having an input descriptor and a tool-specific wrapper that converts the tool output into stand-off XML annotation. Figure 3 shows the interaction of XIRAF with an automatic annotation tool using a wrapper.

The input descriptor associated with a tool is used to select regions in the data that are candidates for processing by that tool. The descriptor may select regions on the basis of the original metadata or annotations added by other tools. For example, both our sentence splitter and our temporal expression tagger use original document metadata to select their input: both select document text, with `//TEXT`. Other tools, such as syntactic parsers and named-entity taggers, require separated sentences as input and thus use the output annotations of the sentence splitter, with the input descriptor `//sentence`. In general, there may be arbitrary dependencies between text-processing tools, which XIRAF takes into account.

In order to add the new annotations generated by a tool to the original document, the output of the tool must be represented using stand-off XML annotation of the input data. Many text processing tools (e.g., parsers or part-of-speech taggers) do not produce XML annotation per se, but their output can be easily converted to stand-off XML annotation. More problematically, text processing tools may actually modify the input text in the course of adding annotations, so that the offsets referenced in the new annotations do not correspond to the original BLOB. Tools make a variety of modifications to their input text: some perform their own tokenization (i.e., inserting whitespaces or other word separators), silently skip parts of the input (e.g., syntactic parsers, when the parsing fails), or replace special symbols (e.g., parentheses with `-LRB-` and `-RRB-`). For many of the available text processing tools, such possible modifications are not fully documented.

XIRAF, then, must map the output of a processing tool back to the original BLOB before adding the new annotations to the original document. This re-alignment of the output of the processing tools with the original BLOB is one of the major hurdles in the development of our system. We approach the problems systematically. We compare the text data in the output of a given tool with the data that was given to it as input and re-align input and output offsets of markup elements using an edit-distance algorithm with heuristically chosen weights of character edits. After re-aligning the output with the original BLOB and adjusting the offsets accordingly, the actual data returned by the tool is discarded and only the stand-off markup is added to the existing document annotations.

5 Question Answering

XQuesta, our corpus-based question-answering system for English and Dutch, makes use of the multi-dimensional approach to linguistic annotation embodied in XIRAF. The system analyzes an incoming question to determine the required answer type and keyword queries for retrieving relevant snippets from the corpus. From these snippets, candidate answers are extracted, ranked, and returned.

The system consults Dutch and English newspaper corpora. Using XIRAF, we annotate the corpora with named entities (including type information), temporal expressions (normalized to ISO values), syntactic chunks, and syntactic parses (dependency parses for Dutch and phrase structure

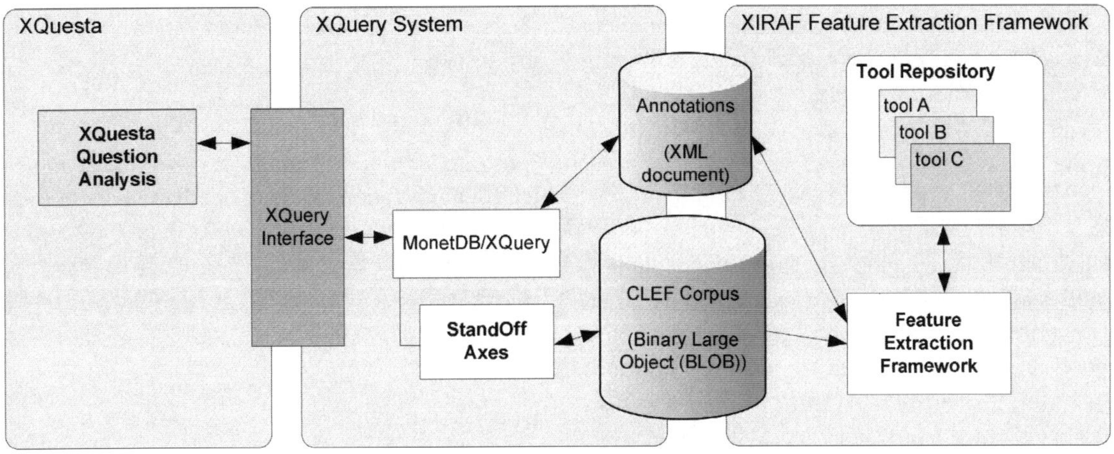

Figure 2: XIRAF Architecture

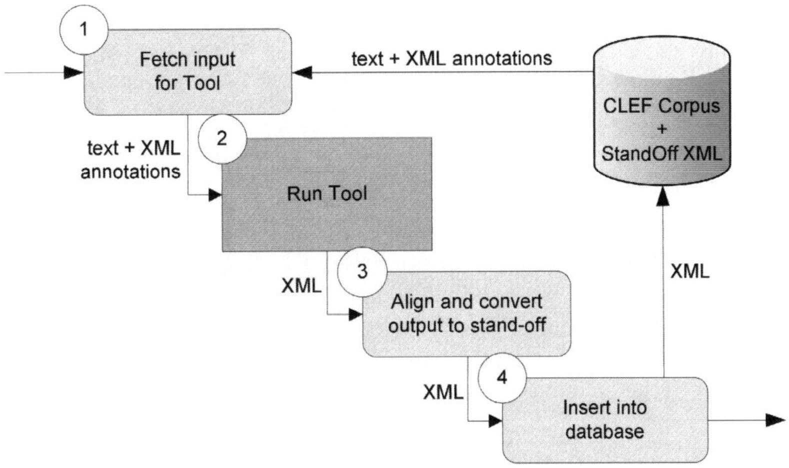

Figure 3: Tool Wrapping Example

parses for English).

XQuesta's question analysis module maps questions to both a keyword query for retrieval of relevant passages and a query for extracting candidate answers. For example, for the question *How many seats does a Boeing 747 have?*, the keyword query is *Boeing 747 seats*, while the extraction query is the pure XPath expression:

```
//phrase[@type="NP"][.//WORD
[@pos="CD"]][so-contains(.,
"seat")]
```

This query can be glossed: find `phrase` elements of type NP that dominate a `word` element tagged as a cardinal determiner and that also contain the string "seat". Note that `phrase` and `word` elements are annotations generated by a single tool (the phrase-structure parser) and thus in the same annotation layer, which is why standard XPath can be used to express this query.

For the question *When was Kennedy assassinated?*, on the other hand, the extraction query is an XPath expression that uses a StandOff axis:

```
//phrase[@type="S" and headword=
"assassinated" and so-contains(.,
"Kennedy")]/select-narrow::timex
```

This query can be glossed: find temporal expressions whose textual extent is contained inside a sentence (or clause) that is headed by *assassinated* and contains the string "Kennedy". Note that `phrase` and `timex` elements are generated by different tools (the phrase-structure parser and the temporal expression tagger, respectively), and therefore belong to different annotation layers. Thus, the `select-narrow::` axis step must be used in place of the standard `child::` or `descendant::` steps.

As another example of the use of the StandOff axes, consider the question *Who killed John*

F. Kennedy?. Here, the keyword query is *kill John Kennedy*, and the extraction query is the following (extended) XPath expression:

```
//phrase[@type="S" and headword=
"killed" and so-contains(.,
 "Kennedy")]/phrase[@type="NP"]/
select-wide::ne[@type="per"]
```

This query can be glossed: find person named-entities whose textual extent overlaps the textual extent of an NP phrase that is the subject of a sentence phrase that is headed by *killed* and contains the string "Kennedy". Again, `phrase` elements and `ne` elements are generated by different tools (the phrase-structure parser and named-entity tagger, respectively), and therefore belong to different annotation layers. In this case, we further do not want to make the unwarranted assumption that the subject NP found by the parser properly contains the named-entity found by the named-entity tagger. Therefore, we use the `select-wide::` axis to indicate that the named-entity which will serve as our candidate answer need only overlap with the sentential subject.

How do we map from questions to queries like this? For now, we use hand-crafted patterns, but we are currently working on using machine learning methods to automatically acquire question-query mappings. For the purposes of demonstrating the utility of XIRAF to QA, however, it is immaterial how the mapping happens. What is important to note is that queries utilizing the Stand-Off axes arise naturally in the mapping of questions to queries against corpus data that has several layers of linguistic annotation.

6 Conclusion

We have described a scalable and flexible system for processing documents with multi-dimensional markup. We use stand-off XML annotation to represent markup, which allows us to combine multiple, possibly overlapping annotations in one XML file. XIRAF, our framework for managing the annotations, invokes text processing tools, each accompanied with an input descriptor specifying what data the tool needs as input, and a wrapper that converts the tool's output to stand-off XML. To access the annotations, we use an efficient XPath/XQuery engine extended with new Stand-Off axes that allow references to different annotation layers in one query. We have presented examples of such concurrent extended XPath queries in the context of our corpus-based Question Answering system.

Acknowledgments

This research was supported by the Netherlands Organization for Scientific Research (NWO) under project numbers 017.001.190, 220-80-001, 264-70-050, 612-13-001, 612.000.106, 612.000.207, 612.066.302, 612.069.006, 640.-001.501, and 640.002.501.

References

W. Alink. 2005. XIRAF – an XML information retrieval approach to digital forensics. Master's thesis, University of Twente, Enschede, The Netherlands, October.

P.A. Boncz, T. Grust, S. Manegold, J. Rittinger, and J. Teubner. 2005. Pathfinder: Relational XQuery Over Multi-Gigabyte XML Inputs In Interactive Time. In *Proceedings of the 31st VLDB Conference*, Trondheim, Norway.

P.A. Boncz. 2002. *Monet: A Next-Generation DBMS Kernel For Query-Intensive Applications*. Ph.d. thesis, Universiteit van Amsterdam, Amsterdam, The Netherlands, May.

F.J. Burkowski. 1992. Retrieval Activities in a Database Consisting of Heterogeneous Collections of Structured Text. In *Proceedings of the 1992 SIGIR Conference*, pages 112–125.

A. Dekhtyar and I.E. Iacob. 2005. A framework for management of concurrent xml markup. *Data Knowl. Eng.*, 52(2):185–208.

S. DeRose. 2004. Markup Overlap: A Review and a Horse. In *Extreme Markup Languages 2004*.

T. Grust. 2002. Accelerating XPath Location Steps. In *Proceedings of the 21st ACM SIGMOD International Conference on Management of Data*, pages 109–120.

I.E. Iacob, A. Dekhtyar, and W. Zhao. 2004. XPath Extension for Querying Concurrent XML Markup. Technical report, University of Kentucky, February.

V. Jijkoun, E. Tjong Kim Sang, D. Ahn, K. Müller, and M. de Rijke. 2005. The University of Amsterdam at QA@CLEF 2005. In *Working Notes for the CLEF 2005 Workshop*.

K.C. Litkowksi. 2003. Question answering using XML-tagged documents. In *Proceedings of the Eleventh Text REtrieval Conference (TREC-11)*.

K.C. Litkowksi. 2004. Use of metadata for question answering and novelty tasks. In *Proceedings of the Twelfth Text REtrieval Conference (TREC 2003)*.

P. Ogilvie. 2004. Retrieval Using Structure for Question Answering. In *The First Twente Data Management Workshop (TDM'04)*, pages 15–23.

W. Piez. 2004. Half-steps toward LMNL. In *Proceedings of the fifth Conference on Extreme Markup Languages*.

C.M. Sperberg-McQueen and C. Huitfeldt. 2000. GODDAG: A Data Structure for Overlapping Hierarchies. In *Proc. of DDEP/PODDP 2000*, volume 2023 of *Lecture Notes in Computer Science*, pages 139–160, January.

XMark. 2006. XMark – An XML Benchmark Project. `http://monetdb.cwi.nl/xml/`.

Annotation and Disambiguation of Semantic Types in Biomedical Text: a Cascaded Approach to Named Entity Recognition

Dietrich Rebholz-Schuhmann, Harald Kirsch, Sylvain Gaudan, Miguel Arregui
European Bioinformatics Institute (EBI),
Wellcome Trust Genome Campus, Hinxton, Cambridge, UK
{rebholz,kirsch,gaudan,arregui}@ebi.ac.uk

Goran Nenadic
School of Informatics
University of Manchester
Manchester, UK
g.nenadic@manchester.ac.uk

Abstract

Publishers of biomedical journals increasingly use XML as the underlying document format. We present a modular text-processing pipeline that inserts XML markup into such documents in every processing step, leading to multi-dimensional markup. The markup introduced is used to identify and disambiguate named entities of several semantic types (protein/gene, Gene Ontology terms, drugs and species) and to communicate data from one module to the next. Each module independently adds, changes or removes markup, which allows for modularization and a flexible setup of the processing pipeline. We also describe how the cascaded approach is embedded in a large-scale XML-based application (EBIMed) used for on-line access to biomedical literature. We discuss the lessons learnt so far, as well as the open problems that need to be resolved. In particular, we argue that the pragmatic and tailored solutions allow for reduction in the need for overlapping annotations — although not completely without cost.

1 Introduction

Publishers of biomedical journals have widely adopted XML as the underlying format from which other formats, such as PDF and HTML, are generated. For example, documents in XML format are available from the National Library of Medicine[1] (Medline abstracts and Pubmed[2] Central documents), and from BioMed Central[3] (full text journal articles). Other publishers are heading into the same direction. Such documents contain logical markup to organize meta-information such as title, author(s), sections, headings, citations, references, etc. Inside the text of a document, XML is used for physical markup, e.g. text in italic or boldface, subscript and superscript insertions, etc. Manually generated semantic markup is available only on the document level (e.g. MeSH terms).

One of the most distinguished feature of scientific biomedical literature is that it contains a large amount of terms and entities, the majority of which are explained in public electronic databases. Terms (such as names of genes, proteins, gene products, organisms, drugs, chemical compounds, etc.) are a key factor for accessing and integrating the information stored in literature (Krauthammer and Nenadic, 2004). Identification and markup of names and terms in text serves several purposes:

(1) The users profit from highlighted semantic types, e.g. protein/gene, drug, species, and from links to the defining database for immediate access and exploration.

(2) Identified terms facilitate and improve statistical and NLP based text analysis (Hirschman et al., 2005; Kirsch et al., 2005).

In this paper we describe a cascaded approach to named-entity recognition (NER) and markup in biomedicine that is embedded into EBIMed[4], an on-line service to access the literature (Rebholz-Schuhmann et al., forthcoming). EBIMed facilitates both purposes mentioned above. It keeps the annotations provided by publishers and inserts XML annotations while processing the text. Named entities from different resources are identified in the text. The individual modules provide annotation of protein names with unique identifiers, disambiguation of protein names that are ambiguous acronyms, annotation of drugs, Gene Ontology[5] terms and species. The identification of protein named entities can be further used in an alternative pipeline to identify events

[1] National Library of Medicine, http://www.nlm.nih.gov/
[2] PubMed, http://www.pubmed.org
[3] BioMed Central Ltd, http://www.biomedcentral.com/

[4] EBIMed, www.ebi.ac.uk/Rebholz-srv/ebimed
[5] GO, Gene Ontology, http://geneontology.org, (GO consortium, 2005).

such as protein-protein interactions and associations between terms and mutations (Blaschke et al., 1999; Rzhetsky et al., 2004; Rebholz-Schuhmann et al., 2004; Nenadic and Ananiadou, 2006).

The rest of the paper is organised as follows. In Section 2 we briefly discuss problems with biomedical NER. The cascaded approach and an online text mining system are described in sections 3 and 4 respectively. We discuss the lessons learnt from the on-line application and remainig open problems in Section 5, while conclusions are presented in Section 6.

2 Biomedical Named Entity Recognition

Terms and named-entities (NEs) are the means of scientific communication as they are used to identify the main concepts in a domain. The identification of terminology in the biomedical literature is one of the most challenging research topics both in the NLP and biomedical communities (Hirschman et al., 2005; Kirsch et al., 2005).

Identification of named entities (NEs) in a document can be viewed as a three-step procedure (Krauthammer and Nenadic, 2004). In the first step, single or multiple adjacent words that indicate the presence of domain concepts are recognised (*term recognition*). In the second step, called *term categorisation*, the recognised terms are classified into broader domain classes (e.g. as genes, proteins, species). The final step is *mapping* of terms into referential databases. The first two steps are commonly referred to as *named entity recognition (NER)*.

One of the main challenges in NER is a huge number of new terms and entities that appear in the biomedical domain. Further, terminological variation, recognition of boundaries of multiword terms, identification of nested terms and ambiguity of terms are the difficult issues when mapping terms from the literature to biomedical database entries (Hirschman et al., 2005; Krauthammer and Nenadic, 2004).

On one hand, NER in the biomedical domain (in particular the recognition part) profits from large, freely available terminological resources, which are either provided as ontologies (e.g. Gene Ontology, ChEBI[6], UMLS[7]) or result from biomedical databases containing named entities (e.g. UniProt/Swiss-Prot[8]). On the other hand, combining sets of terms from different terminological resources leads to naming conflicts such as homonymous use of names and terminological ambiguities. The most obvious problem is when the same span of text is assigned to different semantic types (e.g. *'rat'* denotes a species and a protein). In this case, there are three types of ambiguities:

(**Amb1**) A name is used for different entries in the same database, e.g. the same protein name serves for a given protein in different species (Chen et al., 2005).

(**Amb2**) A name is used for entries in multiple databases and thus represents different types, e.g. *'rat'* is a protein and a species.

(**Amb3**) A name is not only used as a biomedical term but also as part of common English (in contrast to the biomedical terminology), e.g. *'who'* and *'how'*, which are used as protein names.

In some cases (i.e. Amb2), broader classification can help to disambiguate between different entries (e.g. differentiate between *'CAT'* as a protein, animal or medical device). However, it is ineffective in situations where names can be mapped to several different entries in the same data source. In such situations, disambiguation on the resource level is needed (see, for example, (Liu et al., 2002) for disambiguation of terms associated with several entries in the UMLS Metathesaurus).

In many solutions, the three steps in biomedical NER (namely, recognition, categorisation and mapping to databases) are merged within one module. For example, using an existing terminological database for recognition of NEs, effectively leads to complete term identification (in cases where there are no ambiguities). Some researchers, however, have stressed the advantages of tackling each step as a separate task, pointing at different sources and methods needed to accomplish each of the subtasks (Torii et al., 2003; Lee et al., 2003). Also, in the case of modularisation, it is easier to integrate different solutions for each specific problem. However, it has been suggested that whether a clear separation into single steps would improve term identification is an open issue (Krauthammer and Nenadic, 2004). In this paper we discuss a cascaded, modular approach to biomedical NER.

3 Biomedical NER based on XML annotation: Modules in a pipeline

In this Section we present a modular approach to identification, disambiguation and annotation of

[6] ChEBI, Chemical Entities of Biological Interest, http://www.ebi.ac.uk/chebi/m

[7] UMLS, Unified Medical Language System http://www.nlm.nih.gov/research/umls/, (Browne et al., 2003).

[8] UniProt, http://www.ebi.uniprot.org/, (Bairoch et al., 2005); Swiss-Prot, http://ca.expasy.org/sprot/

several biomedical semantic types in the text. Full identification of NEs and resolving ambiguities in particular, may require a full parse tree of a sentence in addition to the analysis of local context information. On the other hand, full parse trees may be only derivable after NEs are resolved. Methods to efficiently overcome these problems are not yet available today and in order to come up with an applicable solution, it was necessary to choose a more pragmatic approach.

We first discuss the basic principles and design of the processing pipeline, which is based on a pragmatic cascade of modules, and then present each of the modules separately.

3.1 Modular design of a text processing pipeline

Our methodology is based on the idea of separating the process into clearly defined functions applied one after another to text, in a processing *pipeline* characterized by the following statements:

(P1) The complete text processing task consists of separate and independent modules.

(P2) The task is performed by running all modules exactly once in a fixed sequence.

(P3) Each module operates continuously on an input *stream* and performs its function on stretches or "windows" of text that are usually much smaller than the whole input. As soon as a window is processed, the module produces the resulting output.

(P4) After the startup phase, all modules run in parallel. Incoming requests for annotation are accepted by a master process that ensures that all required modules are approached in the right order.

(P5) Communication of information between the modules is strictly downstream and all meta-information is contained in the data stream itself in the form of XML markup.

An instance of a processing pipeline (which is actually embedded in EBIMed) is presented in Figure 1. The modules M-1 to M-8 are run in this order, and no communication between them is needed apart from streaming the text from the output of one module to the input of another. The text contains the meta-data as XML markup. The modules are described below.

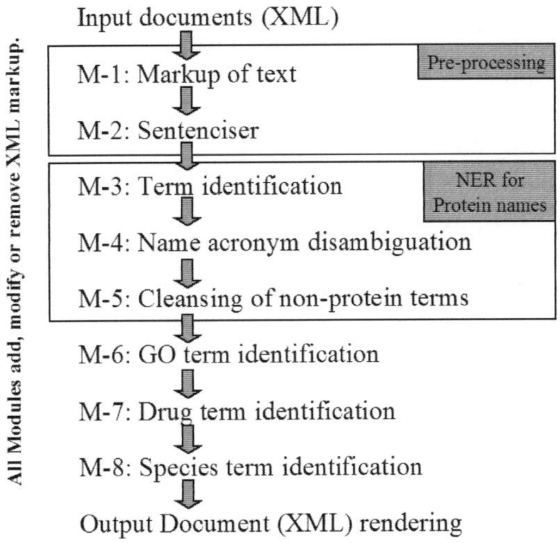

Figure 1. A processing pipeline embedded in EBIMed

Although this is the standard pipeline for EBIMed, it is possible to re-arrange the modules to favour identification of specific semantic types. More precisely, in our modular approach, after identification of a term in the text, disambiguation only decides whether the term is of that type or not. If it is not, the specific annotation is removed and left to the downstream modules to tag the term differently. While this requires *n* identification steps, adding identification of new types is independent of modules already present. However, the prioritization of semantic types is enforced by the order of the associated term identification modules.

3.2 Input documents and pre-processing

Input documents are XML-formatted Medline abstracts as provided from the National Library of Medicine (NLM). The XML structure of Medline abstracts includes meta information attached to the original document, such as the journal, author list, affiliations, publication dates as well as annotations inserted by the NLM such as creation date of the Medline entry, list of chemicals associated with the document, as well as related MeSH headings.

The text processing modules are only concerned with the document parts that consist of natural language text. In Medline abstracts, these stretches of text are marked up as *ArticleTitle* and *AbstractText*. Inside these elements we add another XML element, called *text*, to flag natural language text independent of the original input document format (module M-1 in Figure 1). Thereby the subsequent text processing modules become independent of the document structure: other document types, e.g. BioMed Central full text papers, can easily be fed into the pipeline providing a simple adaptation of the input pre-processor.

As a final pre-processing step (M-2), sentences are identified and marked using the <SENT> tag.

3.3 Finding protein names in text

For identification of protein names (M-3 in Figure 1), we use an existing protein repository. UniProt/Swiss-Prot contains roughly 190,000 protein/gene names (PGNs) in database entries that also annotate proteins with protein function, species and tissue type. PGNs from UniProt/Swiss-Prot are matched with regular expressions which account for morphological variability. These terms are tagged using the <z:uniprot> tag (see Figure 2). The list of identifiers (*ids* attribute) contains the accession numbers of the mentioned protein in the UniProt/Swiss-Prot database. All synonyms from a database entry are kept, and in the case of homonymy, where one name refers to several database entries, all accession numbers are stored. The pair consisting of the database name and the accession number(s) forms a unique identifier (UID) that represents the semantics of the term and can be trivially rewritten into a URL pointing to the database entry. Each entity also contains the attribute *fb* which provides the frequency of the term in the British National Corpus (BNC).

3.4 Resolving (some) protein name ambiguities

The approach to finding names that we presented can create three types of ambiguities mentioned above in Section 2.

In the current implementation, **Amb1** (ambiguity within a given resource) is not resolved. Rather, the links to *all* entries in the same database are maintained. **Amb2** and **Amb3** are partially resolved for protein/gene names as explained below (steps M-4 and M-5). Note that **Amb2** is resolved on "first-come first-serve" basis, meaning that an annotation introduced by one module is not overwritten by a subsequent module.

Many protein names are indeed or at least look like abbreviations. It has been proved that ambiguities of abbreviations and acronyms found in Medline abstracts can be automatically resolved with high accuracy (Yu et al., 2002; Schwartz and Hearst, 2003; Gaudan et al., 2005).

```
<SENT sid="2" pm="."> Aberrant
Wnt signaling, which results from
mutations of either <z:uniprot
fb="0" ids="P26233,P35222,P35223,
P35224,Q02248, Q9WU82">beta-
catenin</z:uniprot> or adenomat-
ous polyposis coli (<z:uniprot
fb="28" ids="P25054">APC </z:uni-
prot>), renders <z:uniprot fb="0"
ids= "P26233,P35222, P35223,
P35224,Q02248, Q9WU82"> beta-
catenin</z:uniprot> resistant to
degradation, and has been associ-
ated with multiple types of human
cancers
</SENT>
```

Figure 2. XML annotation of UniProt/Swiss-Prot proteins .

In our approach (Gaudan et al., 2005) all acronyms from Medline have been gathered together with their expanded forms, called senses. In addition all morphological and syntactical variants of a known expanded form have been extracted from Medline. Expanded forms were categorised into classes of semantically equivalent forms. Feature representations of Medline abstracts containing the acronym and the expanded form were used to train support vector machines (SVMs). Disambiguation of acronyms to their senses in Medline abstracts based on the SVMs was achieved at an accuracy of above 98%. This was independent from the presence of the expanded form in the Medline abstract. This disambiguation solution lead to the solution integrated into the processing pipeline.

A potential protein has to be evaluated against three possible outcomes: either a name is an acronym and can be resolved as (a) a protein or (b) not a protein, or (c) a name cannot be resolved. To distinguish cases (a) and (b) the document content is processed to identify the expanded form of the acronym and to check whether the expanded form refers to a protein name. In case of (c), the frequency of the name in the British National Corpus (BNC) is compared with a threshold. If the frequency is higher than the threshold, the name is assumed not to be a protein name. The threshold was chosen not to exclude important protein names that have already entered common English (such as *insulin*).

The disambiguation module (M-4) runs on the results of the previous module that performs protein-name matching and indiscriminately assumes each match to be a protein name. The module M-4 marks up all known acronym expansions in the text and combines the two pieces of information: a marked up protein name is looked up in the list of abbreviations. If the abbreviation has an expansion that is marked up in the vicinity **and** denotes a protein name, the abbreviation is verified as a protein name (case (a) above) by adding an attribute with a suitable value to the protein tag. The annotation also includes the normalised form of the acronym, which serves as an identifier for further database lookups. Similarly, if the expansion is clearly not a protein name, the same attribute is used with the according value.

Finally, the module M-5 removes the protein name markup if the name is either (b) clearly not a protein, or in case (c) has a BNC frequency beyond the threshold.

3.5 Finding other names in text

Further modules (M-6, M-7 and M-8 in Fig. 1) perform matching and markup for drugs from MedlinePlus[9], species from Entrez Taxonomy[10] and terms from the Gene Ontology (GO). As for proteins, the semantic type is signified by the element name and a unique ID referencing the source database is added as an attribute. Disambiguation for these names and terms is, however, not yet available.

Finding GO ontology terms in text can be difficult, as these names are typically "descriptions" rather than real terms (e.g. GO:0016886, *ligase activity, forming phosporic ester bonds*), and therefore are not likely to appear in text frequently (McCray et al., 2002; Verspoor et al., 2003; Nenadic et al., 2004).

Figure 3 shows an example of a sentence annotated for semantic types and POS information using the pipeline from the Figure 1. Note that POS tags are inside the type tags although type annotation has been performed prior to the POS tagging.

3.6 Other modules in the pipeline

The modular text processing pipeline of EBIMed is currently being extended to include other modules. The part-of-speech tagger (POS-tagger) is a separate module and combines tokenization and POS annotation. It leaves previously annotated entities as single tokens, even for multi-word terms, and assigns a noun POS tag to every named entity.

Shallow parsing is introduced as another layer in the multidimensional annotation of biomedical documents. After the NER modules, the shallow parsing modules extract events of protein-protein interactions. Shallow parsing basically annotates noun phrases (NP) and verb groups. Noun phrases that contain a protein name receive a modified NP tag (Protein-NP) to simplify finding of protein-protein interaction phrases. Patterns of Protein-NPs in conjunction with selected verb groups are annotated as final result.

```
<abs id='1' db='unknown'>
<text><SENT sid="0" pm="."><tagged>
<tok><sur> </sur><lem cat="bos"
mor=""></lem></tok>
<z:uniprot fb="0" ids="P50144,P50145">
<tok><sur>Cholecystokinin</sur><lem
cat="n" mor=":e">cholecystokinin</lem>
</tok> </z:uniprot>
<tok><sur>and</sur><lem cat="cnj"
mor=":K">and</lem></tok>
<z:uniprot fb="4" ids="O02686,P01350">
<tok><sur>gastrin</sur><lem cat="n"
mor=":e">gastrin</lem></tok>
</z:uniprot>
<tok><sur>differed</sur><lem cat="v"
mor=":V:P">differ</lem></tok>
<tok><sur>in</sur><lem cat="prep"
mor="">in</lem></tok>
<tok><sur>stimulatin</sur><lem cat="n"
mor=":e:m">stimulatin</lem></tok>
<z:uniprot fb="4" ids="O02686,P01350">
<tok><sur>gastrin</sur><lem cat="n"
mor=":e">gastrin</lem></tok>
</z:uniprot>
<z:go ids="GO:0046903"
onto="biological_process">
<tok><sur>secretion</sur><lem cat="n"
mor=":e">secretion</lem></tok>
</z:go>
<tok><sur>in</sur><lem cat="prep"
mor="">in</lem></tok>
<z:species ids="9986">
<tok><sur>rabbit</sur><lem cat="n"
mor=":e">rabbit</lem></tok>
</z:species>
<tok><sur>gastric</sur><lem cat="adj"
mor=":b">gastric</lem></tok>
<tok><sur>glands</sur><lem cat="n"
mor=":m">gland</lem></tok>
<tok><sur>.</sur><lem cat="eos"
mor=""></lem></tok>
</tagged></SENT>
</text>
</abs>
```

Figure 3. XML annotation of a sentence containing different semantic types and POS tags.

[9] MedlinePlus, National Library of Medicine, http://www.nlm.nih.gov/medlineplus/

[10] Entrez Taxonomy, National Center for Biotechnology Information, http://www.ncbi.nlm.nih.gov/entrez/

4 EBIMed

This cascaded approach to NER has been incorporated into EBIMed, a system for mining biomedical literature.

EBIMed is a service that combines document retrieval with co-occurrence-based summarization of Medline abstracts. Upon a keyword query, EBIMed retrieves abstracts from EMBL-EBI's installation of Medline and filters for biomedical terminology. The final result is organised in a view displaying pairs of concepts. Each pair co-occurs in at least one sentence in the retrieved abstracts. The findings (e.g. UniProt/Swiss-Prot proteins, GO annotations, drugs and species) are listed in conjunction with the UniProt/Swiss-Prot protein that appears in the same biological context. All terms, retrieved abstracts and extracted sentences are automatically linked to contextual information, e.g. entries in biomedical databases.

The annotation modules are also available via HTTP request that allows for specification of which modules to run (cf. Whatizit[11]). Note that with suitable pre-processing to insert the `<text>` tags, even well formed HTML can be processed.

5 Lessons Learnt so far

Our text mining solution EBIMed successfully applies multi-dimensional markup in a pipeline of text processing modules to facilitate online retrieval and mining of the biomedical literature. The final goal is semantic annotation of biomedical terms with UID, and – in the next step – shallow parsing based text processing for relationship identification. The following lessons have been learnt during design, implementation and use of our system.

The end-users expect to see the original document at all times and therefore we have to rely on proper formatting of the original and the processed text. Consequently, when adding semantic information, all other meta-information must be preserved to allow for proper rendering as similar as possible to the original document. Therefore, our approach does not remove any pre-existing annotations supplied by the publisher, i.e. the original document could be recovered by removing all introduced markup.

All modules only process sections of the document containing the natural language text, which improves modularisation. The document structure is irrelevant to single modules and facilitates reading and writing to the input and output stream, respectively, without taking notice of the beginning and/or the end of a single document. All information exchanged between modules is contained in the data stream. This facilitates running all the modules in a given pipeline in parallel, after an initial start-up. Even more, the modules can be distributed on separate machines with no implementation overheads for the communication over the network. Adding more modules with their own processors does not significantly impair overall runtime behaviour for large datasets and leads to fast text processing throughput combined with a reasonable — albeit not yet perfect — quality, which allows for new and practically useful text mining solutions such as EBIMed.

Modularisation of the text processing tasks leads to improved scalability and maintainability inherent to all modular software solutions. In the case of the presented solution, the modular approach allows for a selection of the setup and ordering of the modules, leading to a flexible software design, which can be adapted to different types of documents and which allows for an (incremental) replacement of methods to improve the quality of the output. This can also facilitate improved interoperability of XML-based NLP tools.

Semantic annotation of named entities and terms blends effectively with logical markup, simply because there is no overlap between document structure and named entities and terms. On the other hand, some physical markup (such as *<i>* in the BMC corpus) is in some documents used to highlight names or terms of a semantic type, e.g. gene names. With consistent semantic markup, this kind of physical tags could be abandoned to be replaced by external style information. However, some semantic annotations still must be combined with physical markup as in the term ***B**-sup* that initially was annotated by a publisher as *<b>B</b>-sup* and that now (after NER) would be marked as `<z:uniprot><b>B</b>-sup</z:uniprot>`.

Matching of names of a semantic type, e.g. protein/gene, is done on a "longest of the left-most" basis and prioritization of semantic types is enforced by the order of the term identification modules. Both choices lead to the result that overlapping annotations are preempted and that annotations automatically endorse a link to a unique identifier, unless there are ambiguity on the level of biomedical resource.. This type of ambiguity is not resolved in our text processing solution. Instead, for a given biomedical term, links to all entries referring to this term in the same database are kept.

[11] http://www.ebi.ac.uk/Rebholz-srv/whatizit/pipe

One approach to the disambiguation of **Amb2** (multiple resources) and **Amb3** (common English words) ambiguities would be to integrate all terms into one massive dictionary, identify the strings in the text and then disambiguate between *n* semantic types. This would require the disambiguation module be trained to distinguish all semantic types. If a new type is added, the disambiguation module would need to be retrained, which limits the possibilities for expansion and tailoring of text mining solutions.

Open Problems: We consider two categories of open problems: *NLP-based* and *XML-based* problems.

Bio NLP-based problems include challenges in recognition and disambiguation of biomedical names in text. One of the main issues in our approach is annotation of compound and nested terms. The presented methodology can lead to the following annotations:

1. the head noun belongs to the same semantic type, but is not part of the protein name (as represented in the terminological resource):
`<z:uniprot>Wnt-2</z:uniprot> protein`
2. the head noun belongs to a different semantic type not covered by any of the available terminological resources:
`<z:uniprot>WNT8B</z:uniprot> mRNA`
3. a compound term consists of terms from different semantic types, but its semantic type is not known:
`<z:uniprot fb="0" ids="…">beta-catenin</z:uniprot> <z:go ids="…" onto= "…">binding </z:go> domain`

Therefore, an important open problem is the annotation of nested terms where an entity name is part of a larger term that may or may not be in one of the dictionaries. Once the inner term is marked up with inline annotation, simple string pattern matching (utilised in our approach) cannot be used easily to find the outer, because the XML structure is in the way. A more effective solution could be a combination of inline with stand-off annotation.

Further, in a more complex case such as in
`htr-wnt-<uniprot>A protein</uniprot>`

neither `wnt` nor `htr` refer to a single protein but to a protein family, and whereas `A protein` is a known protein, this is not the case for `wnt-A`. The most obvious annotation `<uniprot>htr-wnt-A protein</uniprot>` cannot be resolved by the terminology from the UniProt/Swiss-Prot database, as it simply does not exist in the database.

More work is also needed on disambiguation of terms that correspond to common English words.

Annotation (i.e. XML)-based problems mainly relate to an open question whether different tag names should be used for various semantic types, or semantic types should be represented via attributes of a generalised *named entity or term* tag. In EBIMed, specific tags are used to denote specific semantic types. A similar challenge is how to treat and make use of entities such as in-line references, citations and formulas (typically annotated in journals), which are commonly ignored by NLP modules.

The most important issue, however, is how to represent still unresolved ambiguities, so that annotations might be modified at a later stage, e.g. when POS information or even the full parse tree is available. This also includes the issues on kind of information that should be made available for later processing. For example, as (compound) term identification is done before POS tagging, an open question is whether POS information should be assigned to individual components of a compound term (in addition to the term itself), since this information could be used to complete NER or adjust the results in a later stage.

6 Conclusions

In this paper, we have described a pipeline of XML-based modules for identification and disambiguation of several semantic types of biomedical named entities. The pipeline processes and semantically enriches documents by adding, changing or removing annotations. More precisely, the documents are augmented with UIDs referring to referential databases. In the course of the processing, the number of annotated NEs increases and the quality of the annotation improves. Thus, one of the main issues is to represent still unresolved ambiguities consistently, so that the following modules can perform both identification and disambiguation of new semantic types. As subsequent modules try to add new semantic annotations, prioritization of semantic types is enforced by the order of the term identification modules.

We have shown that such approach can be employed in a real-world, online information mining system EBIMed. The end-users expect to view the original layout of the documents at all times, and thus the solution needs to provide an efficient multidimensional markup that preserves and combines existing markup (from publishers) with semantic NLP-derived tags. Since, in the biomedical domain, it is essential to provide links from term and named-entity occurrences to referential databases, EBIMed provides identification and disambiguation of such entities and integrates text with other knowledge sources.

The existing solution to annotate only longest non-overlapped entities is useful for real world use scenarios, but we also need ways to improve annotations by representing nested and overlapped terms.

Acknowledgements

The development of EBIMed is supported by the Network of Excellence "Semantic Interoperability and Data Mining in Biomedicine" (NoE 507505). Medline abstracts are provided from the National Library of Medicine (NLM, Bethesda, MD, USA) and PubMed is the premier Web portal to access the data.

Sylvain Gaudan is supported by an "E-STAR" fellowship funded by the EC's FP6 Marie Curie Host fellowship for Early Stage Research Training under contract number MESTCT- 2004-504640. Goran Nenadic acknowledges supported from the UK BBSRC grant "Mining Term Associations from Literature to Support Knowledge Discovery in Biology" (BB/C007360/1).

EBI thanks IBM for the grant of an IBM eServer BladeCenter for use in its research work.

References

A. Bairoch, R. Apweiler, C.H. Wu, W.C. Barker, B. Boeckmann, S. Ferro, E. Gasteiger, H. Huang, R. Lopez, M. Magrane, M.J. Martin, D.A. Natale, C. O'Donovan, N. Redaschi and L.S. Yeh. 2005. The Universal Protein Resource (UniProt). *Nucleic Acids Research,* 33(Database issue):D154-9.

C. Blaschke, M.A. Andrade, C. Ouzounis and A. Valencia. 1999. Automatic extraction of biological information from scientific text: Protein-protein interactions. *Proc. ISMB*, 7:60–7.

A.C. Browne, G. Divita, A.R Aronson and A.T. McCray. 2003. UMLS language and vocabulary tools. *AMIA Annual Symposium Proc.*, p. 798.

L. Chen, H. Liu and C. Friedman. 2005. Gene name ambiguity of eukaryotic nomenclature. *Bioinformatics*, 21(2):248-56

S. Gaudan, H. Kirsch and D. Rebholz-Schuhmann. 2005. Resolving abbreviations to their senses in Medline. *Bioinformatics,* 21(18):3658-64

GO Consortium. 2006. The Gene Ontology (GO) project in 2006. *Nucleic Acids Research,* 34(suppl_1):D322-D326.

L. Hirschman, A. Yeh, C. Blaschke and A. Valencia. 2005. Overview of BioCreAtIvE: critical assessment of information extraction for biology. *BMC Bioinformatics*, 6 Suppl 1:S1.

H. Kirsch, S. Gaudan and D. Rebholz-Schuhmann. 2005. Distributed modules for text annotation and IE applied to the biomedical domain. *International Journal Medical Informatics.* (doi:10.1016/j.ijmedinf.2005.06.011)

M. Krauthammer and G. Nenadic. 2004. Term identification in the biomedical literature. *Journal Biomedical Informatics*, 37(6):512-26.

K. Lee, Y. Hwang, and H. Rim. 2003. Two-Phase Biomedical NE Recognition based on SVMs. *Proc. of NLP in Biomedicine, ACL 2003*. p. 33-40.

H. Liu, S.B. Johnson, and C. Friedman, 2002. Automatic resolution of ambiguous terms based on machine learning and conceptual relations in the UMLS. *J Am Med Inform Assoc*, 2002. 9(6): p. 621-36.

A. McCray, A. Browne and O. Bodenreider O. 2002. The lexical properties of Gene ontology (GO). *Proceedings of AMIA 2002*. 2002:504-8.

G. Nenadic, I. Spasic, and S. Ananiadou. 2005. Mining Biomedical Abstracts: What's in a Term?, *LNAI* Vol. 3248, pp. 797-806, Springer-Verlag

G. Nenadic and S. Ananiadou. 2006. Mining Semantically Related Terms from Biomedical Literature. *ACM Transactions on ALIP*, 01/2006 (Special Issue Text Mining and Management in Biomedicine)

xD. Rebholz-Schuhmann, H. Kirsch, M. Arregui, S. Gaudan, M. Rynbeek and P. Stoehr. (forthcoming) Identification of proteins and their biological context from Medline: EBI's text mining service EBIMed.

D. Rebholz-Schuhmann, S. Marcel, S. Albert, R. Tolle, G. Casari and H. Kirsch. 2004. Automatic extraction of mutations from Medline and cross-validation with OMIM. *Nucleid Acids Research*, 32(1):135–142.

A. Rzhetsky, I. Iossifov, T. Koike, M. Krauthammer, P. Kra, et al. 2004. GeneWays: A system for extracting, analyzing, visualizing, and integrating molecular pathway data. *Journal Biomedical Informatics*, 37:43–53.

A.S. Schwartz and M.A. Hearst. 2003. A simple algorithm for identifying abbreviation definitions in biomedical text. *Proceedings of Pac Symp Biocomput*. 2003. p. 451-62.

M. Torii, S. Kamboj and K. Vijay-Shanker. 2003. An Investigation of Various Information Sources for Classifying Biological Names. *Proceedings of NLP in Biomedicine, ACL 2003*. p. 113-120

CM Verspoor, C. Joslyn and G. Papcun. 2003. The Gene ontology as a source of lexical semantic knowledge for a biological natural language processing application. *Proc. of Workshop on Text Analysis and Search for Bioinformatics,* SIGIR 03

H. Yu, G. Hripcsak and C. Friedman. 2002. Mapping abbreviations to full forms in biomedical articles. *J Am Med Inform Assoc*, 2002. 9(3): p. 262-72.

Tools to Address the Interdependence between Tokenisation and Standoff Annotation

Claire Grover and **Michael Matthews** and **Richard Tobin**
School of Informatics
University of Edinburgh
{C.Grover, M.Matthews, R.Tobin}@ed.ac.uk

Abstract

In this paper we discuss technical issues arising from the interdependence between tokenisation and XML-based annotation tools, in particular those which use stand-off annotation in the form of pointers to word tokens. It is common practice for an XML-based annotation tool to use word tokens as the target units for annotating such things as named entities because it provides appropriate units for stand-off annotation. Furthermore, these units can be easily selected, swept out or snapped to by the annotators and certain classes of annotation mistakes can be prevented by building a tool that does not permit selection of a substring which does not entirely span one or more XML elements. There is a downside to this method of annotation, however, in that it assumes that for any given data set, in whatever domain, the optimal tokenisation is known before any annotation is performed. If mistakes are made in the initial tokenisation and the word boundaries conflict with the annotators' desired actions, then either the annotation is inaccurate or expensive retokenisation and reannotation will be required. Here we describe the methods we have developed to address this problem. We also describe experiments which explore the effects of different granularities of tokenisation on NER tagger performance.

1 Introduction

A primary consideration when designing an annotation tool for annotation tasks such as Named Entity (NE) annotation is to provide an interface that makes it easy for the annotator to select contiguous stretches of text for labelling (Carletta et al., 2003; Carletta et al., in press). This can be accomplished by enabling actions such as click and snapping to the ends of word tokens. Not only do such features make the task easier for annotators, they also help to reduce certain kinds of annotator error which can occur with interfaces which require the annotator to sweep out an area of text: without the safeguard of requiring annotations to span entire tokens, it is easy to sweep too little or too much text and create an annotation which takes in too few or too many characters. Thus the tokenisation of the text should be such that it achieves an optimal balance between increasing annotation speed and reducing annotation error rate. In Section 2 we describe a recently implemented XML-based annotation tool which we have used to create an NE-annotated corpus in the biomedical domain. This tool uses standoff annotation in a similar way to the NXT annotation tool (Carletta et al., 2003; Carletta et al., in press), though the annotations are recorded in the same file, rather than in a separate file.

To perform annotation with this tool, it is necessary to first tokenise the text and identify sentence and word tokens. We have found however that conflicts can arise between the segmentation that the tokeniser creates and the segmentation that the annotator needs, especially in scientific text where many details of correct tokenisation are not apparent in advance to a non-expert in the domain. We discuss this problem in Section 3 and illustrate it with examples from two domains, biomedicine and astrophysics.

In order to meet requirements from both the annotation tool and the tokenisation needs of the annotators, we have extended our tool to allow

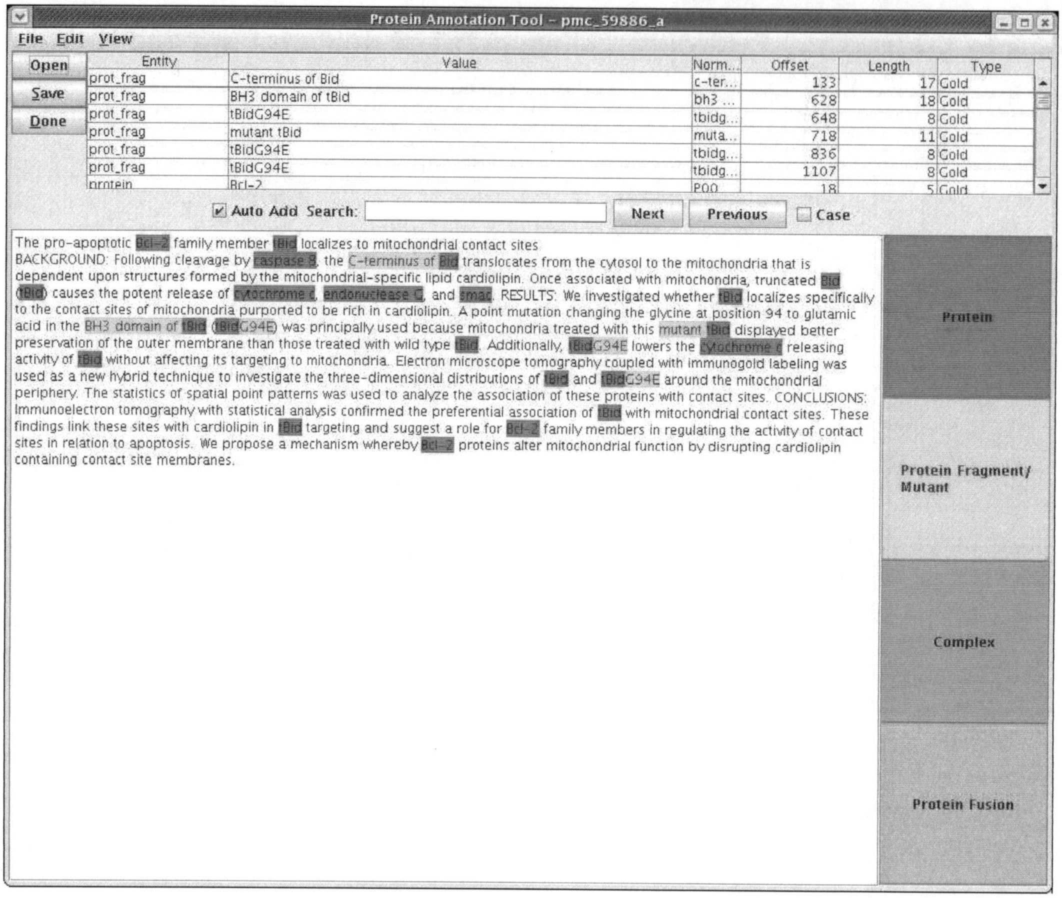

Figure 1: Screenshot of the Annotation Tool

the annotator to override the initial tokenisation where necessary and we have developed a method of recording the result of overriding in the XML mark-up. This allows us to keep a record of the optimal annotation and ensures that it will not be necessary to take the expensive step of having data reannotated in the event that the tokenisation needs to be redone. As improved tokenisation procedures become available we can retokenise both the annotated material and the remaining unannotated data using a program which we have developed for this task. We describe the extension to the annotation tool, the XML representation of conflict and the retokenisation program in Section 4.

2 An XML-based Standoff Annotation Tool

In a number of recent projects we have explored the use of machine learning techniques for Named Entity Recognition (NER) and have worked with data from a number of different domains, including data from biomedicine (Finkel et al., in press; Dingare et al., 2004), law reports (Grover et al., 2004), social science (Nissim et al., 2004), and astronomy and astrophysics (Becker et al., 2005; Hachey et al., 2005). We have worked with a number of XML-based annotation tools, including the the NXT annotation tool (Carletta et al., 2003; Carletta et al., in press). Since we are interested only in written text and focus on annotation for Information Extraction (IE), much of the complexity offered by the NXT tool is not required and we have therefore recently implemented our own IE-specific tool. This has much in common with NXT, in particular annotations are encoded as standoff with pointers to the indices of the word tokens. A screenshot of the tool being used for NE annotation of biomedical text is shown in Figure 1. Figure 2 contains a fragment of the XML underlying the annotation for the excerpt

> "glutamic acid in the BH3 domain of tBid (tBidG94E) was principally used because ....".

```
<body>
 .... <w id='w609'>glutamic</w> <w id='w618'>acid</w> <w id='w623'>in</w> <w id='w626'>the</w>
 <w id='w630'>BH3</w> <w id='w634'>domain</w> <w id='w641'>of</w> <w id='w644'>tBid</w>
 <w id='w649'>(</w><w id='w650'>tBidG94E</w><w id='w658'>)</w> <w id='w660'>was</w>
 <w id='w664'>principally</w> <w id='w676'>used</w> <w id='w681'>because</w> ....
</body>
<ents>
 <ent id='e7' type='prot_frag' sw='w630' ew='w644'>BH3 domain of tBid</ent>
 <ent id='e8' type='protein' sw='w644' ew='w644'>tBid</ent>
 <ent id='e9' type='prot_frag' sw='w650' ew='w650'>tBidG94E</ent>
 <ent id='e10' type='protein' sw='w650' ew='w650' eo='-4'>tBid</ent>
</ents>
```

Figure 2: XML Encoding of the Annotation.

Note that the standoff annotation is stored at the bottom of the annotated file, not in a separate file. This is principally to simplify file handling issues which might arise if the annotations were stored separately. Word tokens are wrapped in w elements and are assigned unique ids in the id attribute. The tokenisation is created using significantly improved upgrades of the XML tools described in Thompson et al. (1997) and Grover et al. (2000)[1]. The ents element contains all the entities that the annotator has marked and the link between the ent elements and the words is encoded with the sw and ew attributes (*start word* and *end word*) which point at word ids. For example, the protein fragment entity with id e7 starts at the first character of the word with id w630 and ends at the last character of the word with id w644.

Our annotation tool and the format for storing annotations that we have chosen are just one instance of a wide range of possible tools and formats for the NE annotation task. There are a number of decision points involved in the development of such tools, some of which come down to a matter of preference and some of which are consequences of other choices. Examples of annotation methods which are not primarily based on XML are GATE (Cunningham et al., 2002) and the annotation graph model of Bird and Liberman (2001). The GATE system organises annotations in graphs where the start and end nodes have pointers into the source document character offsets. This is an adaptation of the TIPSTER architecture (Grishman, 1997). (The UIMA system from IBM (Ferrucci and Lally, 2004) also stores annotations in a TIPSTER-like format.) The annotation graph model encodes annotations as a directed graph with fielded records on the arcs and optional time references on the nodes. This is broadly compatible with our standoff XML representation and with the TIPSTER architecture. Our decision to use an annotation tool which has an underlying XML representation is partly for compatibility with our NLP processing methodology where a document is passed through a pipeline of XML-based components. A second motivation is the wish to ensure quality of annotation by imposing the constraint that annotations span complete XML elements. As explained above and described in more detail in Section 4 the consequence of this approach has been that we have had to develop a method for recording cases where the tokenisation is inconsistent with an annotator's desired action so that subsequent retokenisation does not require reannotation.

3 Tokenisation Issues

The most widely known examples of the NER task are the MUC competitions (Chinchor, 1998) and the CoNLL 2002 and 2003 shared task (Sang, 2002; Sang and De Meulder, 2003). In both cases the domain is newspaper text and the entities are general ones such as person, location, organisation etc. For this kind of data there are unlikely to be conflicts between tokenisation and entity mark-up and a vanilla tokenisation that splits at whitespace and punctuation is adequate. When dealing with scientific text and entities which refer to technical concepts, on the other hand, much more care needs to be taken with tokenisation.

In the SEER project we collected a corpus of abstracts of radio astronomical papers taken from the NASA Astrophysics Data System archive, a digital library for physics, astrophysics, and instru-

[1]Soon to be available under GPL as LT-XML2 and LT-TTT2 from http://www.ltg.ed.ac.uk/

mentation[2]. We annotated the data for the following four entity types:

Instrument-name Names of telescopes and other measurement instruments, e.g. *Superconducting Tunnel Junction (STJ) camera, Plateau de Bure Interferometer, Chandra, XMM-Newton Reflection Grating Spectrometer (RGS), Hubble Space Telescope.*

Source-name Names of celestial objects, e.g. *NGC 7603, 3C 273, BRI 1335-0417, SDSSp J104433.04-012502.2, PC0953+ 4749.*

Source-type Types of objects, e.g. *Type II Supernovae (SNe II), radio-loud quasar, type 2 QSO, starburst galaxies, low-luminosity AGNs.*

Spectral-feature Features that can be pointed to on a spectrum, e.g. *Mg II emission, broad emission lines, radio continuum emission at 1.47 GHz, CO ladder from (2-1) up to (7-6), non-LTE line.*

In the Text Mining programme (TXM) we have collected a corpus of abstracts and full texts of biomedical papers taken from PubMed Central, the U.S. National Institutes of Health (NIH) free digital archive of biomedical and life sciences journal literature[3]. We have begun to annotate the data for the following four entity types:

Protein Proteins, both full names and acronyms, e.g. *p70 S6 protein kinase, Kap-1, p130(Cas).*

Protein Fragment/Mutant Subparts or mutants of proteins e.g. $Bub1^{1-331}$, a domain of Bub1, nup53-δ405-430.

Protein Complex Complexes made up of two or more proteins e.g. Kap95p/Kap60, DOCK2-ELMO1, RENT complex. Note that nesting of protein entities inside complexes may occur.

Fusion Protein Fusions of two proteins or protein fragments e.g. β-catenin-Lef1, GFP-tubulin, GFP-EB1. Note that nesting of protein entities inside fusions may occur.

In both the astronomy and biomedical domains, there is a high density of technical and formulaic language (e.g. from astronomy: $(N(H_2) \simeq 10_{24}cm^{-2})$, 17.8 h_{70}^{-1} kpc, for $\Omega_m = 0.3$, $\Lambda = 0.7$, 30 μJy/beam). This technical nature means that the vanilla tokenisation style that was previously adequate for MUC-style NE annotation in generic newspaper text is no longer guaranteed to be a good basis for standoff NE annotation because there will inevitably be conflicts between the way the tokenisation segments the text and the strings that the annotators want to select. In the remainder of this section we illustrate this point with examples from both domains.

3.1 Tokenisation of Astronomy Texts

In our tokenisation of the astronomy data, we initially assumed a vanilla MUC-style tokenisation which gives strong weight to whitespace as a token delimiter. This resulted in 'words' such *Si[I]>0.4* and *I([OIII])* being treated as single tokens. Retokenisation was required because the annotators wanted to highlight *Si[I]* and *[OIII]* as entities of type Spectral-feature. We also initially adopted the practice of treating hyphenated words as single tokens so that examples such as *AGN-dominated* in the Source-type entity *AGN-dominated NELGs* were treated as one token. In this case the annotator wanted to mark *AGN* as an embedded Source-type entity but was unable to do so. A similar problem occurred with the Spectral-feature *BAL* embedded in the Source-type entity *mini-BAL quasar*.

Examples such as these required us to retokenise the astronomy corpus. We then performed a one-off, ad hoc merger of the annotations that had already been created with the newly tokenised version and then asked the annotators to revisit the examples that they had previously been unable to annotate correctly.

3.2 Tokenisation of Biomedical Texts

Our starting point for tokenisation of biomedical text was to use the finer grained tokenisation that we had developed for the astronomy data in preference to a vanilla MUC-style tokenisation. For the most part this resulted in a useful tokenisation; for example, rules to split at hyphens and slashes resulted in a proper tokenisation of protein complexes such as *Kap95p/Kap60* and *DOCK2-ELMO1* which allowed for the correct annotation of both the complexes and the proteins embedded within them. However, a slash did not always cause a token split and in cases such as *ERK 1/2* the *1/2* was treated as one token which prevented the annotator from marking up *ERK 1* as a protein. A catch-all rule for non-ASCII

[2] http://adsabs.harvard.edu/preprint_service.html

[3] http://www.pubmedcentral.nih.gov/

```
<body>
  .... <w id='w609'>glutamic</w> <w id='w618'>acid</w> <w id='w623'>in</w> <w id='w626'>the</w>
  <w id='w630'>BH3</w> <w id='w634'>domain</w> <w id='w641'>of</w> <w id='w644'>tBid</w>
  <w id='w649'>(</w><w id='w650'>tBid</w><w id='w654'>G94E</w><w id='w658'>)</w>
  <w id='w660'>was</w> <w id='w664'>principally</w> <w id='w676'>used</w>
  <w id='w681'>because</w> ....
</body>
<ents>
  <ent id='e7' type='prot_frag' sw='w630' ew='w644'>BH3 domain of tBid</ent>
  <ent id='e8' type='protein' sw='w644' ew='w644'>tBid</ent>
  <ent id='e9' type='prot_frag' sw='w650' ew='w654'>tBidG94E</ent>
  <ent id='e10' type='protein' sw='w650' ew='w650'>tBid</ent>
</ents>
```

Figure 3: Annotated File after Retokenisation.

characters meant that sequences containing Greek characters became single tokens when sometimes they should have been split. For example, in the string *PKCγK380R* the annotator wanted to mark *PKC* as a protein. Material in parentheses when not preceded by white space was not split off so that in examples such as *coilin(C214)* and *Cdt1(193-447)* the annotators were not able to mark up just the material before the left parenthesis. Sequences of numeric and (possibly mixed-case) alphabetic characters were treated as single tokens, e.g., *tBidG94E* (see Figure 2), *GAL4AD*, *p53TAD*—in these cases the annotators wanted to mark up an initial subpart (*tBid*, *GAL4*, *p53*).

4 Representing Conflict in XML and Retokenisation

Some of the tokenisation problems highlighted in the previous section arose because the NLP specialist implementing the tokenisation rules was not an expert in either of the two domains. Many initial problems could have been avoided by a phase of consultation with the astronomy and biomedical domain experts. However, because they are not NLP experts, it would have been time-consuming to explain the NLP issues to them.

Another approach could have been to use extremely fine-grained tokenisation perhaps splitting tokens on every change in character type.

Another way in which many of the problems could have been avoided might have been to use extremely fine-grained tokenisation perhaps splitting tokens on every change in character type. This would provide a strong degree of harmony between tokenisation and annotation but would be inadvisable for two reasons: firstly, segmentation into many small tokens would be likely to slow annotation down as well as give rise to more accidental mis-annotations because the annotators would need to drag across more tokens; secondly, while larger numbers of smaller tokens may be useful for annotation, they are not necessarily appropriate for many subsequent layers of linguistic processing (see Section 5).

The practical reality is that the answer to the question of what is the 'right' tokenisation is far from obvious and that what is right for one level of processing may be wrong for another. We anticipate that we might tune the tokenisation component a number of times before it becomes fixed in its final state and we need a framework that permits us this degree of freedom to experiment without jeopardising the annotation work that has already been completed.

Our response to the conflict between tokenisation and annotation is to extend our XML-based standoff annotation tool so that it can be used by the annotators to record the places where the current tokenisation does not allow them to select a string that they want to annotate. In these cases they can override the default behaviour of the annotation tool and select exactly the string they are interested in. When this happens, the standoff annotation points to the word where the entity starts and the word where it ends as usual, but it also records start and end character offsets which show exactly which characters the annotator included as part of the entity. The protein entity `e10` in the example in Figure 2 illustrates this technique: the start and end word attributes `sw` and `ew` indicate that the entity encompasses the single token *tBidG94E* but the attribute `eo` (end offset) indicates that the annotator selected only the string *tBid*. Note that the annotator also correctly annotated the entire string *tBidG94E* as a protein fragment. The start and end character offset notation provides a subset of the range descriptions defined in the XPointer draft specification[4].

With this method of storing the annotators' decisions, it is now possible to update the tokenisation component and retokenise the data at any point during the annotation cycle without risk of losing completed annotation and without needing to ask annotators to revisit previous work. We have developed a program which takes as input the original annotated document plus a newly tokenised but unannotated version of it and which causes the correct annotation to be recorded in the retokenised version. Where the retokenisation accords with the annotators' needs there will be a decrease in the incidence of start and end offset attributes. Figure 3 shows the output of retokenisation on our example. The current version of the TXM project corpus contains 38,403 sentences which have been annotated for the four protein named entities described above (50,049 entity annotations). With the initial tokenisation (*Tok1*) there are 1,106,279 tokens and for 719 of the entities the annotators have used start and/or end offsets to override the tokenisation. We have defined a second, finer-grained tokenisation (*Tok2*) and used our retokenisation program to retokenise the corpus. This second version of the corpus contains 1,185,845 tokens and the number of entity annotations which conflict with the new tokenisation is reduced to 99. Some of these remaining cases reflect annotator errors while some are a consequence of the retokenisation still not being fine-grained enough. When using the annotations for training or testing, we still need a strategy for dealing with the annotations that are not consistent with our final automatic tokenisation routine (in our case, the 99 entities). We can systematically ignore the annotations or adjust them to the nearest token boundary. The important point is we we have recorded the mismatch between the tokenisation and the desired annotation and we have options for dealing with the discrepancy.

5 Tokenisation for Multiple Components

So far we have discussed the problem of finding the correct level of granularity of tokenisation purely in terms of obtaining the optimal basis for NER annotation. However, the reason for obtaining annotated data is to provide training material for NLP components which will be put together in a processing pipeline to perform information extraction. Given that statistically trained components such as part-of-speech (POS) taggers and NER taggers use word tokens as the fundamental unit over which they operate, their needs must be taken into consideration when deciding on an appropriate granularity for tokenisation. The implicit assumption here is that there can only be one layer of tokenisation available to all components and that this is the same layer as is used at the annotation stage. Thus, if annotation requires the tokenisation to be relatively fine-grained, this will have implications for POS and NER tagging. For example, a POS tagger trained on a more conventionally tokenised dataset might have no problem assigning a propernoun tag to *Met-tRNA/eIF2·* in

> ... and facilitates loading of the Met-tRNA/eIF2· GTP ternary complex ...

however, it would find it harder to assign tags to members of the 10 token sequence *M et - t RNA / e IF 2 ·*.

Similarly, a statistical NER tagger typically uses information about left and right context looking at a number of tokens (typically one or two) on either side. With a very fine-grained tokenisation, this representation of context will potentially be less informative as it might contain less actual context. For example, in the excerpt

> ... using a Tet-on LMP1 HNE2 cell line ...

assuming a fine-grained tokenisation, the pair of tokens *LMP* and *1* make up a protein entity. The left context would be the sequence *using a Tet - on* and the right context would be *HNE 2 cell line*. Depending on the size of window used to capture context this may or may not provide useful information.

To demonstrate the effect that a finer-grained tokenisation can have on POS and NER tagging, we performed a series of experiments on the NER annotated data provided for the Coling BioNLP evaluation (Kim et al., 2004), which was derived from the GENIA corpus (Kim et al., 2003). (The BioNLP data is annotated with five entities, protein, DNA, RNA, cell_type and cell_line.) We trained the C&C maximum entropy tagger (Curran and Clark, 2003) using default settings to obtain

[4]http://www.w3.org/TR/xptr-xpointer/

	Orig	*Tok1*	*Tok2*
training # sentences	18,546		
eval # sentences	3,856		
training # tokens	492,465	540,046	578,661
eval # tokens	101,028	110, 352	117, 950
Precision	65.14%	62.36%	61.39%
Recall	67.35%	64.24%	63.24%
F1	66.23%	63.27%	62.32%

Table 1: NER Results for Different Tokenisations of the BioNLP corpus

NER models for the original tokenisation (*Orig*), a retokenisation using the first TXM tokeniser (*Tok1*) and a retokenisation using the finer-grained second TXM tokeniser (*Tok2*) (see Section 4). In all experiments we discarded the original POS tags and performed POS tagging using the C&C tagger trained on the MedPost data (Smith et al., 2004). Table 1 shows precision, recall and f-score for the NER tagger trained and tested on these three tokenisations and it can be seen that performance drops as tokenisation becomes more fine-grained.

The results of these experiments indicate that care needs to be taken to achieve a sensible balance between the needs of the annotation and the needs of NLP modules. We do not believe, however, that the results demonstrate that the less fine-grained original tokenisation is necessarily the best. The experiments are a measure of the combined performance of the POS tagger and the NER tagger and the tokenisation expectations of the POS tagger must also have an impact. We used a POS tagger trained on material whose own tokenisation most closely resembles the tokenisation of *Orig* (hyphenated words are not split in the MedPost training data) and it is likely that the low results for *Tok1* and *Tok2* are partly due to the tokenisation mismatch between training and testing material for the POS tagger. In addition, the NER tagger was used with default settings for all runs where the left and right context is at most two tokens. We might expect an improvement in performance for *Tok1* and *Tok2* if the NER tagger was run with larger context windows. The overall message here, therefore, is that the needs of all processors must be taken into account when searching for an optimal tokenisation and developers should beware of bolting together components which have different expectations of the tokenisation—ideally each should be tuned to the same tokenisation.

There is a further reason why the original tokenisation of the BioNLP data works so well. During our experiments with the original data we observed that splitting at hyphens was normally not done (e.g. *monocyte-specific* is one token) but wherever an entity was part of a hyphenated word then it was split (e.g. *IL-2 -independent* where *IL-2* is marked as a protein.) The context of a following word which begins with a hyphen is thus a very clear indicator of entityhood. Although this will improve scores where the training and testing data are marked in the same way, it gives an unrealistic estimate of actual performance on unseen data where we would not expect the hyphenation strategy of an automatic tokeniser to be dependent on prior knowledge of where the entities are. To demonstrate that the *Orig* NER model does not perform well on differently tokenised data, we tested it on the *Tok1* tokenised evaluation set and obtained an f-score of 55.64%.

6 Conclusion

In this paper we have discussed the fact that tokenisation, especially of scientific text, is not necessarily a component that can be got right first time. In the context of annotation tools, especially where the tool makes reference to the tokenisation layer as with XML standoff, there is an interdependence between tokenisation and annotation. It is not practical to have annotators revisit their work every time the tokenisation component changes and so we have developed a tool that allows annotators to override tokenisation where necessary. The annotators' actions are recorded in the XML format in such a way that we can retokenise the corpus and still faithfully reproduce the original annotation. We have provided very specific motivation for our approach from our annotation of the astronomy and biomedical domains but we hope that this method might be taken up as a standard elsewhere as it would provide benefits when sharing corpora—a corpus annotated in this way can be used by a third party and possibly retokenised by them to suit their needs. We also looked at the interdependence between the tokenisation used for annotation and the tokenisation requirements of POS taggers and NER taggers. We showed that it is important to provide a consistent tokenisation throughout and that experimentation is required before the optimal balance can be found. Our retokenisation tools support just this kind of experimentation

Acknowledgements

The work reported here was supported by the ITI Life Sciences Text Mining programme (www.itilifesciences.com), and in part by Edinburgh-Stanford Link Grant (R36759) as part of the SEER project. All Intellectual Property arising from the Text Mining programme is the property of ITI Scotland Ltd.

References

Markus Becker, Ben Hachey, Beatrice Alex, and Claire Grover. 2005. Optimising selective sampling for bootstrapping named entity recognition. In *Proceedings of the ICML-2005 Workshop on Learning with Multiple Views*. Bonn, Germany.

Steven Bird and Mark Liberman. 2001. A formal framework for linguistic annotation. *Speech Communication*, 33(1,2):23–60.

Jean Carletta, Stefan Evert, Ulrich Heid, Jonathan Kilgour, Judy Robertson, and Holger Voormann. 2003. The NITE XML toolkit: flexible annotation for multi-modal language data. *Behavior Research Methods, Instruments, and Computers*, 35(3):353–363.

Jean Carletta, Stefan Evert, Ulrich Heid, and Jonathan Kilgour. in press. The NITE XML toolkit: data model and query. *Language Resources and Evaluation*.

Nancy A. Chinchor. 1998. *Proceedings of the Seventh Message Understanding Conference (MUC-7)*. Fairfax, Virginia.

Hamish Cunningham, Diana Maynard, Kalina Bontcheva, and Valentin Tablan. 2002. GATE: A framework and graphical development environment for robust NLP tools and applications. In *Proceedings of the Association for Computational Linguistics*.

James R. Curran and Stephen Clark. 2003. Language independent NER using a maximum entropy tagger. In *Proceedings of CoNLL-2003*, pages 164–167.

Shipra Dingare, Jenny Finkel, Malvina Nissim, Christopher Manning, and Claire Grover. 2004. A system for identifying named entities in biomedical text: How results from two evaluations reflect on both the system and the evaluations. In *Proceedings of the 2004 BioLink meeting: Linking Literature, Information and Knowledge for Biology, at ISMB 2004*.

David Ferrucci and Adam Lally. 2004. UIMA: an architectural approach to unstructured information processing in the corporate research environment. *Natural Language Engineering*, 10(3-4):327–348.

Jenny Finkel, Shipra Dingare, Christopher Manning, Malvina Nissim, Beatrice Alex, and Claire Grover. in press. Exploring the boundaries: Gene and protein identification in biomedical text. *BMC Bioinformatics*, 6 (Suppl 1).

Ralph Grishman. 1997. TIPSTER Architecture Design Document Version 2.3. *Technical report, DARPA*, `http://www.itl.nist.gov/div894/894.02/related_projects/tipster/`.

Claire Grover, Colin Matheson, Andrei Mikheev, and Marc Moens. 2000. LT TTT—a flexible tokenisation tool. In *LREC 2000—Proceedings of the 2nd International Conference on Language Resources and Evaluation*, pages 1147–1154.

Claire Grover, Ben Hachey, and Ian Hughson. 2004. The HOLJ corpus: Supporting summarisation of legal texts. In *Proceedings of the 5th International Workshop on Linguistically Interpreted Corpora (LINC-04)*. Geneva, Switzerland.

Ben Hachey, Beatrice Alex, and Markus Becker. 2005. Investigating the effects of selective sampling on the annotation task. In *Proceedings of the 9th Conference on Computational Natural Language Learning*. Ann Arbor, Michigan, USA.

Jin-Dong Kim, Tomoko Ohta, Yuka Tateisi, and Jun'ichi Tsujii. 2003. GENIA corpus—a semantically annotated corpus for bio-textmining. *Bioinformatics*, 19(Suppl.1):180–182.

Jin-Dong Kim, Tomoko Ohta, Yoshimasa Tsuruoka, Yuka Tateisi, and Nigel Collier. 2004. Introduction to the Bio-Entity Recognition Task at JNLPBA. In *Proceedings of the International Joint Workshop on NLP in Biomedicine and its Applications*, pages 70–75.

Malvina Nissim, Colin Matheson, and James Reid. 2004. Recognising geographical entities in Scottish historical documents. In *Proceedings of the Workshop on Geographic Information Retrieval at SIGIR 2004*.

Erik F Tjong Kim Sang and Fien De Meulder. 2003. Introduction to the CoNLL-2003 shared task: Language-independent named entity recognition. In *Proceedings of the 2003 Conference on Computational Natural Language Learning*.

Erik F. Tjong Kim Sang. 2002. Introduction to the CoNLL-2002 shared task: Language-independent named entity recognition. In *Proceedings of the 2002 Conference on Computational Natural Language Learning*.

L. Smith, T. Rindflesch, and W. J. Wilbur. 2004. MedPost: a part-of-speech tagger for biomedical text. *Bioinformatics*, 20(14):2320–2321.

Henry Thompson, Richard Tobin, David McKelvie, and Chris Brew. 1997. LT XML. software API and toolkit for XML processing. `http://www.ltg.ed.ac.uk/software/`.

Towards an Alternative Implementation of NXT's Query Language via XQuery

Neil Mayo, Jonathan Kilgour, and Jean Carletta
University of Edinburgh

Abstract

The NITE Query Language (NQL) has been used successfully for analysis of a number of heavily cross-annotated data sets, and users especially value its elegance and flexibility. However, when using the current implementation, many of the more complicated queries that users have formulated must be run in batch mode. For a re-implementation, we require the query processor to be capable of handling large amounts of data at once, and work quickly enough for on-line data analysis even when used on complete corpora. Early results suggest that the most promising implementation strategy is one that involves the use of XQuery on a multiple file data representation that uses the structure of individual XML files to mirror tree structures in the data, with redundancy where a data node has multiple parents in the underlying data object model.

1 Introduction

Computational linguistics increasingly requires data sets which have been annotated for many different phenomena which relate independently to the base text or set of signals, segmenting the data in different, conflicting ways. The NITE XML Toolkit, or NXT (Carletta et al., 2003), has been used successfully on a range of text, spoken language, and multimodal corpora to provide and work with data of this character. Because the original motivation behind it was to make up for a dearth of tools that could be used to hand-annotate and display such data, the initial implementation of data search was required to work well on one data observation at a time — that is, one text, dialogue, or other language event — and to be usable but slow on multiple observations. However, the clear and flexible design of NXT's query language, NQL (Heid et al., 2004; Carletta et al., in press), makes it attractive for larger-scale data analysis, and a number of users have up-translated existing data for the express purpose of improving their search options.

We are now in the process of devising a strategy for re-implementing the NQL processor to serve the needs of this class of user better. In this paper, we describe our requirements for the new implementation, outline the various implementation options that we have, and give early results suggesting how well they meet our requirements. NQL is arguably the most mature of the current special-purpose facilities for searching data sets where the data is not structured as a single tree, and therefore experiences with implementing it are likely to provide lessons for search facilities that are still to come.

2 NXT and the NITE Query Language

NXT is designed specifically for data sets with multiple kinds of annotation. It requires data to be represented as a set of XML files related to each other using stand-off links, with a "metadata" file that provides two things: a catalogue of files containing the audio or video signals used to capture an observation together with the annotations that describe them, and a specification of the corpus design that describes the annotations and how they relate to each other and to signal. Text corpora are treated as signal-less, with the text as a base level of "annotation" to which other annotations can point. Given data of this type, NXT provides Java libraries for data modelling and search as well as for building graphical user interfaces that can be used to display annotations in synchrony with the signals. NXT also comes with a number of finished GUIs for common tasks, some of which are specific to existing data sets and some of which are configurable to new corpus designs. NXT supports data exploration using a search GUI, callable from any tool, that will run an NQL query and highlight results on the tool's display. Data search is then usually done using one of a battery of command line utilities, that, for instance, count results matching a given query or provide tab-delimited output describing the query matches.

Because the data model and query language for a tool are critical to our implementation choices, we briefly describe them, as well as the current NQL implementation.

2.1 NXT's data handling

In NXT, annotations are described by types and attribute value pairs, and can relate to a synchronized set of signals via start and end times, to representations of the external environment, and to each other. Annotations can describe the behaviour of a single 'agent', if more than one participant is involved for the genre being coded, or they can describe the entire language event; the latter possibility is used for annotating written text as well as for interaction within a pair or group of agents. The data model ties the annotations together into a multi-rooted tree structure that is characterized by both temporal and structural orderings. Additional relationships can be overlaid on this structure using pointers that carry no ordering implications. The same basic data objects that are used for annotations are also used to build sets of objects that represent referents from the real world, to structure type ontologies, and to provide access to other external resources stored in XML, resulting in a rich and flexible system.

Data is stored in a "stand-off" XML representation that uses the XML structure of individual files to mirror the most prominent trees in the data itself, forming 'codings' of related annotations, and pointers between files (represented by `XLinks`) for other relationships. For example, the markup

```
<nt nite:start="1.8" nite:end="2.3"
cat="NP" nite:id="s1_506" wc="2">
<nite:child href="a1.words.xml#id(s1_6)"/>
<nite:child href="a1.words.xml#id(s1_7)"/>
</nt>
```

represents a noun phrase in a syntactic tree, pointing to two words in a different file which constitute the content of that syntactic structure.

This has the useful properties of allowing corpus subsets to be assembled as needed; making it easy to import annotations without perturbing the rest of the data set; and keeping each individual file simple to use in external processing. For instance, the words for a single speaker can be stored in a single file that contains no other data, making it easy to pass through to a part-of-speech tagger. NXT itself provides transparent corpus-wide access to the data, and so tool users need not understand how the data is stored. A 'metadata' file defines the structures of the individual files and the relationships among them, as well as detailing where to find the data and signals on the file system.

2.2 NXT's query language

Search is conducted in NXT by means of a dedicated query language, NQL. A simple query finds n-tuples of data objects (annotations and objects) that satisfy certain conditions. The query expression consists of two parts, separated by a colon (:). In the first part, variables representing the data objects are declared. These either match all data objects (e.g. '($x)' for a variable named '$x') or are constrained to draw matches from a designated set of simple types (e.g. '($w word || sil)', matching data objects of the simple types 'word' or 'sil'). The second part of the query expression specifies a set of conditions that are required to hold for a match, which are combined using negation (logical not, '!'), conjunction (logical and, '&&'), and disjunction (logical or, '||'). Queries return a structure that for each match lists the variables and references the data objects they matched.

NQL has operators that allow match conditions to be expressed for each of the essential properties of a data object such as its identity, its attribute-value pairs, its textual content, its timing, and its relationships via the two types of structural links (child and pointer). The attribute and textual content tests include the ability to match against either the existence or the value of the attribute.

Attribute values or textual content can be tested against explicit values or values of other attributes, using equality, inequality, and the usual ordering tests (conventionally represented as $<$, $<=$, $>=$, and $>$). String values can also be tested against regular expressions.

The temporal operators include the ability to test whether a data object has timing information, and to compare the start or end time with a given point in time. The query language also has operators to test for some common timing relationships between two data objects, such as overlap.

The structural operators test for dominance, precedence, and pointer relationships. Precedence can be tested against all of the orderings in the overlapping annotations.

In addition, identity tests can be used to avoid matches where different variables point to the same data object. It is also possible in NQL to 'bind' variables within the query using existential ('exists') and universal ('forall') quantifiers in the variable declarations (which have the same meaning as in first-order logic). Such bound variables are not returned in the query result.

NXT also supports the sequencing of queries into a 'complex' query using a double colon (::) operator. The results for a complex query are returned not as a flat list but as a tree structure. For example, in a corpus of timed words from two speakers, A and B,

```
  ($wa word):($wa@agent = "A")::
($wb word):($wb@agent="B") && ($wa
overlaps.with $wb)
```

will return a tree showing word overlaps; underneath each top level node, representing an overlapping word from speaker A, will be a set of nodes representing the words from speaker B that overlap that word of speaker A.

2.3 Comparison to other search facilitiies

The kinds of properties that linguists wish to use in searching language data are cumbersome to express in general-purpose query languages. For this reason, there are a number of other query languages designed specifically for language corpora, some of which are supported by implementation. LPath (Bird et al., 2006) and tgrep2 (Rohde, nd) assume the data forms one ordered tree. TigerSearch (Tiger Project, nd) is primarily for single trees, but does allow some out-of-tree relationships; the data model includes "secondary edges" that link a node to an additional parent and that can be labelled, with query language operators that will test for the presence or absence of such an edge, with or without a specific label. ATLAS (National Institute of Standards and Technology, 2000) intends a query language over richer structures, but the structures and query language are still under development.

3 Requirements

We already have a successful NQL implementation as part of NXT, NXT Search. However, as always, there are a number of things that could be improved about it. We are considering a re-implementation with the following aims in mind:

Faster query execution. Although many queries run quite quickly in NXT Search, more complicated queries can take long enough to execute on a large corpus that they have to be scheduled overnight. This is partially due to the approach of checking every possible combination of the variables declared in the query, resulting in a large search space for some queries. Our aim is to have the vast majority of queries that exploit NXT's multi-rooted tree structure run quickly enough on single observations that users will be happy to run them in an interactive GUI environment.

The ability to load more data. NXT loads data into a structure that is 5-7 times the size of the data on disk. A smaller memory representation would allow larger data sets to be loaded for querying. Because it has a "lazy" implementation that only loads annotations when they are required, the current performance is sufficient for many purposes, as this allows all of the annotations relating a single observation to be loaded unless the observation is both long and very heavily annotated. It is too limited (a) when the user requires a query to relate annotations drawn from different observations, for instance, as a convenience when working on sparse phenomena, or when working on multiple-document applications such as the extraction of named entities from newspaper articles; (b) for queries that draw on very many kinds of annotation all at the same time on longer observations; and (c) when the user is in an interactive environment such as a GUI using a wide range of queries on different phenomena. In the last case, our goal could be achieved by memory management that throws loaded data away instead of increasing the loading capacity.

4 XQuery as a Basis for Re-implementation

XQuery (Boag et al., 2005), currently a W3C Candidate Recommendation, is a Turing-complete functional query/programming language designed for querying (sets of) XML documents. It subsumes XPath, which is "a language for addressing parts of an XML document" (Clark and DeRose, 1999). XPath supports the navigation, selection and extraction of fragments of XML documents, by the specification of 'paths' through the XML hierarchy. XQuery queries can include a mixture of XML, XPath expressions, and function calls; and also FLWOR expressions, which provide various programmatical constructs such as *for*, *let*, *where*, *orderby* and *return* keywords for looping and variable assignment. XQuery is designed to make efficient use of the inherent structure of XML to calculate the results of a query.

XQuery thus appears a natural choice for querying XML of the sort over which NQL operates. Although the axes exposed in XPath allow comprehensive navigation around tree structures, NXT's object model allows individual nodes to draw multiple parents from different trees that make up the data; expressing navigation over this multi-tree structure can be cumbersome in XPath alone. XQuery allows us to combine fragments of XML, selected by XPath, in meaningful ways to construct the results of a given query.

There are other possible implementation options that would not use XQuery. The first of these would use extensions to the standard XPath axes to query concurrent markup, as has been demonstrated by (Iacob and Dekhtyar, 2005). We have not yet investigated this option.

The second is to come up with an indexing scheme that allows us to recast the data as a relational database, the approach taken in LPath (Bird et al., 2006). We chose not to explore this option. It is not difficult to design a relational database to match a particular NXT corpus as long as editing is not enabled. However, a key part of NXT's data model permits annotations to descend recursively through different layers of the same set of data types, in order to make it easy to represent things like syntax trees. This makes it difficult to build a generic transform to a relational database - such a transform would need to inspect the entire data set to see what the largest depth is. It also makes it impossible to allow editing, at least without placing some hard limit on the recursion. It is admittedly true that any strategy based on XQuery will also be limited to static data sets for the present, but update mechanisms for XQuery are already beginning to appear and are likely to become part of some future standard.

5 Implementation Strategy

In our investigation, we compare two possible implementation strategies to NXT Search, our existing implementation.

5.1 Using NXT's stand-off format

The first strategy is to use XQuery directly on NXT's stand-off data storage format. The bulk of the work here is in writing libraries of XQuery functions that correctly interpret NXT's stand-off child links in order to allow navigation over the same primary axes as are used in XPath, but with multiple parenthood, and operating over NXT's multiple files. The libraries can resolve the `XLinks` NXT uses both forwards and backwards. Backwards resolution requires functions that access the corpus metadata to find out which files could contain annotations that could stand in the correct relationship to the starting node. Built on top of this infrastructure would be functions which implement the NQL operators.

Resolving ancestors is a rather expensive operation which involves searching an entire coding file for links to a node with a specified identity. Additionally, if a query includes variables which are not bound to a particular type, this precludes the possibility of reducing the search space to particular coding files.

A drawback to using XPath to query a hierarchy which is serialised to multiple annotation files, is that much of the efficiency of XPath expressions can be lost through the necessity of resolving XLinks at every child or parent step of the expression. This means that even the descendant and ancestor axes of XPath may not be used directly but must be broken down into their constituent single-step axes.

In addition to providing a transparent interface for navigating the data, it may be necessary to provide additional indexing of the data, to increase efficiency and avoid the duplication of calculations. An alternative is to overcome the standoff nature of the data by resolving links explicitly, as described in the following section.

5.2 Using a redundant data representation

The second strategy makes use of the classic trade-off between memory and speed by employing a redundant data representation that is both easy to calculate from NXT's data storage format and ensures that most of the navigation required exercises common parts of XPath, since these are the operations upon which XQuery implementations will have concentrated their resources.

The particular redundancy we have in mind relies on NXT's concept of "knitting" data. In NXT's data model, every node may have multiple parents, but only one set of children. Where multiple parents exist, at most one will be in the same file as the child node, with the rest connected by `XLinks`. "Knitting" is the process of starting with one XML file and recursively following children and child links, storing the expanded result as an XML file. The redundant representation we used is then the smallest set of expanded files that contains within it every child link from the original data as an XML child. .

Although this approach has the advantage of using XPath more heavily than our first approach, it has the added costs of generating the knitted data and handling the redundancy. The knitting stylesheet that currently ships with NXT is very slow, but a very fast implementation of the knitting process that works with NXT format data has been developed and is expected as part of an upcoming LTXML release (University of Edinburgh Language Technology Group, nd). The cost of dealing with redundancy depends on the branching structure of the corpus. To date, most corpora with multiple parenthood have a number of quite shallow trees that do not branch themselves but all point to the same few base levels (e.g. orthography), suggesting we can at least avoid exponential expansion.

6 Tests

For initial testing, we chose a small set of queries which would allow us to judge potential implementations in terms of whether they could do everything we need to do, whether they would give the correct results, and how they would perform against our stated requirements. This allows us to form an opinion whilst only writing portions of the code required for a complete NQL implementation. Our set of queries is therefore designed to involve all of the basic operations required to exploit NXT's ability to represent multi-rooted trees and to traverse a large amount of data, so that they are computationally expensive and could return many results. In the tests, we ran the queries over the NXT translation for the Penn Treebank syntax annotated version of one Switchboard dialogue (Carletta et al., 2004), sw4114. The full dialogue is approximately 426Kb in physical size, and contains over 1101 word elements.

6.1 Test queries

Our test queries were as follows.

- Query 1 (Dominance):
  ```
  (exists $e nt)($w word):
  $e@cat="NP" && $e^$w
  ```
  (words dominated by an NP-category nt)

- Query 2 (Complex query with precedence and dominance):
  ```
  ($w1 word)($w2 word):
  TEXT($w1)="the" && $w1<>$w2
  ::
  (exists $p nt): $p@cat="NP"
  && $p^$w1 && $p^$w2
  ```
  (word pairs where the word "the" precedes the second word with respect to a common NP dominator)

- Query 3 (Eliminative):
  ```
  ($a word)(forall $b
  turn):!($b^$a)
  ```
  (words not dominated by any turn)

In the data, the category "nt" represents syntactic non-terminals. The third query was chosen because it is particularly slow in the current NQL implementation, but is easily expressed as a path and therefore is likely to execute efficiently in XPath implementations.

Although NXT's object model also allows for arbitrary relationships between nodes using pointers with named roles, increasing speed for queries over them is only a secondary concern, and we know that implementing operators over them is possible in XQuery because it is very similar to resolving stand-off child links. For this reason, none of our test queries involve pointers.

6.2 Test environment

For processing XQuery, we used Saxon (www.saxonica.com), which provides an API so that it can be called from Java. There are several available XQuery interpreters, and they will differ in their implementation details. We chose Saxon because it appears to be most complete and is well-supported. Alternative interpreters, Galax (www.galaxquery.org) and Qexo (www.gnu.org/software/qexo/), provided only incomplete implementations at the time of writing.

6.3 Comparability of results

It is not possible in a test like this to produce completely comparable results because the different implementation strategies are doing very different things to arrive at their results. For example, consider our second query. Apart from some primitive optimizations, on this and all queries, NXT Search does an exhaustive search of all possible k-tuples that match the types given in the query, varying the rightmost variable fastest. Our XQuery implementation on stand-off data first finds matches to $w1, $w2, and $np; then calls a function that calculates the ancestries for matches to $w1 and $w2; for each ($w1, $w2) pair, computes the intersection of the two ancestries; and finally filters this intersection against the list of $np matches.

On the other hand, the implementation on the knitted data is shown in figure 1. It first sets variables representing the XML document containing our knitted data and all distinct nt elements within that document which both have a category attribute "NP" and have further `word` descendants. It then sets a variable to represent the sequence of results. The results are calculated by taking each `NP`-type element and checking its `word` descendants for those pairs where a word "the" precedes another word. The implementation also applies the condition that the `NP`-type element must not have another `NP` element as an ancestor — this is to remove duplicates introduced by the way we find the initial set of `NP`s.

In addition to the execution strategies, the methods used to start off processing were quite different. For each of the implementations, we did whatever gave the best performance. For the XQuery-based implementations, this meant writing a Java class to start up a static context for the execution of the query and reusing it to run the query repeatedly. For NXT, it meant using a shell script to run the command-line utility `SaveQueryResults` repeatedly on a set of observations, exiting each time.

Figure 1: An XQuery rewritten for knitted data; containing more direct XPath expressions.

```
let $doc := doc("data/knitted/swbd/sw4114.syntax.xml"),
    $nps := $doc//nt[@cat="NP"][descendant::word] union (),
    $result := (
        for $np in $nps return (
            let $w2 := $np//word, $w1 := $w2[text()="the"]
            for $a in $w1, $b in $w2
            where (struct:node-precedes($a, $b)
                and not($np/ancestor::nt[@cat="NP"]))
            (: only return for the uppermost common NP ancestor :)
            return (element match {$a, $b})
        )
    ) union ()
return element result {attribute count count($result), $result}
```

Our aim in performing the comparison is to assess what is *possible* in each approach rather than to do the same thing in each, and this is why we have attempted to achieve best possible performance in each context rather than making the conditions as similar as possible. In all cases, the figures we report are the mean timings over five runs of what the Linux `time` command reports as 'real' time.

7 Speed Results

The results of our trial are shown in the following table. Timings which are purely in seconds are given to 2 decimal places; those which extend into the minutes are given to the nearest second. "NXT" means NXT Search; "XQ" is the condition with XQuery using stand-off data; and "XQ-K" is the condition with XQuery using the redundant knitted data.

	Query		
Impl	Q1	Q2	Q3
NXT	3.38s	1m24	18.25s
XQ	10.21s	3m24	14.42s
XQ-K	2.03s	2.17s	2.47s

Although it would be wrong to read too much into our simple testing, these results do suggest some tentative conclusions. The first is that using XQuery on NXT's stand-off data format is unlikely to increase execution speed except for queries that are computationally very expensive for NXT, and may decrease performance for other queries. If users show any tolerance for delays, it is more likely to be for the delays to the former, and therefore this does not seem a winning strategy. On the other hand, using XQuery on the knitted data provides useful (and sometimes impressive) gains across the board.

It should be noted that our results are based upon a single XQuery implementation and are inevitably implementation-specific. Future work will also attempt to make comparisons with alternatives, including those provided by XML databases.

7.1 Memory results

To explore our second requirement, the ability to load more data, we generated a series of corpora which double in size from an initial set of 4 children with 2 parents.

We ran both NXT Search and XQuery in Saxon on these corpora, with the Java Virtual Machine initialised with increasing amounts of memory, and recorded the maximum corpus size each was able to handle. Both query languages were exercised on NXT stand-off data, with the simple task of calculating parent/child relationships. Results are shown in the following table.

	Max corpus size (nodes, disk space)	
Mem Mb	**NXT**	**XQuery/Saxon**
500	$3*2^{17}$, 28Mb	$3*2^{19}$, 111Mb
800	$3*2^{18}$, 56Mb	$3*2^{20}$, 224Mb
1000	$3*2^{18}$, 56Mb	$3*2^{20}$, 224Mb

These initial tests suggest that at its best, the XQuery implementation in Saxon can manage around 4 times as much data as NXT Search. It is interesting to note that the full set of tests took about 19 minutes for XQuery, but 18 hours for NXT Search. That is, Saxon appears to be far more efficient at managing large data sets. We also discovered that the NXT results were different when a different query was used; we hope to elaborate these results more accurately in the future.

We did not specifically run this test on the implementation that uses XQuery on knitted data because the basic characteristics would be the same as for the XQuery implementation with stand-off data. The size of a knitted data version will depend on the amount of redundancy that knitting creates. Knitting has the potential to increase the amount of memory required greatly, but it is worth noting that it does not always do so. The knitted version of the Switchboard dialogue used for these tests is actually smaller than the stand-off version, because the original stand-off stores terminals (words) in a separate file from syntax trees even though the terminals are defined to have only one parent. That is, there can be good reasons for using stand-off annotation, but it does have its own costs, as `XLinks` take space.

7.2 Query rewriting

In the testing described far, we used the existing version of NXT Search. Rather than writing a new query language implementation, we could just invest our resources in improvement of NXT Search itself. It is possible that we could change the underlying XML handling to use libraries that are more memory-efficient, but this is unlikely to give real scalability. The biggest speed improvements could probably be made by re-ordering terms before query execution. Experienced query authors can often speed up a query if they rewrite the terms to minimize the size of the search space, assuming they know the shape of the underlying data set. Although we do not yet have an algorithm for this rewriting, it roughly involves ignoring the "exists" quantifier, splitting the query into a complex one with one variable binding per subquery, sequencing the component queries by increasing order of match set size, and evaluating tests on the earliest subquery possible. For example, consider the query

```
($w1 word):text($w1)="the" ::
($p nt):$p@cat eq "NP" && $p^$w1 ::
($w2 word): $p^$w2 && $w1<>$w2
```

This query, which bears a family resemblance to query 2, takes 4.31s, which is a considerable improvement. Of course, the result tree is a different shape from the one specified in the original query, and so this strategy for gaining speed improvements would incur the additional cost of rewriting the result tree after execution.

7.2.1 Discussion

Our testing suggests that if we want to make speed improvements, creating a new NQL implementation that uses XQuery on a redundant data representation is a good option. Although not the result we initially expected, it is perhaps unsurprising. This XQuery implementation strategy draws more heavily on XPath than the stand-off strategy, and XPath is the most well-exercised portion of XQuery. The advantages do not just come from recasting our computations as operations over trees. XPath allows us, for instance, to write a single expression that both binds a variable and performs condition tests on it, rather than requiring us to first bind the variable and then loop through each combination of nodes to determine which satisfy the constraints. Using a redundant data representation increases memory requirements, but the XQuery-based strategies use enough less memory that the redundancy in itself will perhaps not be an issue. In order to settle this question, we must think more carefully about the size and shape of current and potential NXT corpora.

Our other option for making speed improvements is to augment NXT Search with a query rewriting strategy. This needs further evaluation because the improvements will vary widely with the query being rewritten, but our initial test worked surprisingly well. However, augmenting the current NXT Search in this way will not reduce its memory use, and it is not clear whether this improvement can readily be made by other means.

Acknowledgments

This work has been funded by a grant from Scottish Enterprise via the Edinburgh-Stanford Link. We are grateful to Stefan Evert for designing NQL and for discussing its specification with us, and to Jan-Torsten Milde and Felix Sasaki for making available to us their own initial experiments suggesting that this re-implementation would be worth attempting.

References

[Bird et al.2006] Steven Bird, Yi Chen, Susan Davidson, Haejoong Lee, and Yifeng Zheng. 2006. Designing and evaluating an XPath dialect for linguistic queries. In *22nd International Conference on Data Engineering*, Atlanta, USA.

[Boag et al.2005] Scott Boag, Don Chamberlin, Mary F. Fernandez, Daniela Florescu, Jonathan Robie, Jrme Simon, and Mugur Stefanescu. 2005. Xquery 1.0: An XML Query Language, November. http://www.w3.org/TR/xquery/; accessed 18 Jan 06.

[Carletta et al.2003] J. Carletta, Stefan Evert, Ulrich Heid, Jonathan Kilgour, Judy Robertson, and Holger Voormann. 2003. The NITE XML Toolkit: flexible annotation for multi-modal language data. *Behavior Research Methods, Instruments, and Computers*, 35(3):353–363.

[Carletta et al.2004] Jean Carletta, Shipra Dingare, Malvina Nissim, and Tatiana Nikitina. 2004. Using the NITE XML Toolkit on the Switchboard Corpus to study syntactic choice: a case study. In *Fourth Language Resources and Evaluation Conference*, Lisbon, Portugal.

[Carletta et al.in press] J. Carletta, S. Evert, U. Heid, and J. Kilgour. in press. The NITE XML Toolkit: data model and query language. *Language Resources and Evaluation Journal.*

[Clark and DeRose1999] James Clark and Steve DeRose. 1999. Xml path language (xpath) version 1.0, 16 November. http://www.w3.org/TR/xpath; accessed 18 Jan 06.

[Heid et al.2004] Ulrich Heid, Holger Voormann, Jan-Torsten Milde, Ulrike Gut, Katrin Erk, and Sebastian Pad. 2004. Querying both time-aligned and hierarchical corpora with NXT Search. In *Fourth Language Resources and Evaluation Conference*, Lisbon, Portugal.

[Iacob and Dekhtyar2005] Ionut E. Iacob and Alex Dekhtyar. 2005. Towards a query language for multihierarchical xml: Revisiting xpath. In *Eighth International Workshop on the Web and Databases (WebDB 2005)*, Baltimore, Maryland, USA, 16-17 June.

[National Institute of Standards and Technology2000] National Institute of Standards and Technology. 2000. ATLAS Project. http://www.nist.gov/speech/atlas/; last update 6 Feb 2003; accessed 18 Jan 06.

[Rohdend] Doug Rohde. n.d. Tgrep2. http://tedlab.mit.edu/ dr/Tgrep2/; accessed 18 Jan 06.

[Tiger Projectnd] Tiger Project. n.d. Linguistic interpretation of a German corpus. http://www.ims.uni-stuttgart.de/projekte/TIGER/; last update 17 Nov 2003; accessed 1 Mar 2004.

[University of Edinburgh Language Technology Groupnd] University of Edinburgh Language Technology Group. n.d. LTG Software. http://www.ltg.ed.ac.uk/software/; accessed 18 Jan 2006.

Multi-dimensional Annotation and Alignment in an English-German Translation Corpus

Silvia Hansen-Schirra
Computational Linguistics & Applied Linguistics, Translation and Interpreting
Saarland University, Germany
hansen@coli.uni-sb.de

Stella Neumann
Applied Linguistics, Translation and Interpreting
Saarland University, Germany
st.neumann@mx.uni-saarland.de

Mihaela Vela
Applied Linguistics, Translation and Interpreting
Saarland University, Germany
m.vela@mx.uni-saarland.de

Abstract

This paper presents the compilation of the CroCo Corpus, an English-German translation corpus. Corpus design, annotation and alignment are described in detail. In order to guarantee the searchability and exchangeability of the corpus, XML stand-off mark-up is used as representation format for the multi-layer annotation. On this basis it is shown how the corpus can be queried using XQuery. Furthermore, the generalisation of results in terms of linguistic and translational research questions is briefly discussed.

1 Introduction

In translation studies the question of how translated texts differ systematically from original texts has been an issue for quite some time with a surge of research in the last ten or so years. Example-based contrastive analyses of small numbers of source texts and their translations had previously described characteristic features of the translated texts, without the availability of more large-scale empirical testing. Blum-Kulka (1986), for instance, formulates the hypothesis that explicitation is a characteristic phenomenon of translated versus original texts on the basis of linguistic evidence from individual sample texts showing that translators explicitate optional cohesive markers in the target text not realised in the source text. In general, explicitation covers all features that make implicit information in the source text clearer and thus explicit in the translation (cf. Steiner 2005).

Building on example-based work like Blum-Kulka's, Baker put forward the notion of translation universals (cf. Baker 1996) which can be analysed in corpora of translated texts regardless of the source language in comparison to original texts in the target language. Olohan and Baker (2000) therefore analyse explicitation in English translations concentrating on the frequency of the optional *that* versus zero-connector in combination with the two verbs *say* and *tell.* While being extensive enough for statistical interpretation, corpus-driven research like Olohan and Baker's is limited in its validity to the selected strings.

More generally speaking, there is a gap between the abstract research object and the low level features used as indicators. This gap can be reduced by operationalising notions like explicittation into syntactic and semantic categories, which can be annotated and aligned in a corpus. Intelligent queries then produce linguistic evidence with more explanatory power than low level data obtained from raw corpora. The results are not restricted to the queried strings but extend to more complex units sharing the syntactic and/ or semantic properties obtained by querying the annotation.

This methodology serves as a basis for the CroCo project, in which the assumed translation property of explicitation is investigated for the language pair English – German. The empirical evidence for the investigation consists in a corpus of English originals, their German translations as well as German originals and their English translations. Both translation directions are represented in eight registers. Biber's calculations, i.e. 10 texts per register with a length of at least 1,000 words, serve as an orientation for the size of the sub-corpora (cf. Biber 1993). Altogether the CroCo Corpus comprises one million words. Additionally, reference corpora are included for German and English. The reference corpora are register-neutral including 2,000 word samples from 17 registers (see Neumann & Hansen-Schirra 2005 for more details on the CroCo corpus design).

The CroCo Corpus is tokenised and annotated for part-of-speech, morphology, phrasal categories and grammatical functions. Furthermore, the following (annotation) units are aligned: words, grammatical functions, clauses and sentences. The annotation and alignment steps are described in section 2.

Each annotation and alignment layer is stored separately in a multi-layer stand-off XML representation format. In order to empirically investigate the parallel corpus (e.g. to find evidence for explicitation in translations), XQuery is used for posing linguistic queries. The query process itself works on each layer separately, but can also be applied across different annotation and alignment layers. It is described in more detail in section 3. This way, parallel text segments and/or parallel annotation units can be extracted and compared for translations and originals in German and English.

2 CroCo XML

The annotation in CroCo extends to different levels in order to cover possible linguistic evidence on each level. Thus, each kind of annotation (part-of-speech, morphology, phrase structure, grammatical functions) is realised in a separate layer. An additional layer is included which contains comprehensive metainformation in separate header files for each text in the corpus. The file containing the indexed tokens (see section 2.1) includes an **xlink** attribute referring to this header file as depicted in Figure 2.1. The metadata are based on the TEI guidelines[1] and include register information. The complex multilingual structure of the corpus in combination with the multi-layer annotation requires indexing the corpus. The indexing is carried out on the basis of the tokenised corpus. Index and annotation layers are kept separate using XML stand-off mark-up. The mark-up builds on XCES[2]. Different formats of the multiple annotation and alignment outputs are converted with Perl scripts. Each annotation and alignment unit is indexed. The respective annotations and alignments are linked to the indexed units via XPointers.

The following sections describe the different annotation layers and are exemplified for the German original sentence in (1) and its English translation in (2)[3].

```
(1) Ich spielte viele Möglichkeiten
durch, stellte mir den Täter in
verschiedenen Posen vor, ich und
die Pistole, ich und die Giftfla-
sche, ich und der Knüppel, ich und
das Messer.
```

```
(2) I ran through numerous possibi-
lities, pictured the perpetrator in
various poses, me with the gun, me
with the bottle of poison, me with
the bludgeon, me with the knife.
```

2.1 Tokenisation and indexing

The first layer to be presented here is the tokenisation layer. Tokenisation is performed in CroCo for both German and English by TnT (Brants 2000), a statistical part-of-speech tagger. As shown in Figure 2.1 each token annotated with the attribute **strg** has also an **id** attribute, which indicates the position of the word in the text. This **id** represents the anchor for all XPointers pointing to the tokenisation file by an **id** starting with a "t". The file is identified by the **name** attribute. The **xml:lang** attribute indicates the language of the file, **docType** provides information on whether the present file is an original or a translation.

```
<document
xmlns:xlink="http://www.w3.org/1999/
xlink" name="GO.tok.xml" xml:lang="de"
docType="ori">
<header xlink:href="GO.header.xml"/>
 <tokens>
  <token id="t64" strg="Ich"/>
  <token id="t65" strg="spielte"/>
  <token id="t66" strg="viele"/>
  <token id="t67"
   strg="Möglichkeiten"/>
  <token id="t68" strg="durch"/>
  <token id="t69" strg=","/>
</tokens>
</document>
```

Figure 2.1. Tokenisation and indexing

Similar index files necessary for the alignment of the respective levels are created for the units chunk, clause and sentence. These units stand in

[1] http://www.tei-c.org
[2] http://www.xml-ces.org
[3] All examples are taken from the CroCo Corpus.

a hierarchical relation with sentences consisting of clauses, clauses consisting of chunks etc.

2.2 Part-of-speech tagging

The second layer annotated for both languages is the part-of-speech layer, which is provided again by TnT[4]. The token annotation of the part-of-speech layer starts with the **xml:base** attribute, which indicates the index file it refers to. The part-of-speech information for each token is annotated in the **pos** attribute, as shown in Figure 2.2. The attribute **strg** in the token index file and **pos** in the tag annotation are linked by an **xlink** attribute pointing to the **id** attribute in the index file. For example, the German token pointing to "t65" in the token index file whose **strg** value is *stellte* is a finite verb (with the PoS tag vvfin).

```
<document
xmlns:xlink="http://www.w3.org/1999/
xlink" name="GO.tag.xml">
 <tokens xml:base="GO.tok.xml">
  <token pos="pper" xlink:href="#t64"/>
  <token pos="vvfin"
   xlink:href="#t65"/>
  <token pos="pidat"
   xlink:href="#t66"/>
  <token pos="nn" xlink:href="#t67"/>
  <token pos="ptkvz"
   xlink:href="#68"/>
  <token pos="yc" xlink:href="#t69"/>
</tokens>
</document>
```

Figure 2.2. PoS tagging

2.3 Morphological annotation

Morphological information is particularly relevant for German due to the fact that this language carries much syntactic information within morphemes rather than in separate function words like English. Morphology is annotated in CroCo with MPro, a rule-based morphology tool (Maas 1998). This tool works on both languages. As shown in Figure 2.3 each token has morphological attributes such as **person**, **case**, **gender**, **number** and **lemma.** As before, the **xlink** attribute refers back to the index file, thus providing the connection between the morphological attributes and the **strg** information in the index file.

For the morphological annotation of the German token "t65" in Figure 2.3 the **strg** value is determined by following the XPointer "t65" to the token index file, i.e. *spielte*. The **pos** value is retrieved by searching in the tag annotation for the file with the same **xml:base** value. The matching tag, in this case vvfin, carries the same XPointer “t65”.

```
<document
xmlns:xlink="http://www.w3.org/1999/
xlink" name="GO.morph.xml">
 <tokens xml:base="GO.tok.xml">
  <token strg="Ich" per="1" case="nom"
   nb="sg" gender="f;m" lemma="ich"
   lb="ich" xlink:href="#t64"/>
  <token strg="spielte" vtype="fiv"
   tns="past" per="3" nb="sg"
   lemma="spielen" lb="spielen" comp=
   "spielen" xlink:href="#t65"/>
  <token strg="viele" case="nom;acc"
   nb="plu" gender="f" lemma="viel"
   lb="viel" comp="viel" deg="base"
   xlink:href="#t66"/>
  <token strg="Möglichkeiten" case=
   "nom;acc" nb="plu" gender="f" lemma=
   "möglichkeit" lb="möglich" comp=
   "möglichkeit" xlink:href="#t67"/>
  <token strg="durch" lemma="durch"
   lb="durch" pref="vzs"
   xlink:href="#t68"/>
  <token strg="," lemma="," lb=","
   xlink:href="#t69"/>
 </tokens>
</document>
```

Figure 2.3. Morphological annotation

2.4 Phrase chunking and annotation of grammatical functions

Moving up from the token unit to the chunk unit, first we have to index these units again before we can annotate them. The chunk index file assigns an **id** attribute to each chunk within the file. The problem of discontinuous phrase chunks is solved by listing child tags referring to the individual tokens which make up the chunk via **xlink** attributes. Figure 2.4 shows that the VP “ch14” in the German phrase annotation consists of “t70” (*stellte*) and “t77” (*vor*).

```
<document xmlns:xlink=
"http://www.w3.org/1999/xlink"
name="GO.chunk.xml">
 <chunks xml:base="GO.tok.xml">
  <chunk id="ch13">
   <tok xlink:href="#t66"/>
   <tok xlink:href="#t67"/>
  </chunk>
  <chunk id="ch14">
   <tok xlink:href="#t70"/>
  </chunk>
  <chunk id="ch15">
   <tok xlink:href="#t71"/>
  </chunk>
  <chunk id="ch16">
   <tok xlink:href="#t72"/>
   <tok xlink:href="#t73"/>
  </chunk>
```

[4] For German we use the STTS tag set (Schiller et al. 1999), and for English the Susanne tag set (Sampson 1995).

```
  <chunk id="ch17">
   <tok xlink:href="#t74"/>
   <chunk id="ch18">
    <tok xlink:href="#t75"/>
    <tok xlink:href="#t76"/>
   </chunk>
  </chunk>
  <chunk id="ch19">
    <tok xlink:href="#t77"/>
  </chunk>
 </chunks>
</document>
```

Figure 2.4. Chunk indexing

The phrase structure annotation (see Figure 2.5) assigns the **ps** attribute to each phrase chunk identified by MPro. XPointers link the phrase structure annotation to the chunk index file. It should be noted that in CroCo the phrase structure analysis is limited to higher chunk nodes, as our focus within this layer is more on complete phrase chunks and their grammatical functions.

```
<document
 xmlns:xlink="http://www.w3.org/1999/
 xlink" name="GO.ps.xml">
 <chunks xml:base="GO.chunk.xml">
  <chunk ps="NP" xlink:href="#ch13"/>
  <chunk ps="VPFIN"
   xlink:href="#ch14"/>
  <chunk ps="NP" xlink:href="#ch15"/>
  <chunk ps="NP" xlink:href="#ch16"/>
  <chunk ps="PP" xlink:href="#ch17"/>
  <chunk ps="NP" xlink:href="#ch18"/>
  <chunk ps="VPPRED"
   xlink:href="#ch19"/>
 </chunks>
</document>
```

Figure 2.5. Phrase structure annotation

The annotation of grammatical functions is again kept in a separate file (see Figure 2.6). Only the highest phrase nodes are annotated for their grammatical function with the attribute **gf**. The XPointer links the annotation of each function to the chunk **id** in the chunk index file. From this file in turn the string can be retrieved in the token annotation. For example, the English chunk "ch13" carries the grammatical function of direct object (DOBJ). It is identified as an NP in the phrase structure annotation by comparing the **xml:base** attribute value of the two files and the XPointers.

```
<document
xmlns:xlink="http://www.w3.org/1999/
xlink" name="GO.gf.xml">
 <chunks xml:base="GO.chunk.xml">
  <chunk gf="DOBJ" xlink:href="#ch13"/>
  <chunk gf="FIN" link:href="#ch14"/>
  <chunk gf="IOBJ" xlink:href="#ch15"/>
  <chunk gf="DOBJ" xlink:href="#ch16"/>
  <chunk gf="ADV" xlink:href="#ch17"/>
  <chunk gf="PRED" xlink:href="#ch19"/>
 </chunks>
</document>
```

Figure 2.6. Annotation of grammatical functions

2.5 Alignment

In the examples shown so far, the different annotation layers linked to each other all belonged to the same language. By aligning words, grammatical functions, clauses and sentences, the connection between original and translated text is made visible. The use of this multi-layer alignment will become clearer from the discussion of a sample query in section 3.

For the purpose of the CroCo project word alignment is realised with GIZA++ (Och & Ney 2003), a statistical alignment tool. Chunks and clauses are aligned manually with the help of MMAX II (Müller & Strube 2003), a tool allowing assignment of own categories and linking units. Finally, sentences are aligned using WinAlign, an alignment tool within the Translator's Workbench by Trados (Heyn 1996).

The alignment procedure produces four new layers. It follows the XCES standard. Figure 2.7 shows the chunk alignment of (1) and (2). In this layer, we align on the basis of grammatical functions instead of phrases since this annotation includes the information of the phrase chunking as well as on the semantic relations of the chunks. The grammatical functions are mapped onto each other cross-linguistically and then aligned according to our annotation and alignment scheme. The **trans.loc** attribute locates the chunk index file for the aligned texts in turn. Furthermore, the respective language as well as the **n** attribute organising the order of the aligned texts are given. We thus have an alignment tag for each language in each chunk pointing to the chunk index file. As can be seen from Figure 2.7, chunks which do not have a matching equivalent receive the value "#undefined", a phenomenon that will be of interest in the linguistic interpretation on the basis of querying the corpus.

```
<document
xmlns:xlink="http://www.w3.org/1999/
xlink" name="gfAlign.xml">
<translations xml:base="/CORPUS/">
<translation trans.loc="GO.chunk.xml"
xml:lang="de" n="1"/>
<translation
trans.loc="ETrans.chunk.xml"
xml:lang="en" n="2"/>
```

```
</translations>
 <chunks>
  <chunk>
   <align xlink:href="#ch14"/>
   <align xlink:href="#ch16"/>
  </chunk>
  <chunk>
   <align xlink:href="#ch15"/>
   <align xlink:href="#undefined"/>
  </chunk>
  <chunk>
   <align xlink:href="#ch16"/>
   <align xlink:href="#ch17"/>
  </chunk>
  <chunk>
   <align xlink:href="#ch17"/>
   <align xlink:href="#ch18"/>
  </chunk>
  <chunk>
   <align xlink:href="#ch19"/>
   <align xlink:href="#undefined"/>
  </chunk>
 </chunks>
</document>
```

Figure 2.7. Chunk alignment

3 Querying the CroCo Corpus

The comprehensive annotation including the alignment described in section 2 is the basis for the interpretation to be presented in what follows. We concentrate on two types of queries into the different alignment layers that are assumed relevant in connection with our research question.

3.1 Crossing lines and empty links

From the linguistic point of view we are interested in those units in the target text which do not have matches in the source text and vice versa, i.e. **empty links**, or whose alignment crosses the alignment of a higher level, i.e. **crossing lines**. We analyse for instance stretches of text contained in one sentence in the source text but spread over two sentences in the target text, as this probably has implications for the overall information contained in the target text. We would thus pose a query retrieving all instances where the alignment of the lower level is not parallel to the higher level alignment but points into another higher level unit. In the example below the German source sequence (3) as well as the English target sequence (4) both consist of three sentences. These sentences are each aligned as illustrated by dashed boxes in Figure 3.1.

```
(3) Aus dem Augenwinkel sah ich,
wie eine Schwester dem Bettnachbarn
das Nachthemd wechselte. Sie rieb
den Rücken mit Franzbranntwein ein
und massierte den etwas jüngeren
Mann, dessen Adern am ganzen Körper
bläulich hervortraten. Ihre Hände
ließen ihn leise wimmern.
```

```
(4) Out of the corner of my eye I
watched a nurse change his
neighbor's nightshirt and rub his
back with alcoholic liniment. She
massaged the slightly younger man,
whose veins stood out blue all over
his body. He whimpered softly under
her hands.
```

In German the first two sentences are subdivided into two clauses each. The English target sentences are co-extensive with the clauses contained in each sentence. This means that two English clauses have to accommodate four German clauses. Figure 3.1 shows that the German clause 3 (*Sie rieb den Rücken mit Franzbranntwein ein*) in sentence 2 is part of the bare infinitive complementation (*...and rub his back with alcoholic liniment*) in the English sentence 1. The alignment of this clause points out of the aligned first sentence, thus constituting crossing lines.

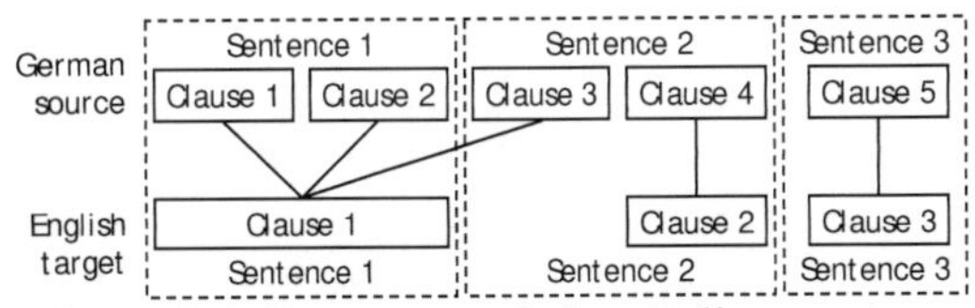

Figure 3.1. Sentence and clause alignment

The third sentence also contains a crossing line, in this case on the levels of chunk and word alignment: The words *Ihre Hände* in the German subject chunk are aligned with the words *her hands* in the English adverbial chunk. However, this sentence is particularly interesting in view of empty links. The query asks for units not matching any unit in the parallel text, i.e. for **xlink** attributes whose values are "#undefined" (cf. section 2.5). In Figure 3.2, the empty links are marked by a black dot.

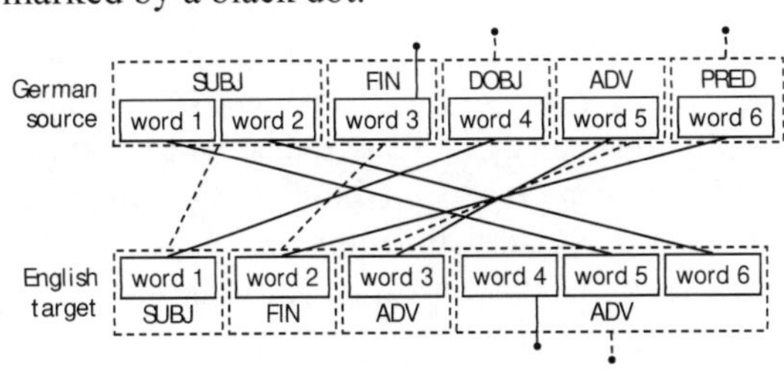

Figure 3.2. Chunk and word alignment

Our linguistic interpretation is based on a functional view of language. Hence, the finite *ließen* (word 3) in the German sentence is interpreted as a semi-auxiliary and thus as the finite part of the verbal group. Therefore, *wimmern* (word 6) receives the label PRED, i.e. the non-finite part of the verb phrase, in the functional analysis. This German word is linked to word 2 (*whimpered*) in the target sentence, which is assigned FIN, i.e. the finite verb in the layer of grammatical functions. As FIN exists both in the source and in the target sentences, this chunk is aligned. The German functional unit PRED does not have an equivalent in the target text and gets an empty link. Consequently, word 3 in the source sentence (*ließen*) receives an empty link as well. This mismatch will be interpreted in view of our translation-oriented research. In the following subsection we will see how these two phenomena can be retrieved automatically.

3.2 Corpus exploitation using XQuery

Since the multi-dimensional annotation and alignment is realised in XML, the queries are posed using XQuery[5]. This query language is particularly suited to retrieve information from different sources like for instance individual annotation and alignment files. The use for multi-layer annotation is shown in (Teich et al. 2001).

The query for determining an empty link at word level can be formulated as follows: find all words which do not have an aligned correspondent, i.e. which carry the **xlink** attribute value "#undefined". The same query can be applied on the chunk level, the query returning the grammatical functions that do not have an equivalent in the other language.

```
(5)Ihre Hände ließen ihn leise wim-
mern.
```

```
(6) He whimpered softly under her
hands.
```

Applied to the sentences in (5) and (6) the XQuery in Figure 3.3 returns all German and English words, which receive an empty link due to a missing equivalent in alignment (*ließen* and *under*). This query can be used analogously in all other alignment layers. It implies the call of a self-defined XQuery function (see Figure 3.4), which looks in the correspondent index file for words not aligned.

[5] http://www.w3.org/TR/xquery

```
let $doc := .
for $k in $doc//tokens/token
return
 if ($k/align[1][@xlink:href="#un-
  defined"] and $k/align[2]
  [@xlink:href!="#undefined"])
 then local:getString($k/align[1]/
  @xlink:href,$k/align[2]/@xlink:href,
  $doc//translations/translation
  [@n='2']/@trans.loc)
 else if ($k/align[1][@xlink:href
  !="#undefined"] and $k/align[2]
  [@xlink:href="#undefined"])
 then local:getString($k/align[1]/
  @xlink:href,$k/align[2]/@xlink:href,
  $doc//translations/translation
  [@n='1']/@trans.loc)
 else ()
```

Figure 3.3. XQuery for empty links

```
declare function local:getString
($firstToken as xs:string,$secondTo-
ken as xs:string,$fileName as
xs:string) as element()
 {let $res:=(if(($firstToken eq
  "#undefined") and ($lang eq doc
  ($fileName)//document/@xml:lang))
  then doc($fileName)//tokens/token[@id
  eq substring-after($secondToken,"#")]
  else if (($secondToken eq "#unde-
  fined") and ($lang eq doc($fileName)
  //document/@xml:lang))
  then doc($fileName)//tokens/token[@id
  eq substring-after($firstToken,"#")]
  else ())
return
 <token>{$res/@strg}</token>};
```

Figure 3.4. XQuery function for missing alignment

Querying crossing lines in the German source sentence in (5) and the English target sentence in (6) is based on the annotation at word level as well as on the annotation at the chunk level. As mentioned in section 3.1, crossing lines are identified in (5) and (6) if the words contained in the chunks aligned on the grammatical function layer are not aligned on the word level. This means that the German subject is aligned with the English subject, but the words within the subject chunk are aligned with words in other grammatical functions instead.

In a first step, the query for determining a crossing line requires information about all aligned German chunks with a **xlink** attribute whose value is not "#undefined" and all aligned German words with a **xlink** attribute whose value is not "#undefined". Then all German words that are not aligned on the word level but are aligned as part of chunks on the chunk level are filtered out. Figure 3.6 reflects the respective XQuery.

```
let $doc := .
for $k in $doc//chunks/chunk
let $ch1:=(if($k/align[1][@xlink:href
 !="#undefined"] and $k/align[2]
 [@xlink:href!="#undefined"])
 then doc($doc//translations/trans-
 lation[@n='1']/@trans.loc)//chunks
 /chunk[@id eq substring-after
 ($k/align[1]/@xlink:href,"#")]
 else ())
let $ch2:=(if($k/align[1][@xlink:href
 !="#undefined"] and $k/align[2]
 [@xlink:href!="#undefined"])
 then (doc($doc//translations/transla-
 tion[@n='2']/@trans.loc)//chunks/chunk
 [@id eq substring-after($k/align[2]/
 @xlink:href,"#")])
 else ())
for $i in doc("g2e.tokenAlign.xml")
 //tokens/token
let $tok1:=(if($i/align[1][@xlink:href
 !="#undefined"] and $i/align[2]
 [@xlink:href!="#undefined"])
 then(doc(doc("g2e.tokenAlign.xml")
 //translations/translation[@n='1']
 /@trans.loc)//tokens/token[@id eq
 substring-after($i/align[1]
 /@xlink:href,"#")])
 else ())
let $tok2:=(if($i/align[1][@xlink:href
 !="#undefined"] and $i/align[2]
 [@xlink:href!="#undefined"])
 then(doc(doc("g2e.tokenAlign.xml")
 //translations/translation[@n='2']
 /@trans.loc)//tokens/token[@id eq
 substring-after($i/align[2]
 /@xlink:href,"#")])
 else ())
where(local:containsToken($ch1/tok
 [position()=1],$ch1/tok[last()],$tok1
 /@id) and not(local:containsToken
 ($ch2/tok[position()=1],
 $ch2/tok[last()],$tok2/@id)))
return $tok1
```

Figure 3.6. XQuery for crossing lines

First, the aligned chunks (**$ch1** and **$ch2**) are saved into variables. These values are important in order to detect the span for each of the chunks (**$ch1/tok[position()=1], $ch1/tok[last()]** and **$ch2/tok[position()=1], $ch2/tok[last()]**), and to identify the words making up the source chunks as well as their German or English equivalents. In the second step all words that do not have empty links are saved (**$tok1** and **$tok2**). The last step filters the crossing lines, i.e. word alignments pointing out of the chunk alignment. For this purpose, we define a new function (**local:-containsToken**) which tests whether a word belongs to a chunk or not. By applying **local:containsToken** for the German original and **not-(local:containsToken)** for the English translation, all words in the German chunks whose aligned English equivalent words do not belong to the aligned English chunks are retrieved. The example query returns the German words *Ihre Hände* that are part of the German subject chunk and which are aligned with the English words *her hands* that again are part of the second adverbial chunk.

4 Summary and conclusions

In a broader view, it can be observed that there is an increasing need in richly annotated corpora across all branches of linguistics. The same holds for linguistically interpreted parallel corpora in translation studies. Usually, though, the problem with large-scale corpora is that they do not reflect the complexity of linguistic knowledge we are used to dealing with in linguistic theory. Simple research questions can of course be answered on the basis of raw corpora or with the help of an automatic part-of-speech tagging. Most linguistics and translation scholars are, however, interested in more complex questions like the interaction of syntax and semantics across languages.

The research described here shows the use of comprehensive multi-layer annotation across languages. By relating a highly abstract research question to multiple layers of lexical and grammatical realisations, characteristic patterns of groups of texts, e.g. explicitation in translations and originals in the case of the CroCo project, can be identified on the basis of statistically relevant linguistic evidence.

If we want to enrich corpora with multiple kinds of linguistic information, we need a linguistically motivated model of the linguistic units and relations we would like to extract and draw conclusions based on an annotated and aligned corpus. So the first step for the compilation of a parallel translation corpus is to provide a classification of linguistic units and relations and their mappings across source and target languages. The classification of English and German linguistic units and relations chosen for the CroCo project (i.e. for the investigation of explicitation in translations and originals) is reflected in the CroCo annotation and alignment schemes and thus in the CroCo Corpus annotation and alignment.

From a technical point of view, the representation of a multilingual resource comprehensively annotated and aligned is to be realised in such a way that

- multiple linguistic perspectives on the corpus are possible since different annotations and alignments can be investigated independently or in combination,
- the corpus format guarantees best possible accessibility and exchangeability, and
- the exploitation of the corpus is possible using easily available tools for search and analysis.

We coped with this challenge by introducing a multi-layer stand-off corpus representation format in XML (see section 2), which takes into account not only the different annotation layers needed from a linguistic point of view, but also multiple alignment layers necessary to investigate different translation relations.

We also showed how the CroCo resource can be applied to complex research questions in linguistics and translation studies using XQuery to retrieve multi-dimensional linguistic information (see section 3). Based on the stand-off storage of annotation and alignment layers combined with the possibility to exploit the required layers through intelligent queries, parallel text segments and/or parallel annotation units can be extracted and compared across languages.

In order to make the CroCo resource available to researchers not familiar with the complexities of XML mark-up and the XQuery language, a graphical user interface will be implemented in Java which allows formulating queries without knowledge of the XQuery syntax.

Acknowledgement

The authors would like to thank the reviewers for their excellent comments and helpful feedback on previous versions of this paper.

The research described here is sponsored by the German Research Foundation as project no. STE 840/5-1.

References

Mona Baker. 1996. Corpus-based translation studies: The challenges that lie ahead. In Harold Somers (ed.). *Terminology, LSP and Translation.* Benjamins, Amsterdam:175-186.

Douglas Biber. 1993. Representativeness in Corpus Design. *Literary and Linguistic Computing* 8/4:243-257.

Shoshana Blum-Kulka. 1986. Shifts of cohesion and coherence in Translation. In Juliane House and Shoshana Blum-Kulka (eds.). *Interlingual and Intercultural Communication.* Gunter Narr, Tübingen:17-35.

Thorsten Brants. 2000. TnT - A Statistical Part-of-Speech Tagger. *Proceedings of the Sixth Applied Natural Language Processing Conference ANLP-2000*, Seattle, WA.

Matthias Heyn. 1996. Integrating machine translation into translation memory systems. *European Association for Machine Translation - Workshop Proceedings*, ISSCO, Geneva:111-123.

Heinz Dieter Maas. 1998. Multilinguale Textverarbeitung mit MPRO. *Europäische Kommunikationskybernetik heute und morgen '98*, Paderborn.

Christoph Müller and Michael Strube. 2003. Multi-Level Annotation in MMAX. *Proceedings of the 4th SIGdial Workshop on Discourse and Dialogue*, Sapporo, Japan:198-107.

Stella Neumann and Silvia Hansen-Schirra. 2005. The CroCo Project: Cross-linguistic corpora for the investigation of explicitation in translations. In *Proceedings from the Corpus Linguistics Conference Series*, Vol. 1, no. 1, ISSN 1747-9398.

Franz Josef Och and Hermann Ney. 2003. A Systematic Comparison of Various Statistical Alignment Models. *Journal of Computational Linguistics* Nr.1, vol. 29:19-51.

Maeve Olohan and Mona Baker. 2000. Reporting *that* in Translated English. Evidence for Subconscious Processes of Explicitation? *Across Languages and Cultures* 1(2):141-158.

Geoffrey Sampson. 1995. *English for the Computer. The Susanne Corpus and Analytic Scheme.* Clarendon Press, Oxford.

Anne Schiller, Simone Teufel and Christine Stöckert. 1999. Guidelines für das Tagging deutscher Textkorpora mit STTS, *University of Stuttgart and Seminar für Sprachwissenschaft*, University of Tübingen.

Erich Steiner. 2005. Explicitation, its lexicogrammatical realization, and its determining (independent) variables – towards an empirical and corpus-based methodology. *SPRIKreports* 36:1-43.

Elke Teich, Silvia Hansen, and Peter Fankhauser. 2001. Representing and querying multi-layer annotated corpora. *Proceedings of the IRCS Workshop on Linguistic Databases.* Philadelphia: 228-237.

Querying XML documents with multi-dimensional markup

Peter Siniakov
siniakov@inf.fu-berlin.de
Database and Information Systems Group, Freie Universität Berlin
Takustr. 9, 14195 Berlin, Germany

Abstract

XML documents annotated by different NLP tools accommodate multi-dimensional markup in a single hierarchy. To query such documents one has to account for different possible nesting structures of the annotations and the original markup of a document. We propose an expressive pattern language with extended semantics of the sequence pattern, supporting negation, permutation and regular patterns that is especially appropriate for querying XML annotated documents with multi-dimensional markup. The concept of fuzzy matching allows matching of sequences that contain textual fragments and known XML elements independently of how concurrent annotations and original markup are merged. We extend the usual notion of sequence as a sequence of siblings allowing matching of sequence elements on the different levels of nesting and abstract so from the hierarchy of the XML document. Extended sequence semantics in combination with other language patterns allows more powerful and expressive queries than queries based on regular patterns.

1 Introduction

XML is widely used by NLP tools for annotating texts. Different NLP tools can produce overlapping annotations of text fragments. While a common way to cope with concurrent markup is using stand-off markup (Witt, 2004) with XPointer references to the annotated regions in the source document, another solution is to consolidate the annotations in a single document for easier processing. In that case concurrent markup has to be merged and accommodated in a single hierarchy. There are many ways to merge the overlapping markup so that different nesting structures are possible. Besides, the annotations have to be merged with the original markup of the document (e.g. in case of a HTML document). The problem of merging overlapping markup has been treated in (Siefkes, 2004) and we do not consider it here. Instead we focus on the problem of finding a universal querying mechanism for documents with multi-dimensional markup. The query language should abstract from the concrete merging algorithm for concurrent markup, that is to identify desired elements and sequences of elements independently from the concrete nesting structure.

The development of the query language was motivated by an application in text mining. In some text mining systems the linguistic patterns that comprise text and XML annotations (such as syntactic annotations, POS tags) made by linguistic tools are matched with semistructured texts to find desired information. These texts can be HTML documents that are enriched with linguistic information by NLP tools and therefore contain multi-dimensional markup. The linguistic annotations are specified by XML elements that contain the annotated text fragment as CDATA. Due to the deliberate structure of the HTML document the annotations can be nested in arbitrary depth and vice versa – the linguistic XML element can contain some HTML elements with nested text it refers to. To find a linguistic pattern we have to abstract from the concrete DTD and actual structure of the XML document ignoring irrelevant markup, which leads to some kind of "fuzzy" matching. Hence it is sufficient to specify a sequence of text fragments and known XML elements (e.g. linguistic tags) without knowing by what elements they are nested. During the matching process the nesting markup will be omitted even if the sequence elements are on different nesting levels.

We propose an expressive pattern language with the extended semantics of the sequence pattern, permutation, negation and regular patterns that is especially appropriate for querying XML annotated documents. The language provides a rich tool set for specifying complex sequences of XML elements and textual fragments. We ignore some important aspects of a fully-fledged XML query language such as construction of result sets, aggregate functions or support of all XML Schema structures focusing instead on the semantics of the language.

Some modern XML query languages impose a relational view of data contained in the XML document aiming at retrieval of sets of elements with certain properties. While these approaches are adequate for database-like XML documents, they are less appropriate for documents in that XML is used rather for annotation than for representation of data. Taking the rather textual view of a XML document its querying can be regarded as finding patterns that comprise XML elements and textual content. One of the main differences when querying annotated texts is that the query typically captures parts of the document that go beyond the boundaries of a single element disrupting the XML tree structure while querying a database-like document returns its subtrees remaining within a scope of an element. Castagna (Castagna, 2005) distinguishes path expressions that rather correspond to the database view and regular expression patterns as complementary "extraction primitives" for XML data. Our approach enhances the concept of regular expression patterns making them mutually recursive and matching across the element boundaries.

2 Related Work

After publishing the XML 1.0 recommendation the early proposals for XML query languages focused primarily on the representation of hierarchical dependencies between elements and the expression of properties of a single element. Typically, hierarchical relations are defined along parent/child and ancestor/descendant axis as done in XQL and XPath. XQL (Robie, 1998) supports positional relations between the elements in a sibling list. Sequences of elements can be queried by "immediately precedes" and "precedes" operators restricted on the siblings. Negation, conjunction and disjunction are defined as filtering functions specifying an element. XPath 1.0 (Clark and DeRose, 1999) is closely related addressing primarily the structural properties of an XML document by path expressions. Similarly to XQL sequences are defined on sibling lists. Working Draft for Xpath 2.0 (Berglund et al., September 2005) provides support for more data types than its precursor, especially for sequence types defining set operations on them.

XML_QL (Deutsch et al., 1999) follows the relational paradigm for XML queries, introduces variable binding to multiple nodes and regular expressions describing element paths. The queries are resolved using an XML graph as the data model, which allows both ordered and unordered node representation. XQuery (Boag et al., 2003) shares with XML_QL the concept of variable bindings and the ability to define recursive functions. XQuery features more powerful iteration over elements by FLWR expression borrowed from *Quilt* (Chamberlin et al., 2001), string operations, "if else" case differentiation and aggregate functions. The demand for stronger support of querying annotated texts led to the integration of the full-text search in the language (Requirements, 2003) enabling full-text queries across the element boundaries.

Hosoya and Pierce propose integration of XML queries in a programming language (Hosoya and Pierce, 2001) based on regular patterns Kleene's closure and union with the "first-match" semantics. Pattern variables can be declared and bound to the corresponding XML nodes during the matching process. A static type inference system for pattern variables is incorporated in *XDuce* (Hosoya and Pierce, 2003) – a functional language for XML processing. *CDuce* (Benzaken et al., 2003) extends *XDuce* by an efficient matching algorithm for regular patterns and first class functions. A query language *CQL* based on regular patterns of *CDuce* uses *CDuce* as a query processor and allows efficient processing of *XQuery* expressions (Benzaken et al., 2005). The concept of fuzzy matching has been inroduced in query languages for IR (Carmel et al., 2003) relaxing the notion of context of an XML fragment.

3 Querying by pattern matching

The general purpose of querying XML documents is to identify and process their fragments that satisfy certain criteria. We reduce the problem of querying XML to pattern matching. The patterns specify the query statement describing the desired properties of XML fragments while the matching fragments constitute the result of the query. Therefore the pattern language serves as the query language and its expressiveness is crucial for the capabilities of the queries. The scope for the query execution can be a collection of XML documents, a single document or analogously to XPath a subtree within a document with the current context node as its root. Since in the scope of the query there may be several XML fragments matching the pattern, multiple matches are treated according to the "all-match" policy, i.e. all matching fragments are included in the result set. The pattern language does not currently support construction of new XML elements (however, it can be extended adding corresponding syntactic constructs). The result of the query is therefore a set of sequences of XML nodes from the document. Single sequences represent the XML fragments that match the query pattern. If no XML fragments in the query scope match the pattern, an empty result set is returned.

In the following sections the semantics, main components and features of the pattern language are introduced and illustrated by examples. The complete EBNF specification of the language can be found on `http://page.mi.fu-berlin.de/~siniakov/patlan`.

3.1 Extended sequence semantics

Query languages based on path expressions usually return sets (or sequences) of elements that are conform with the original hierarchical structure of the document. In not uniformly structured XML documents, though, the hierarchical structure of the queried documents is unknown. The elements we may want to retrieve or their sequences can be arbitrarily nested. When retrieving the specified elements the nesting elements can be omitted disrupting the original hierarchical structure. Thus a sequence of elements does no longer have to be restricted to the sibling level and may be extended to a sequence of elements following each other on different levels of XML tree.

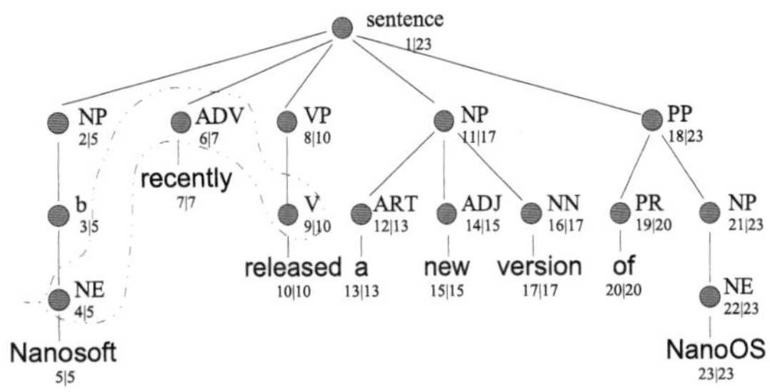

Figure 1: Selecting the sequence (NE ADV V) from a chunk-parsed POS-tagged sentence. XML nodes are labeled with preorder numbered *OID|right bound* (maximum descendant *OID*)

To illustrate the semantics and features of the language we will use the mentioned text mining scenario. In this particular text mining task some information in HTML documents with textual data should be found. The documents contain linguistic annotations inserted by POS tagger and syntactic chunk parser as XML elements that include the annotated text fragment as a text node. The XML output of the NLP tools is merged with the HTML markup so that various nestings are possible. A common technique to identify the relevant information is to match linguistic patterns describing it with the documents. The fragments of the documents that match are likely to contain relevant information. Hence the problem is to identify the fragments that match our linguistic patterns, that is, to answer the query where the queried fragments are described by linguistic patterns. Linguistic patterns comprise sequences of text fragments and XML elements added by NLP tools and are specified in our pattern language. When looking for linguistic patterns in an annotated HTML document, it cannot be predicted how the linguistic elements are nested because nesting depends on syntactic structure of a sentence, HTML layout and the way both markups are merged. Basically, the problem of unpredictable nesting occurs in any document with a heterogeneous structure. Let us assume we would search for a sequence of POS tags: `NE ADV V` in a subtree of a HTML document depicted in fig. 1. Some POS tags are chunked in noun (NP), verb (VP) or prepositional phrases (PP). Named entity "Nanosoft" is emphasized in boldface and therefore nested by the HTML element <b>. Due to the syntactic structure and the HTML markup the elements `NE, ADV` and `V` are on different nesting levels and not children of the same element. According to the extended sequence semantics we can ignore the nesting elements we are not interested in (NP_{OID2} and b_{OID3} when matching NE, VP_{OID8} when matching V) so that the sequence (NE_{OID4}, ADV_{OID6}, V_{OID9}) matches the sequence pattern `NE ADV V`, in short form `NE ADV V` $\cong$ (NE_4, ADV_6, V_9).

By the previous example we introduced the matching relation $\cong$ as a binary relation $\cong \subseteq P \times F$ where P is the set of patterns and F a set of XML fragments. An XML fragment f is a sequence of XML nodes $n_1 \ldots n_n$ that belong to the subtree of the context node (i.e. the node whose subtree is queried, e.g. document root). Each XML node in the subtree is labeled by the pair *OID|right bound*. *OID* is obtained assigning natural numbers to the nodes during the preorder traversal. *Right bound* is the maximum *OID* of a descendant of the node – the *OID* of the rightmost leaf in the rightmost subtree. To match a sequence pattern an XML fragment has to fulfil four important requirements.

1. Consecutiveness: All elements of the sequence pattern have to match the consecutive parts of the XML fragment

2. Order maintenance: Its elements must be in the "tree order", i.e., the *OIDs* of the nodes according to the preorder numbering schema must be in ascending order.

3. Absence of overlaps: No node in the sequence can be the predecessor of any other node in the sequence on the way to the root. E.g. `NP PP NP` $\not\cong$ (NP_{11}, PP_{18}, NP_{21}) because PP_{18} is a predecessor of NP_{21} and therefore subsumes it in its subtree. The semantics of the sequence implies that a sequence element cannot be subsumed by the previous one but has to follow it in another subtree. To determine whether a node m is a predecessor of the node n the *OIDs* of the nodes are compared. The predecessor must have a smaller *OID* according to the preorder numbering scheme, however any node in left subtrees of n has a smaller *OID* too. Therefore the *right bounds* of the nodes can be compared since the *right bound* of a predecessor will be greater or equal to the *right bound* of n while the *right bound* of any element in the left subtree will be smaller:

$$pred(m, n) =$$
$$OID(m) < OID(n) \wedge rightBound(m) \geq rightBound(n)$$

4. Completeness: XML fragment must not contain any gaps, i.e. there should not be a node that is not in the XML fragment, not predecessor of one of the nodes, whose *OID* however lies between the *OIDs* of the fragment nodes. Since such a node is not a predecessor, it must be an element of the sequence; otherwise it is omitted and the sequence is not complete. Hence, the pattern `V NP NP` $\not\cong$ (V_9, NP_{11}, NP_{21}) because the node PR_{19} lying between NP_{11} and NP_{21} is not a predecessor of any of the fragment nodes and not an element of the fragment. If the nodes lying between NP_{11} and NP_{21} cannot be exactly specified, we can use wildcard pattern (see sec. 3.3) to enable matching: `V NP * NP` $\cong$ (V_9, NP_{11}, PR_{19}, NP_{21}):

Using these requirements we can formally specify the semantics of the sequence:
Let $s = s_1 \ldots s_k$ be a sequence pattern and $f = n_1 \ldots n_n$ the matching XML fragment.

$$s \cong f \Leftrightarrow$$

(*I*) $s_1 \cong (n_1 \ldots n_i),\ s_2 \cong (n_{i+1} \ldots n_j), \ldots, s_k \cong (n_l \ldots n_n)$

(*II*) $\forall\ 1 \leq i < n\ OID(n_i) < OID(n_{i+1})$

(*III*) $\nexists\ 1 \leq i < n\ pred(n_i, n_{i+1})$

(*IV*) $\forall\ 1 \leq i < n\ \nexists\ m\ OID(n_i) < OID(m) < OID(n_{i+1}) \wedge$
$\wedge \neg pred(m, n_{i+1})$

The fourth requirement stresses the important aspect of "exhaustive" sequence: we are interested in a certain sequence of known elements that can be arbitrarily nested and captured by some elements that are irrelevant for our sequence (e.g. html layout elements when searching for a sequence of linguistic elements). We call such a sequence an *exhaustive non-sibling sequence* (*ENSS*). It is exhaustive because all predecessors omitted during the matching are covered at some level by the matching descendants so that there is no path to a leaf of the predecessor subtree that leads through an unmatched node. If such a path existed, the fourth requirement would not be met. If the sequence does not begin at the leftmost branch or does not end at the rightmost branch of an omitted predecessor, the subtree of the respective predecessor is not fully covered. In `ADJ NN PR` ≅ (ADJ_{14}, NN_{16}, PR_{19}) the omitted predecessors NP_{11} and PP_{18} are not completely a part of the sequence because they have descendants outside the sequence borders. Nevertheless the sequence is exhaustive since there is no path to a leaf through an unmatched node within its borders.

Another important aspect of *ENSS* is that it can match XML fragments across the element borders. XPath imposes a query context by specifying the path expression that usually addresses a certain element, XQuery restricts it indirect by iterating over and binding variables to certain nodes. Matching *ENSS* there is no additional restriction of the query scope, that is, the sequence can begin and end at any node provided that the *ENSS* requirements are met. The dashed line in the fig. 1 points up the region covered by the sample sequence.

According to the specification of the sequence pattern in the pattern language (cf. appendix ??):
Pattern ::= Pattern′ ′ Pattern*
any pattern can be the element of the sequence. Therefore the sequence can also contain textual elements, which is especially important when processing annotated texts. Textual nodes represent leaves in an XML tree and are treated as other XML nodes so that arbitrary combinations of XML elements and text are possible: `"released" NP "of" NE` ≅ ("released"$_{10}$, NP_{11}, "of"$_{20}$, NE_{22})

Exhaustive sequence allows a much greater abstraction from the DTD of a document than the usually used sequence of siblings. The expressiveness of the language significantly benefits from the combination of backtracking patterns (cf. sec. 3.3) with exhaustive sequence.

3.2 Specification of XML nodes

Patterns matching single XML nodes are the primitives that the more complex patterns are composed from. The pattern language supports matching for document, element, attribute, text and CDATA nodes while some DOM node types such as entities and processing instructions are not supported. Some basic patterns matching element and text nodes have been already used as sequence elements in the previous section. Besides the simple addressing of an element by its name it is possible to specify the structure of its subtree:
Pattern ::=′ \′XML-Tag(′[′Pattern′]′)?
A pattern specifying an element node will match if the element has the name corresponding to the XML-Tag and the pattern in the square brackets matches the XML fragment containing the sequence of its children. E.g. `\PP[ PR NE]` ≅ (PP_{18}) because the name of the element is identical and `PR NE` ≅ (PR_{19}, NE_{22}). As this example shows, the extended sequence semantics applies also when the sequence is used as the inner pattern of another pattern. Therefore the specification of elements can benefit from the *ENSS* because we again do not have to know the exact structure of their subtrees, e.g. their children, but can specify the nodes we expect to occur in a certain order.

Attribute nodes can be accessed by element pattern specifying the attribute values as a constraint: `\V {@normal="release"}` ≅ (V_9), assumed that the element V_9 has the attribute "normal" that stores the principal form of its textual content. Besides equality tests, numeric comparisons and boolean functions on string attribute values can be used as constraints.

Patterns specifying textual nodes comprise quoted strings:
Pattern ::= QuotedString
and match a textual node of an XML element if it has the same textual content as the quoted string. Textual patterns can be used as ele-

ments of any other patterns as already demonstrated in the previous section. An element may be, for instance, described by a complex sequence of text nodes combined with other patterns: `\sentence[NE * \V{@normal=release} \NP[* "new" "version"] "of" NE *]` ≅ (sentence_1)
The pattern above can already be used as a linguistic pattern identifying the release of a new product version.

3.3 Backtracking patterns and variables

In contrast to the database-like XML documents featuring very rigid and repetitive structures annotated texts are distinguished by a very big structural variety. To handle this variety one needs patterns that can cover several different cases "at once". So called backtracking patterns have this property and constitute therefore a substantial part of the pattern language. Their name comes from the fact that during the matching process backtracking is necessary to find a match.

The pattern language features complex and primitive patterns. Complex patterns consist of at least one inner element that is a pattern itself. Primitive patterns are textual patterns or XML attribute and element specifications if the specification of the inner structure of the element is omitted, e.g. `"released"`, `NP`. If at least one of the inner patterns does not match, the matching of the complex pattern fails. Backtracking patterns except for wildcard pattern are complex patterns.

Let us assume, we look for a sequence `"released" NE` and do not care what is between the two sequence elements. In the subtree depicted in fig. 1 no XML fragment will match because there are several nodes between "released"_{10} and NE_{22} and the completeness requirement is not met. If we include the wildcard pattern in the sequence, `"released" * NE` ≅ ("released"_{10} NP_{11} PR_{19} NE_{22}), the wildcard pattern matches the nodes lying between V_9 and NE_{22}. Thus, every time we do not know what nodes can occur in a sequence or we are not interested in the nodes in some parts of the sequence, we can use wildcard pattern to specify the sequence without losing its completeness. Wildcard pattern matches parts of the sequence that are in turn sequences themselves. Therefore it matches only those XML fragments that fulfil the *ENSS* requirements II-IV. Since there are often multiple possibilities to match a sequence on different levels, wildcard matches nodes that are at the highest possible level such as NP_{11} in the previous example.

If one does not know whether an XML fragment occurs, but wants to account for both cases the option pattern should be used:
Pattern ::=' ('Pattern')?'
Pattern ::=' ('Pattern')*'
Kleene closure differs from the option by the infinite number of repetitions. It matches a sequence of any number of times repeated XML fragments that match the inner pattern of the Kleene closure pattern. Since Kleene closure matches sequences, the *ENSS* requirements have to be met by matching XML fragments. Let $O = (\mathsf{p})?$ be an option, $K = (\mathsf{p})^*$ a Kleene closure pattern, $f \in F$ an XML fragment:

$$O \cong f \quad \Leftrightarrow \quad \mathsf{p} \cong f \ \vee \ \{\} \cong f$$
$$K \cong f \quad \Leftrightarrow \quad \{\} \cong f \ \vee \ \mathsf{p} \cong f \ \vee \ \mathsf{p}\,\mathsf{p} \cong f \ \vee \ \ldots$$

where f fulfils *ENSS* requirements I-IV.
The option pattern matches either an empty XML fragment or its inner pattern.

An alternative occurrence of two XML fragments is covered by the union pattern:
Pattern ::=' ('Pattern('|'Pattern)+')'
Different order of nodes in the sequence can be captured in the permutation pattern:
Pattern ::=' ('Pattern Pattern+')%'
Let $U = (\mathsf{p}_1|\mathsf{p}_2)$ be a union pattern, $P = (\mathsf{p}_1, \ldots, \mathsf{p}_n)\%$ a permutation pattern

$$U \cong f \quad \Leftrightarrow \quad \mathsf{p}_1 \cong f \vee \mathsf{p}_2 \cong f$$
$$P \cong f \quad \Leftrightarrow \quad \mathsf{p}_1\ \mathsf{p}_2 \ldots \mathsf{p}_n \cong f \ \vee\ \mathsf{p}_1\ \mathsf{p}_2 \ldots \mathsf{p}_n\ \mathsf{p}_{n-1} \cong f\ \vee \cdots$$
$$\cdots \vee\ \mathsf{p}_1\ \mathsf{p}_n \ldots \mathsf{p}_2 \cong f\ \vee\ \cdots \vee\ \mathsf{p}_n\ \mathsf{p}_{n-1} \ldots \mathsf{p}_2\ \mathsf{p}_1 \cong f$$

Permutation can not be expressed by regular constructs and is therefore not a regular expression itself.

The backtracking patterns can be arbitrarily combined to match complex XML fragments. E.g. the pattern `((PP | PR)? NP)%` matches three XML fragments: (NP_2), (NP_{11}, PP_{18}) and (PR_{19}, NP_{21}). Using the backtracking patterns recursively enlarges the expressivity of the patterns a lot allowing to specify very complex and variable structures without significant syntactic effort.

Variables can be assigned to any pattern Pattern ::= Pattern′ =:′ String accomplishing two functions. Whenever a variable is referenced within a pattern by the reference pattern Pattern ::=′ \$′String′\$′ it evaluates to the pattern it was assigned to. The pattern `(NP)*=:noun_phrase * $noun_phrase$` $\cong$ (NP_2, ADV_6, VP_8, NP_{11}) so that the referenced pattern matches NP_{11}. A pattern referencing the variable v matches XML fragments that match the pattern that has been assigned to v. To make the matching results more persistent and enable further processing variables can be bound to the XML fragment that matched the pattern the variable is assigned to. After matching the pattern `\sentence[NE=:company * \V{@normal=release} \NP[* "new" "version"] "of" NE=:product *]` $\cong$ ($sentence_1$) the variable `company` refers to NE_4(Nanosoft) and `product` is bound to NE_{22}(NanoOS). The relevant parts of XML fragment can be accessed by variables after a match has been found. Assigning variable to the wildcard pattern can be used to extract a subsequence between two known nodes: `"released" * =:direct_object "of"` $\cong$ ("released"$_{10}$ NP_{11} "of"$_{20}$) with the variable `direct_object` bound to NP_{11}.
Let $A = \mathsf{p} =: \mathsf{v}$ be an assignment pattern:

$$A \cong f \Leftrightarrow \mathsf{p} \cong f$$

Matching backtracking patterns can involve multiple matching variants of the same XML fragment, which usually leads to different variable bindings for each matching variant. As opposed to multiple matchings when different fragments match the same pattern discussed above, the first-match policy is applied when the pattern ambiguously matches a XML fragment. For instance,two different matching variants are possible for the pattern `(NP)?:=noun_phrase (NP |PR)*:=noun_prep` $\cong$ (NP_{11}, PR_{19}). In the first case `(NP)?:=noun_phrase` $\cong$ (NP_{11}) so that `noun_phrase` is bound to NP_{11} and `noun_prep` to PR_{19}. In the second case `(NP)?:=noun_phrase` $\cong$ {} and `(NP | PR)*:=noun_prep` $\cong$ (NP_{11}, PR_{19}) so that `noun_phrase` is bound to {} and `noun_prep` to (NP_{11}, PR_{19}). In such cases the first found match is returned as the final result. The order of processing of single patterns is determined by a convention.

3.4 Negation

When querying an XML document it is often useful not only to specify what is expected but also to specify what should not occur. This is an efficient way to exclude some unwanted XML fragments from the query result because sometimes it is easier to characterize an XML fragment by not wanted rather than desirable properties. Regular languages (according to Chomsky's classification) are not capable of representing that something should not appear stating only what may or has to appear. In the pattern language the absence of some XML fragment can be specified by negation .

As opposed to most XML query languages negation is a pattern and not a unary boolean operator. Therefore it has no boolean value, but matches the empty XML fragment. Since the negation pattern specifies what should not occur, it does not "consume" any XML nodes during the matching process so that we call it "non-substantial" negation. The negation pattern `!(p)` matches the empty XML fragment if its inner pattern `p` does not occur in the current context node. To underline the difference to logical negation, consider the double negation. The double negation `!(!(p))` is not equivalent to p, but matches an empty XML element if `!(p)` matches the current context node, which is only true if the current context node is empty. Since the negation pattern only specifies what should not occur, the standalone usage of negation is not reasonable. It should be used as an inner pattern of other complex patterns. Specifying a sequence `VP *=:wildcard_1 !(PR) *=:wildcard_2 NP` we want to identify sequences starting with VP and ending with NP where PR is not within a sequence. Trying to find a match for the sequence starting in VP_8 and ending in NP_{21} there are multiple matching variants for wildcard patterns. Some of them enable the matching of the negation pattern binding PR to one of the wildcards, e.g. `wildcard_1` is bound to (NP_{11}, PR_{19}), `!(PR)` $\cong$ {}, `wildcard_2` is bound to {}. However, there is a matching variant when the negated pattern is matched with PR_{19} (`wildcard_1` is bound to NP_{11}, `wildcard_2` is bound to {}). We would certainly not want the sequence (VP_8, NP_{11}, PR_{19}, NP_{21}) to match our pattern because the occurrence of PR in the sequence should be avoided. Therefore we define the semantics of the negation so that there is no matching variant that enables the occurrence of negated pattern:

Let P_1 !(p) P_2 be a complex pattern comprising negation as inner pattern. P_1 and P_2 are the left and right syntactic parts of the pattern and may be not valid patterns themselves (e.g. because of unmatched parentheses). The pattern obtained from the concatenation of both parts P_1 P_2 is a valid pattern because it is equivalent to the replacing of the negation by an empty pattern.

$$\mathsf{P}_1 \;!(\mathsf{p})\; \mathsf{P}_2 \cong f \Leftrightarrow$$
$$\mathsf{P}_1\;\mathsf{p}\;\mathsf{P}_2 \ncong f \wedge \mathsf{P}_1\;\mathsf{P}_2 \cong f$$

Requiring $\mathsf{P}_1\;\mathsf{p}\;\mathsf{P}_2 \ncong f$ guarantees that no matching variant exists in that the negated pattern p occurs. Since !(p) matches an empty fragment, the pattern $\mathsf{P}_1\mathsf{P}_2$ has to match complete f. It is noteworthy that the negation is the only pattern that influences the semantics of a complex pattern as its inner pattern. Independent of its complexity any pattern can be negated allowing very fine-grained specification of undesirable XML fragments.

4 Conclusion

XML documents with multi-dimensional markup feature a heterogeneous structure that depends on the algorithm for merging of concurrent markup. We present a pattern language that allows to abstract from the concrete structure of a document and formulate powerful queries. The extended sequence semantics allows matching of sequences across element borders and on different levels of the XML tree ignoring nesting levels irrelevant for the query. The formal specification of the sequence semantics guarantees that the properties of "classic" sibling sequence such as ordering, absence of gaps and overlaps between the neighbors are maintained. The combination of fully recursive backtracking patterns with the *ENSS* semantics allows complex queries reflecting the complicated positional and hierarchical dependencies of XML nodes within a multi-dimensional markup. Negation enhances the expressivity of the queries specifying an absence of a pattern in a certain context.

References

V. Benzaken, G. Castagna, and A. Frisch. 2003. CDuce: an XML-centric general-purpose language. In *In ICFP '03, 8th ACM International Conference on Functional Programming*, pages 51–63.

V. Benzaken, G. Castagna, and C. Miachon. 2005. A full pattern-based paradigm for XML query processing. In *Proceedings of the 7th Int. Symposium on Practical Aspects of Decl. Languages*, number 3350.

A. Berglund, S. Boag, D. Chamberlin, M. Fernndez, M. Kay, J. Robie, and J. Simon. September 2005. XML Path Language (XPath) 2.0. `http://www.w3.org/TR/2005/WD-xpath20-20050915/`.

S. Boag, D. Chamberlin, M. Fernandez, D. Florescu, J. Robie, J. Simon, and M. Stefanescu. 2003. XQuery 1.0: An XML Query Language. `http://www.w3c.org/TR/xquery`.

David Carmel, Yoelle S. Maarek, Matan Mandelbrod, Yosi Mass, and Aya Soffer. 2003. Searching XML documents via XML fragments. In *SIGIR '03: Proceedings of the 26th annual int. ACM SIGIR conference*, pages 151–158, New York,USA. ACM Press.

G. Castagna. 2005. Patterns and types for querying XML. In *DBPL - XSYM 2005 joint keynote talk*.

Don Chamberlin, Jonathan Robie, and Daniela Florescu. 2001. Quilt: An XML query language for heterogeneous data sources. *LNCS*, 1997:1–11.

J. Clark and S. DeRose. 1999. XML Path Language (XPath). `http://www.w3.org/TR/Xpath`.

Alin Deutsch, Mary F. Fernandez, D. Florescu, A.Y. Levy, and D. Suciu. 1999. A query language for XML. *Computer Networks*, 31(11-16):1155–1169.

H. Hosoya and P.C. Pierce. 2001. Regular expression patern matching for XML. In *In POPL '01, 25th Symposium on Principles of Prog. Languages*.

Haruo Hosoya and Benjamin C. Pierce. 2003. XDuce: A statically typed XML processing language. *ACM Trans. Inter. Tech.*, 3(2):117–148.

XQuery and XPath Full-Text Requirements. 2003. `http://www.w3.org/TR/2003/WD-xquery-full-text-requirements-20030502/`.

Jonathan Robie. 1998. The design of XQL. `http://www.ibiblio.org/xql/xql-design.html`.

C. Siefkes. 2004. A shallow algorithm for correcting nesting errors and other well-formedness violations in XML-like input. In *Extreme Markup Languages*.

A. Witt. 2004. Multiple hierarchies: new aspects of an old solution. In *Extreme Markup Languages 2004*.

SYSTEM DEMONSTRATIONS

Annotating text using the Linguistic Description Scheme of MPEG-7: The DIRECT-INFO Scenario

Thierry Declerck, Stephan Busemann
Language Technology Lab
DFKI GmbH
Saarbrücken, Germany
{declerck|busemann}@dfki.de

Herwig Rehatschek, Gert Kienast
Institute for Information Systems & Information Management,
JRS GmbH
Graz, Austria
{rehatschek|kienast}@joanneum.at

Abstract

We describe the way we adapted a text analysis tool for annotating with the Linguistic Description Scheme of MPEG-7 text related to and extracted from multimedia content. Practically applied in the DIRECT-INFO EC R&D project we show how such linguistic annotation contributes to semantic annotation of multimodal analysis systems, demonstrating also the use of the XML schema of MPEG-7 for supporting cross-media semantic content annotation.

1 Introduction

In the R&D project DIRECT-INFO the concrete business case of sponsorship tracking was targeted. The scenario investigated within the project was that sponsors want to know how often their brands are mentioned in connection with the sponsored company. The visual detection of a brand (e.g. in videos) is not sufficient to meet the requirements of this business case. Multimodal analysis and fusion – as implemented within DIRECT-INFO – is needed in order to fulfill these requirements (Rehatschek, 2004).

Within this context text analysis has been applied to documents reporting on entities, like football teams, that have close relations to large sponsoring companies. In the text analysis component of the system we had to detect if an entity was mentioned positively, negatively or neutrally. Besides all the processing and annotation issues to positive or negative mentions, we had to make our results available to a global MPEG-7 document, which is encoding the annotation results of various analysis of the modalities involved (logo detection, speech recognition, text analysis etc.). This global MPEG-7 document was the input for a fusion component.

In the next sections we describe the Text Analysis (TA) component of DIRECT-INFO. We then briefly describe the linguistic description scheme (LDS) of MPEG-7 and show the annotation generated by the TA. Finally we briefly discuss the role the LDS, and generally speaking MPEG-7, can play in supporting an interoperable cross-media annotation strategy. It seems to us, that LDS is offering a good mean for adding semantic metadata to image/video, but not for a real semantic integration of text and media content annotation, which in the case of DIRECT-INFO was performed by an additional fusion component.

2 The detection of positive/negative mentioning

Our work in DIRECT-INFO has been dedicated in enhancing an already existing tool for linguistic annotation. This tool, called SCHUG (Shallow and CHunk-based Unification Grammar tool), is annotating texts considering both linguistic constituency and dependency structures (T. Declerck, M. Vela 2005).

A first development step was dedicated in creating specialized lexicons for various types of lexical categories (like nouns, adjectives and verbs) that can bear the property of being intrinsically positive or negative in a specific domain, as can be seen just below in the case of soccer:

```
command => {POS => Noun, INT => "positive"}
dominate => {POS => Verb, INT => "positive"}
weak => {POS => Adj, INT => "negative"}
```

Considering a sentence like "ManU takes the command in the game against the weak Spanish team", the head-noun of the direct object (linguistically speaking) "the command" gets from the access to the specialized DIRECT-INFO lexicon a tag "INTERPRETATION" with value "positive". Whereas the adjective "weak" in the PP-adjunct "in the game against the weak Spanish team" gets an "INTERPRETATION" tag with value "negative".

Once the words in the sentence have been lexically tagged with respect to their interpretation, the computing of the pos./neg. interpretation at the level of linguistic fragments and then at the level of the sentences can start. For this we have defined heuristics along the lines of the dependency structures delivered by the linguistic analysis. So in the case of the NP "the weak Spanish team", the head noun "team", as such a neutral expression, is getting the "INTERPRETATION" tag with the value "negative", since it is modified by a "negative" adjective. In case the reference resolution algorithm of the linguistic tools has been able to specify that the "Spanish team" is in fact "Real Madrid" this entity gets a negative "INTERPRETATION" tag.

The head noun of the NP realizing the subject of the sentence, "ManU" gets a positive mention tag, since it is the subject of a positive verb and direct object combination (the NP "the command" having a positive reading, whereas the verb "takes" has a neutral reading).

A last aspect to be mentioned here concerns the treatment of the so-called polarity items. Specific words in natural language intrinsically carry a negation or position force (or scope). So the words *not*, *none* or *no* have an intrinsic negation force and negate the words and fragments in the context in which those specific words are occurring. The context that is negated by such words can be also called the "scope" (or the range) of the negation. Consider for example the sentence: "I would definitely pay £15 million to get Owen, *not even* a decent striker, instead..." Our tools are able to detect that the NP "decent striker" is negated, and therefore the positive reading of "decent striker" is being ruled out.

3 Metadata Description

The different content analysis modules of the DIRECT-INFO system extract different types of metadata, ranging from low-level audiovisual feature descriptions to semantic metadata. The global metadata description must be rich and has to clearly interrelate the various analysis results, as it is the input of the fusion component.

4.1 Using MPEG-7 for Detailed Description of Audiovisual Content

In DIRECT-INFO the MPEG-7 standard is used for metadata description. It is an excellent choice for describing audiovisual content because of its comprehensiveness and flexibility. The comprehensiveness results from the fact that the standard has been designed for a broad range of applications and thus employs very general and widely applicable concepts. The standard contains a large set of tools for diverse types of annotations on different semantic levels. The flexibility of MPEG-7, which is provided by a high level of generality, makes it usable for a broad application area without imposing strict constraints on the metadata models of these applications. The flexibility is very much based on the structuring tools and allows the description to be modular and on different levels of abstraction. MPEG-7 supports fine grained description, and it is possible to attach descriptors to arbitrary segments on any level of detail of the description.

Among the descriptive tools developed within the MPEG-7 framework, one is concerned with the use of natural language for adding metadata to the content description of image and video: the so-called Linguistic Description Scheme (LDS).

4.2 MPEG-7: The Linguistic Description Scheme (LDS)

MPEG-7 foresees four kinds of textual annotation that can be attached as metadata to some audio-video content. The natural language expression used here is "Spain scores a goal against Sweden. The scoring player is Morientes".

Free Text Annotation: Here only tags are put around the text:

```
<TextAnnotation>
   <FreeTextAnnotation xml:lang="en">
   Spain scores a goal against Sweden.
   The scoring player is Morientes.
   </FreeTextAnnotation>
</TextAnnotation>
```

Key Word Annotation: Key Words are extracted from text and correspondingly annotated:

```
<TextAnnotation>
   <KeywordAnnotation>
      <Keyword>score</Keyword>
      <Keyword>Sweden</Keyword>
      <Keyword>Spain</Keyword>
      <Keyword>Morientes</Keyword>
   </KeywordAnnotation>
</TextAnnotation>
```

Structured Annotation: Question/Answering like semantics is associated to the text:

```
<TextAnnotation>
  <StructuredAnnotation>
    <Who><Name>Spain</Name></Who>
    <WhatAction><Name>score
goal</Name></WhatAction>
    <Where><Name>A Coruña,
Spain</Name></Where>
    <When><Name>March 25,
1998<Name></When>
  </StructuredAnnotation>
</TextAnnotation>
```

Dependency Structure: Here the full linguistic apparatus is used for annotating the text:

```
<TextAnnotation>
 <DependencyStructure>
  <Sentence>
   <Phrase operator="subject">
    <Head type="noun">Spain</Head>
   </Phrase>
   <Head type="verb" base-
Form="score">scored</Head>
   <Phrase operator="object">
    <Head type="article noun">a
goal</Head>
   </Phrase>
   <Phrase>
    <Head
type="preposition">against</Head>
   <Phrase>
    <Head>Sweden</Head></Phrase>
   </Phrase>
  </Sentence>
 </DependencyStructure>
</TextAnnotation>[1]
```

4 MPEG-7 Format of the Text Analysis component in DIRECT-INFO

On the base of the linguistic analysis of our dependency parser, we generate the "structured annotation" of the MPEG-7 Linguistic Description Scheme. We think that this kind of annotation is the most practical of LDS for adding semantics to multimedia content, since it is probably more intuitive for the media expert as the underlying linguistic dependency structure. At the same time it seems also straightforward to go first for a (internal) dependency analysis, since it is then relatively easy to map automatically dependency units to the "Who", "WhatAction" and other tags of LDS.

The MPEG-7 output of the TA module of DIRECT-INFO looks like:

```
<MediaInformation>
 <MediaProfile>
  <MediaFormat>
   <Content href="http://www.direct-
info.net/mpeg7/cs/ContentCS.2004.xml/di.
content.writtenText">
     <Name>Written text</Name>
   </Content>
  </MediaFormat>
  <MediaInstance>
   <InstanceIdentifier/>
   <MediaLocator>
    <!-- essence id-->
    <MediaUri>5543</MediaUri>
   </MediaLocator>
  </MediaInstance>
 </MediaProfile>
</MediaInformation>
<StructuralUnit href="http://www.direct-
info.net/mpeg7/cs/StructuralUnitCS.2004.
xml/di.vis.pdf">
 <Name>PDF</Name>
</StructuralUnit>
 <!-- more than one page can be stored
within a file -->
<SpatialDecomposition criteria="Page">
 <StillRegion id="TA_PAGE1">
  <StructuralUnit
href="http://www.direct-
info.net/mpeg7/cs/StructuralUnitCS.2004.
xml/di.vis.page">
   <Name>Page</Name>
  </StructuralUnit>
 <SpatialDecomposition   crite-
ria="TextAnalysis" gap="true" over-
lap="false">
  <StillRegion>
   <StructuralUnit
href="http://www.direct-
info.net/mpeg7/cs/StructuralUnitCS.2004.
xml/di.vis.textAnal  ysisAnnotation">
    <Name>Text analysis annota-
tion</Name>
   </StructuralUnit>
   <TextAnnotation>
    <StructuredAnnotation>
     <WhatObject
href="http://www.direct-
info.net/mpeg7/cs/LogoCS.2004.xml/di.ta.
object.juventus">
      <Name
xml:lang="it">Juventus</Name>
     </WhatObject
     <WhatAction
href="http://www.direct-
info.net/mpeg7/cs/TextAnalysisCS.2004.xm
l/di.ta.action.teamMentioned">
<Name xml:lang="it">mentioning of
team</Name>
     </WhatAction>
     <Why>
      <Name xml:lang="it">
295 771120 Con DVD Auto da Sogno Porsche
e 10, con calendario ufficiale 2006 Ju-
ventus o Milan" o Inter o Palermo o
Fiorentina o Totti" o Wrestling" e 6, 9
Euro 1, Poste Italiane Sped . in A.P
      </Name>
     </Why>
     <How href="http://www.direct-
info.net/mpeg7/cs/TextAnalysisCS.2004.xm
l/di.ta.mentioning.neut">
     <Name xml:lang="it">neut</Name>
    </How>
   </StructuredAnnotation>
  </TextAnnotation>
</StillRegion>
```

Without going into too much detail here, it is enough to stress that in the first part of the annotation, the link to the general multimedia and multimodal repository is ensured. We have to

[1] These examples are taken from a former and excellent online tutorial on MPEG-7 by Philippe Salembier.

deal with a PDF document that should be processed by a Text Analysis tool. The "essence" ID is giving information about the location where the application relevant data is stored and where the results of the Text Analysis should be stored. All this metadata is ensuring the combination of the results of the analysis of various modalities dealing with one application relevant dataset (for example the combination of the logo detection of a brand and the related positive or negative mentioning of a team sponsored by this brand). For reason of place, we can not show and comment here the complete (and multimodal) MPEG-7 annotation, but details are given in (G. Kienast, 2005).

The second part of the annotation gives the results of the combined linguistic and "structured" analysis we are dealing with. As mentioned above, in the case of DIRECT-INFO, results of text analysis are accessed via the structured annotation of the Linguistic Description Schema of MPEG-7.

5 Conclusions and future Work

In the DIRECT-INFO project we managed to include results of text analysis in an automated fashion into a MPEG-7 description, which was dealing with the XML representation of the analysis of various modalities. Using corresponding metadata, it was possible to ensure the encoding/annotation of the related results in one file and to facilitate the access to the separated annotation using XPath. As such the DIRECT-INFO MPEG-7 annotation schema is offering a practicable multi-dimensional annotation scheme, if we consider a "dimensions" as being the output of the analysis of various modalities. MPEG-7 proved to be generic and flexible enough for combining, saving and accessing various types of annotation.

Limitations of MPEG-7 were encountered when the task was about fusion or merging of information encoded in the various descriptors (or features), and this task was addressed in a posterior step, whereas the encoding scheme of MPEG-7 was not longer helpful, in defining for example relations between the annotation resulting from the different modules or for defining constraints between those annotation. There seems to be a need for a higher level of representation for annotation resulting from the analysis of distinct media, being low-level features for images or high-level semantic features for texts.

The need of an "ontologization" of multimedia features has been already recognized and projects are already dealing with this, like AceMedia. Initial work in relating multimodal annotation in DIRECT-INFO will be further developed in K-Space, a new Network of Excellence, which goal is to provide for support in semantic inference for both automatic and semi-automatic annotation and retrieval of multimedia content. K-Space aims at closing the "semantic gap" between the low-level content descriptions and the richness and subjectivity of semantics in high-level human interpretations of audiovisual media.

6 Acknowledgements

The R&D work presented in this paper was partially conducted within the DIRECT-INFO project, funded under the 6th Framework Programme of the European Community within the strategic objective "Semantic-based knowledge management systems" (IST FP6-506898). Actual work on interoperability of media, language and semantic annotation is being funded by the Network of Excellence K-Space (IST FP6-027026).

References

T. Declerck, J. Kuper, H. Saggion, A. Samiotou, P. Wittenburg, J. Contreras. Contribution of NLP to the Content Indexing of Multimedia Documents. In *Lecture Notes in Computer Science Volume 3115 / 2004* Pages 610-618,Springer-Verlag Heidelberg, 6 2004.

T. Declerck, M. Vela, "Linguistic Dependencies as a Basis for the Extraction of Semantic Relations", in Proceedings of the ECCB'05 Workshop on Biomedical Ontologies and Text Processing, Madrid (2005)

G. Kienast, A. Horti, András, H. Rehatschek, S. Busemann, T. Declerck, V. Hahn and R. Cavet. "DIRECT INFO: A Media Monitoring System for Sponsorship Tracking." In *Proceedings of the ACM SIGIR Workshop on Multimedia Information Retrieval*. 2005.

H. Rehatschek: "DIRECT-INFO: Media monitoring and multimodal analysis for time critical decisions". Proceedings of the 5th International Workshop on Image Analysis for Multimedia Interactive Services (WIAMIS), ISBN-972-98115-7-1, Lisbon, April 2004.

AceMedia project: http://www.acemedia.org/aceMedia

DIRECT-INFO project: http://www.direct-info.net/

K-Space project: http://kspace.qmul.net/

MPEG-7: http://www.chiariglione.org/mpeg/

Tools for hierarchical annotation of typed dialogue

Myroslava O. Dzikovska, Charles Callaway, Elaine Farrow
Human Communication Research Centre, University of Edinburgh
2 Buccleuch Place, Edinburgh, EH8 9LW, United Kingdom,
{mdzikovs,ccallawa,efarrow}@inf.ed.ac.uk

1 Introduction

We discuss a set of tools for annotating a complex hierarchical and linguistic structure of tutorial dialogue based on the NITE XML Toolkit (NXT) (Carletta et al., 2003). The NXT API supports multi-layered stand-off data annotation and synchronisation with timed and speech data. Using NXT, we built a set of extensible tools for detailed structure annotation of typed tutorial dialogue, collected from a tutor and student typing via a chat interface. There are several corpora of tutoring done with such chat-style communication techniques (Shah et al., 2002; Jordan and Siler, 2002), however, our annotation presents a special problem because of its detailed hierarchical structure. We applied our annotation methodology to annotating corpora in two different tutoring domains: basic electricity and electronics, and symbolic differentiation.

2 Data Structures

Our corpus has two sources of overlapping annotations: the turn structure of the corpus and situational factors annotation. The data are naturally split into turns whenever a participant presses their "submit" button. Timing information is associated with individual turns, representing the time when the entire message was sent to the other participant, rather than with individual words and sounds as it would be in spoken corpora.

However, turns are too large to be used as units in the annotation for dialogue phenomena. For example, the single turn "Well done. Let's try a harder one." consists of two utterances making different dialogue contributions: positive tutorial feedback for the previous student utterance and a statement of a new tutorial goal. Thus, turns must be segmented into smaller units which can serve as a basis for dialogue annotation. We call these utterances by analogy with spoken language, because they are often fragments such as "well done" rather than complete sentences.

Thus, the corpus has two inherently overlapping layers: the turn segmentation layer, grouping utterances into turns, and the dialogue structure layer built up over individual utterances. The NXT toolkit supports such overlapping annotations, and we built two individual tools to support corpus annotation: an utterance segmentation tool and a tutorial annotation tool.

Additionally, the corpus contains annotation done by the tutor herself at collection time which we call "situational factors". The tutors were asked to submit a set of these factors after each turn describing the progress and state of the student, such as answer correctness, confidence and engagement. The factors were submitted separately from dialogue contributions and provide another layer of dialogue annotation which has to be coordinated with other annotations. The factors are typically related to the preceding student's utterance, but the link is implicit in the submission time.[1] Currently we include the factors in the tool's transcript display based on the submission time, so they are displayed after the appropriate turn in the transcript allowing the annotators to visually synchronise them with the dialogue. We also provide an option to annotators for making them visible or not. In the future we plan to make factors a separate layer of the annotation linked by pointers with the preceding student and tutor turns.

[1] The factor interface was designed to be quick to use and minimally impact the dialogue flow, so the submission timings are generally reliable.

3 Utterance Segmentation

We process the raw data with an automatic segmenter/tokenizer which subdivides turns into individual utterances, and utterances into tokens, providing an initial segmentation for the annotation. However, perfect automatic segmentation is not possible, because punctuation is often either inconsistent or missing in typed dialogue and this task therefore requires human judgement. The output of our automatic segmentation algorithm was verified and corrected by a human annotator.

A screen-shot of the interface we developed for segmentation verification is displayed in Figure 1. With the aid of this tool, it took 6 person-hours to check and correct the automatically segmented utterances for the 18 dialogues in our corpus.

4 Tutorial Annotation

To provide a detailed analysis of tutorial dialogue and remediation strategies, we employ a hierarchical annotation scheme which encodes the recursive dialogue structure. Each tutorial session consists of a sequence of tasks, which may be either teaching specific domain concepts or doing individual exercises. Each task's structure includes one or more of the following: giving definitions, formulating a question, obtaining the student answer and remediation by the tutor.

Generally speaking, the structure of tutorial dialogue is governed by the task structure just as in task-oriented dialogue (Grosz and Sidner, 1986). However, the specific annotation structure differs depending on the tutoring method. In our basic electricity and electronics domain, a tutorial session consists of a set of "teach" segments, and within each segment a number of "task" segments. Task segments usually contain exercises in which the student is asked a question requiring a simple (one- or two-line) answer, which may be followed by a long remediation segment to address the conceptual problems revealed by the answer.

In contrast, in our calculus domain the students have to do multi-step procedures to differentiate complex math expressions, but most of the remediations are very short, fixing the immediate problem and letting the student continue on with the procedure. Thus even though the dialogue is hierarchically structured in both cases, the annotation schemes differ depending on the domain. We developed a generic tool for annotating hierarchical dialogue structure which can be configured with the specific annotation scheme.

The tool interface (Figure 2) consists of a transcript of a session and a linked tree representation. Individual utterances displayed in the transcript are leaves of the tree. It is not possible to display them as tree leaves directly as would be done in syntactic trees, because they are too large to fit in graphical tree display. Instead, a segment is highlighted in a transcript whenever it is selected in the tutorial structure, and a hotkey is provided to expand the tree to see all annotations of a particular utterance in the transcript.

The hierarchical tree structure is supported by a schema which describes the annotations possible on each hierarchical tree level. Since the multi-layered annotation scheme is quite complex, the tool uses the annotation schema to limit the number of codes presented to the annotator to be only those consistent with the tree level. For example, in our basic electricity domain annotation described above, there are about 20 codes at different level, but an annotator will only have "teach" as an option for assigning a code to a top tree level, and only "task" and "test" (with appropriate subtypes) for assigning codes immediately below the teach level, based on the schema defined for the domain.

5 Transcript Segmentation

We had to conduct several simpler data analyses where the utterances in the transcript are segmented according to their purpose. For example, in tutorial differentiation the dialogue concentrates on 4 main purposes: general discussion, introducing problems, performing differentiation proper, or doing algebraic transformations to simplify the resulting expressions. In another analysis we needed to mark the segments where the student was making errors and the nature of those errors.

We developed a generic annotation tool to support such segmentation annotation over the utterance layer. The tool is configured with the name of the segment tag and colours indicating different segment types. The annotator can enter a segment type, and use a freetext field for other information. A screenshot of the annotation tool with utterance purposes marked is given in Figure 3.

6 Data Analysis

The NITE query language (NQL) enables us to access the data as a directed acyclic graph to correlate simple annotations, such as finding out the

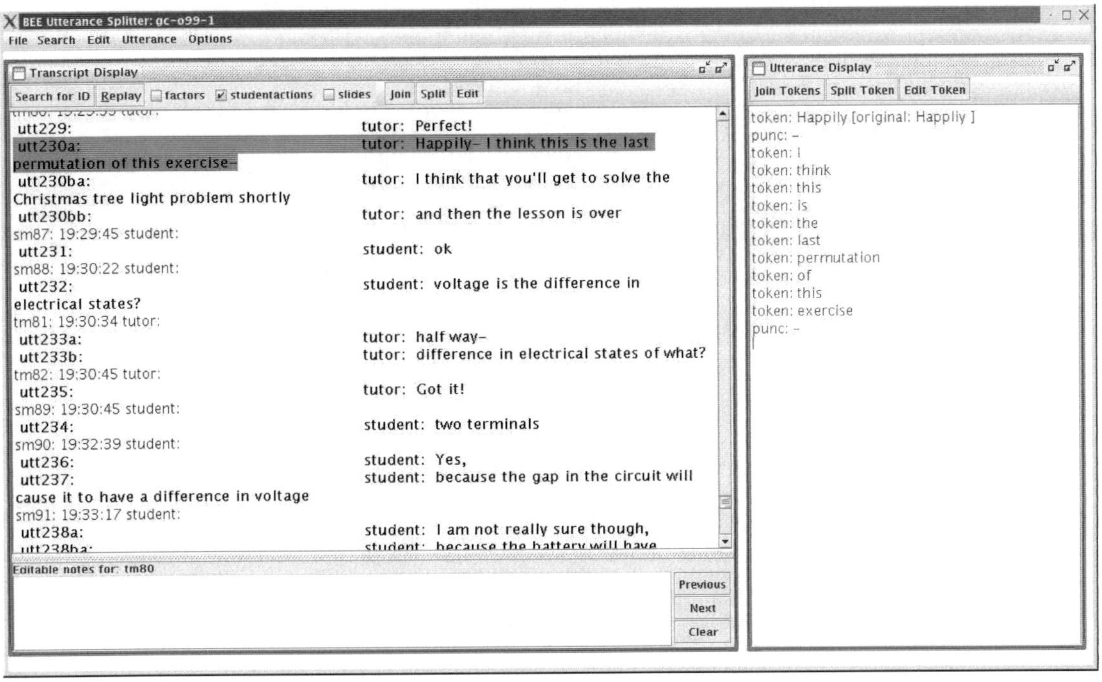

Figure 1: Utterance Segmentation Tool.

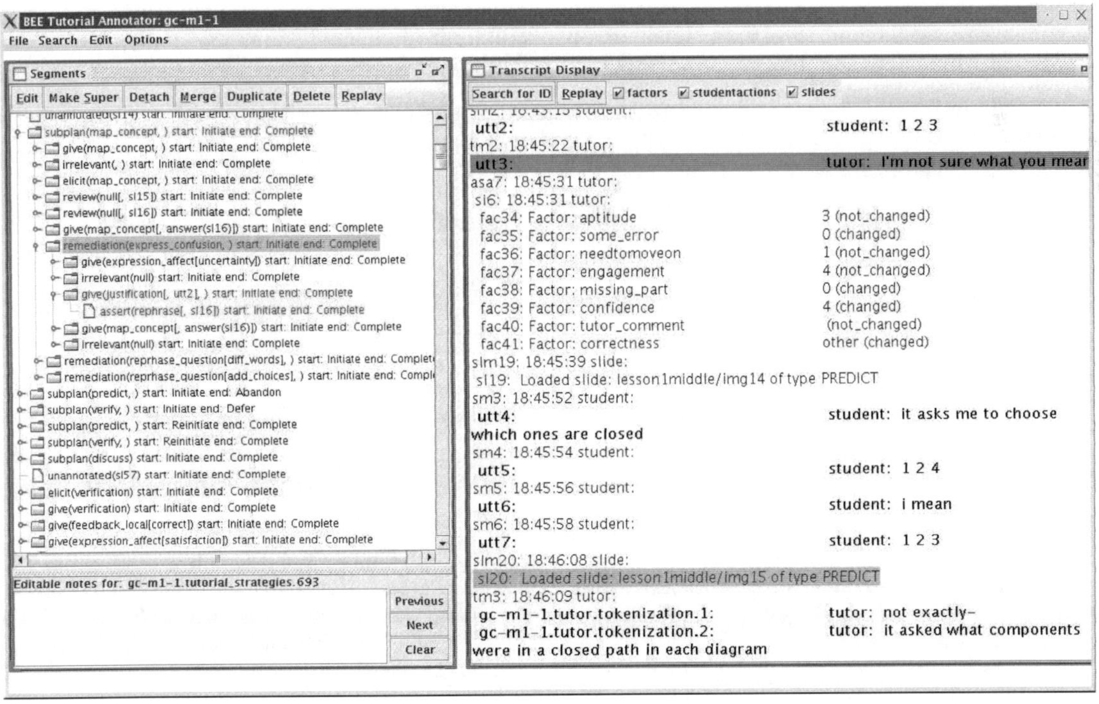

Figure 2: Tutorial Strategy Annotation Tool.

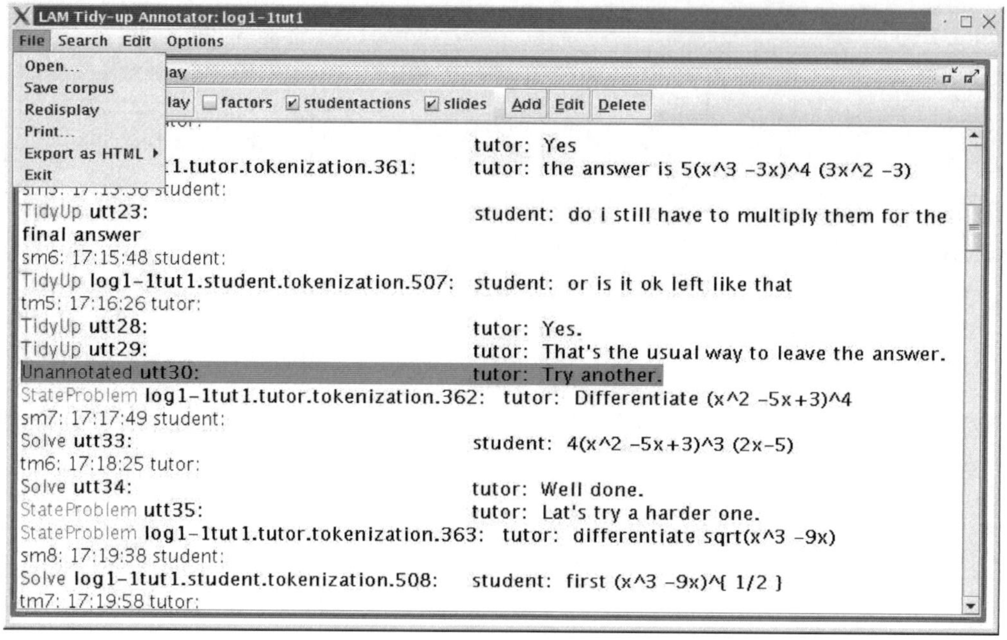

Figure 3: Segmentation tool. The segment labels are shown on the left.

number of turns which contain only mathematical expressions but no words. We use the NITE query interface for simpler analysis tasks such as finding all instances of specific tags and tag combinations.

However, we found the query language less useful for coordinating the situational factors annotated by tutors with other annotation. Each set of factors submitted is normally associated with the first student turn which precedes it, but the factors were not linked to student utterances explicitly. NQL does not have a "direct precedence" operator.[2] Thus it is easier derive this information using the JAVA API. To make the data analysis simpler, we are planning to add a pointer layer, generated automatically based on timing information, which will use explicit pointers between the factor submissions and preceding tutor and student turns.

7 Conclusions

We presented a set of tools for hierarchically annotating dialogue structure, suitable for annotating typed dialogue. The turns in these dialogues are complex and overlap with dialogue structure, and our toolset supports segmenting turns into smaller utterance units and annotating hierarchical dialogue structure over the utterances, as well as providing simpler segmentation annotation.

[2] It's possible to express the query in NQL using its precedence operator "≪" as "`($f factor) ($u utterance) (forall $u1 utterance) : (($f ≪ $u) && ($f ≪ u1)) → (u ≪ u1)`". However, this is very inefficient since it must check all utterance pairs in the corpus to determine direct precedence, especially if it needs to be included as part of a bigger query.

Acknowledgements

This material is based upon work supported by a grant from The Office of Naval Research number N000149910165 and European Union 6th framework programme grant EC-FP6-2002-IST-1-507826 (LeActiveMath).

References

Jean Carletta, J. Kilgour, T. O'Donnell, S. Evert, and H. Voormann. 2003. The NITE object model library for handling structured linguistic annotation on multimodal data sets. In *Proceedings of the EACL Workshop on Language Technology and the Semantic Web.*

Barbara J. Grosz and Candace L. Sidner. 1986. Attention, intentions, and the structure of discourse. *Comput. Linguist.*, 12(3):175–204.

Pamela Jordan and Stephanie Siler. 2002. Student initiative and questioning strategies in computer-mediated human tutoring dialogues. In *Proceedings of ITS 2002 Workshop on Empirical Methods for Tutorial Dialogue Systems.*

Farhana Shah, Martha W. Evens, Joel Michael, and Allen Rovick. 2002. Classifying student initiatives and tutor responses in human keyboard-to-keyboard tutoring sessions. *Discourse Processes*, 33(1).

ANNIS: Complex Multilevel Annotations in a Linguistic Database

Michael Götze and Stefanie Dipper
Department of Linguistics, University of Potsdam
14415 Potsdam, Germany
{goetze,dipper}@ling.uni-potsdam.de

Abstract

We present *ANNIS*, a linguistic database that aims at facilitating the process of exploiting richly annotated language data by naive users. We describe the role of the database in our research project and the project requirements, with a special focus on aspects of multilevel annotation. We then illustrate the usability of the database by illustrative examples. We also address current challenges and next steps.

1 Introduction

Until recently, working with data that is annotated at multiple levels with different types of annotation required rather advanced computer skills, which cannot be expected from the majority of potentially interested users.

We present *ANNIS*, a linguistic database that aims at providing the infrastructure for supporting linguists in their work on multilevel annotations. We describe and illustrate the current state of our work and sketch the next steps.

In sec. 2, we present the research scenario *ANNIS* is developed for, show the role of the linguistic database therein, and sketch the major requirements it aims to fulfill. We then describe the architecture and current functionality, and discuss the way difficult aspects of multidimensional annotations are treated (sec. 3). In sec. 4, we illustrate the work with the database by three exemplary approaches. Finally, we sketch our next steps.

2 Background

Research Scenario

The database *ANNIS* is being developed in the Collaborative Research Center SFB 632 on Information Structure, which consists of 13 individual research projects from disciplines such as theoretical linguistics, psycholinguistics, first and second language acquisition, typology and historical linguistics.[1] In the research center, data of various languages is collected and annotated at the levels of phonology, morphology, syntax, semantics, and pragmatics—levels that contribute in ways yet to be determined to the information structural partitioning of discourse and utterances.

For annotation, task-specific tools are being used, e.g. *EXMARaLDA, annotate, RSTTool*, and *MMAX*.[2] Data is then converted into a standoff data interchange format, which is fed into the linguistic database *ANNIS*. *ANNIS* aims at providing functionalities for exploring and querying the data, offering suitable means for both visualization and export.

User Requirements

Central requirements evolving out of the scenario sketched above and, as we believe, for multilevel annotation in general are *Data heterogeneity*, *Data reuse*, and *Accessibility* (cf. (Dipper and Götze, 2005)).

Data heterogeneity is a result of: (i) the language data to be annotated, varying with respect to size (single sentences vs. narrations), modality (monologue vs. dialogue, text vs. speech) and language; (ii) the annotations, which use different

[1] http://www.sfb632.uni-potsdam.de/. For more information about *ANNIS*, see http://www.sfb632.uni-potsdam.de/annis/ and (Dipper et al., 2004).

[2] http://www.rrz.uni-hamburg.de/exmaralda/
http://www.coli.uni-saarland.de/projects/sfb378/negra-corpus/
http://www.wagsoft.com/RSTTool
http://mmax.eml-research.de/

data structures (attribute-value pairs, trees, pointers, etc.); and (iii) data formats that stem from different task-specific annotation tools.

Data reuse must be supported, e.g. for further or re-annotation, statistical analyses, or reuse of the data in other tools.

Accessibility of both tools and data is an obvious prerequisite for data reuse.

In the following section, we will address those aspects that are particularly relevant for these requirements and discuss their treatment in *ANNIS*.

3 ANNIS

3.1 Main Features

ANNIS is a Java servlet application that can be accessed via standard web browsers. In its current state, it is not database-backed; data is read into memory and exploited for querying and visualization in memory.[3]

Data format and interoperability The data model must be suffiently expressive for capturing the data heterogeneity sketched above, including the representation of overlapping segments, intersecting hierarchies, and alternative annotations (e.g., for ambiguous annotations). It should further facilitate the addition of new annotations.

In our approach, we use a flexible standoff XML format, the SFB-standard interchange format, as the interface format (Dipper, 2005). In this format, primary data is stored in a file that optionally specifies a header, followed by a tag `<body>`, which contains the source text. The format makes use of generic XML elements to encode data structures and annotations: `<mark>` (markable) tags specify text positions or spans of text (or spans of other markables) that can be annotated by linguistic information. Trees and graphs are encoded by `<struct>` (structure) and `<rel>` (relation) elements, which specify local subtrees. `<feat>` (feature) tags specify the information that is annotated to markables or structures, which are referred to by `xlink` attributes. Each type of annotation is stored in a separate file, hence, competing or ambiguous annotations can be represented in a straightforward way: by distributing them over different files.

Our format allows us to represent different kinds of annotations in a uniform way. We provide importers for the export format of the annotation tools *annotate, EXMARaLDA, RST Tool,* and *MMAX*. Our *PCC* corpus (see sec. 4) imports and synchronizes the following annotations, which have been annotated by these tools: syntax, information structure, rhetorical structure, and coreference.

Visualization Suitable means for visualizing information is crucial for exploring and interpreting linguistic data. Due to the high degree of data heterogeneity, special attention has been paid to the support of visualizing various data structures. In addition, annotations may refer to segments of different sizes, e.g. syntax vs. discourse structure. Furthermore, richness of information in multilevel annotations has to be taken into account; this requires a certain degree of user-adaptivity, allowing the user to modify the way information of interest is displayed.

In *ANNIS*, we start from a basic interactive tier-based view, which allows for a compact simultaneous representation of many annotation types and whose appearance can be modified by the user in a format file. In addition, a discourse view helps the user to orient him/herself in the discourse. Further views can be added.

Query support Among the numerous requirements for a good query facility for multilevel annotation, expressiveness, efficiency, and user-friendly query-formulation appear to be the most relevant. Even a very brief discussion of these issues would go beyond the limits of this paper, the reader is instead referred to (Heid et al., 2004).

Currently, *ANNIS* uses a query language prototype which allows the user to query text and annotations, by means of regular expressions and wildcards, and various common relational operators (e.g. for stating relations in tree structures, such as dominance or sibling relations). However, the set for querying sequential relations is not sufficiently expressive, and querying co-reference relations is not supported yet. Furthermore, user support for formulating queries is rather poor.

3.2 Open Issues

Data alignment Alignment of annotations created by different annotation tools appears to be most suitable at the level of tokens. However, tools often come with their own tokenizers and mismatches do occur frequently. We currently use a

[3] For a more elaborate discussion of the basic concepts of *ANNIS*, see (Dipper et al., 2004).

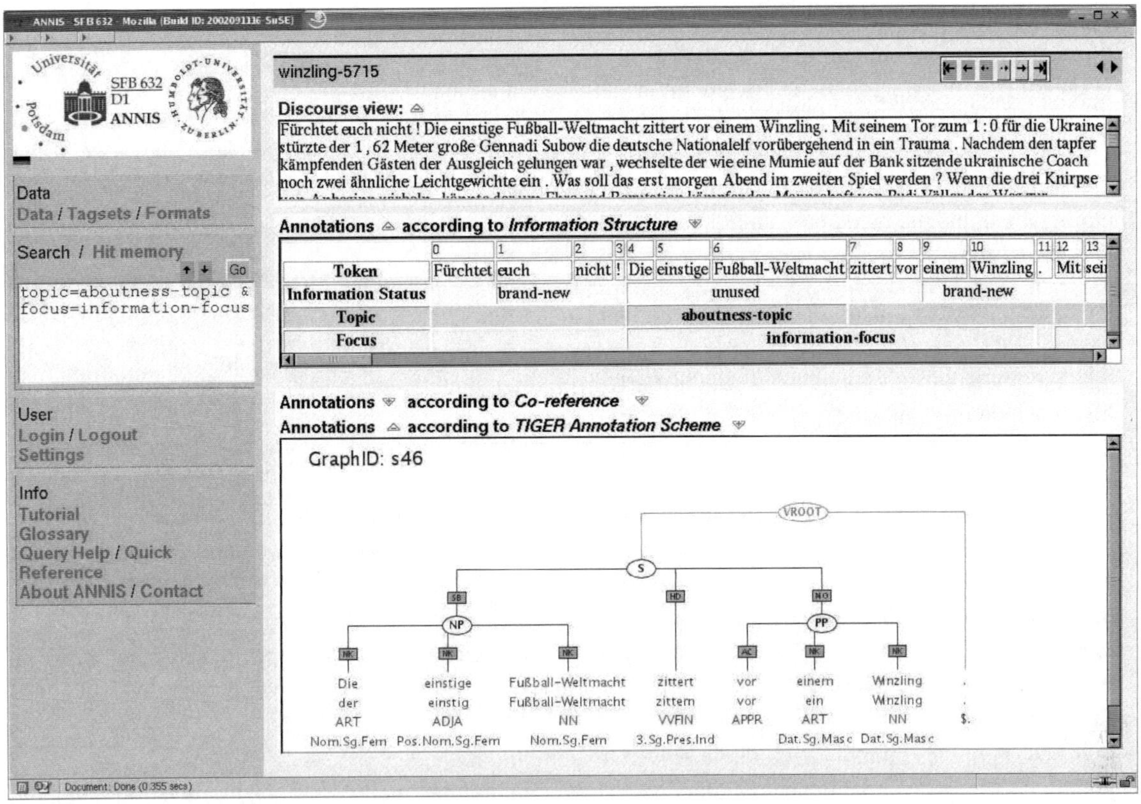

Figure 1: The ANNIS user interface, displaying data from the *PCC*

simple script that checks for text and token identity in the standoff files that we generate from the output of the individual tools. However, all mismatches have to be corrected manually. At least for white-space differences, an automatic fixing procedure should be feasible (similar to the one implemented by (Witt et al., 2005)).

Efficient Querying Current querying is restricted to rather small amounts of data, and complex queries may take some time until finishing the search.

Overlapping elements and intersecting hierarchies The query language does not yet support comfortable searching for overlapping elements. However, exactly what kinds of queries on overlapping segments or intersecting relations should be supported is an open question.

4 Use Cases

We illustrate the use of *ANNIS* in linguistic research, exemplified with research questions from three different linguistic areas.

Historical investigations The project B4: *The role of information structure in the development of word order regularities in Germanic* investigates the verb-second phenomenon, which occurred in certain Germanic languages only (e.g., it did in Modern German, but not in Modern English). One of their findings is that verb placement in the Old High German translation of Tatian correlates with discourse relations: verb-initial sentences usually occur in narrative contexts and signal continuation of the story. In contrast, verb-second sentences indicate subordinative relations (Hinterhölzl and Petrova, 2005).

Typological studies In the research project *D2: Typology of Information Structure* (cf., e.g., (Götze et al., To appear)), a typological questionnaire is designed, with which language data can be elicited using largely language-independent methods. Currently, data from 13 different languages is elicited and annotated with information from various linguistic levels (morphosyntax, phonology, semantics, and information structure).

An interesting query might look for nominal phrases (*const=np*) that are new in the discourse (*given=new*) and belong to the (information-) focus of a sentence (*focus=ans*), e.g. for investigating the phonological realization of these.

The according query has the form: *const=np & given=new & focus=ans & #1_=_#2.*[4]

Queries in *ANNIS* can be restricted to subsets of a corpus, by queries such as *focus=ans & doc=*81-11**, which searches for all answer foci in the data that has been elicited by means of the task 81-11 in the questionnaire, yielding matching data from all languages in our database.

Discourse studies The Potsdam Commentary Corpus, *PCC* (Stede, 2004), consists of 173 newspaper commentaries, annotated for morphosyntax, coreference, discourse structure according to Rhetorical Structure Theory, and information structure.

A question of interest here is the information-structural pattern of sentences introducing discourse segments that elaborate on another part of the discourse: *elaboration & rel=satellite & (cat=vroot & aboutness-topic) & #1 > #2 & #2_=_#3.* Another research issue is the relationship of coreference and discourse structure. However, querying for coreference relations is not supported yet.

5 Future Work

Currently we are working on integrating a native XML database into our system. To make processing more efficient, we are developing an internal inline representation of the standoff interchange format, encoding overlapping segments by means of milestones or fragments (Barnard et al., 1995).

Furthermore, the query language will be extended to cover different kinds of queries on sequential relations as well as coreference relations. Finally, we will add basic statistical means to the query facility, which, e.g., can point to rare and, hence, potentially interesting feature combinations.

6 Demo

In our demonstration of *ANNIS*, we will show example data from the PCC, Old High German, and data elicited by the typological questionnaire. We then illustrate by means of example queries how the researchers make use of our database in their daily work, as described above. This includes presenting the visualization and querying facilities of *ANNIS*.

[4]The expression *#n* refers to the *n*th constraint stated in the query; the binary operator _=_ requires extensional identity (Dipper et al., 2004).

References

David Barnard, Lou Burnard, Jean-Pierre Gaspart, Lynne A. Price, C. M. Sperberg-McQueen, and Giovanni Batista Varile. 1995. Hierarchical encoding of text: Technical problems and SGML solutions. *Text Encoding Initiative: Background and Context. Special Issue of Computers and the Humanities*, 29(211–231).

Stefanie Dipper and Michael Götze. 2005. Accessing heterogeneous linguistic data — generic XML-based representation and flexible visualization. In *Proceedings of the 2nd Language & Technology Conference 2005*.

Stefanie Dipper, Michael Götze, Manfred Stede, and Tillmann Wegst. 2004. ANNIS: A linguistic database for exploring information structure. In Shinichiro Ishihara, Michaela Schmitz, and Anne Schwarz, editors, *Interdisciplinary Studies on Information Structure (ISIS)*, volume 1, pages 245–279. Universitätsverlag Potsdam, Potsdam, Germany.

Stefanie Dipper. 2005. XML-based stand-off representation and exploitation of multi-level linguistic annotation. In *Proceedings of Berliner XML Tage 2005 (BXML 2005)*, pages 39–50, Berlin, Germany.

Michael Götze, Torsten Roloff, Stavros Skopeteas, and Ruben Stoel. To appear. Exploring a cross-linguistic production data corpus. In *Proceedings of the Sixth International Tbilisi Symposium on Language, Logic and Computation*. Batumi, Georgia.

Ulrich Heid, Holger Voormann, Jan-Torsten Milde, Ulrike Gut, Katrin Erk, and Sebastian Padó. 2004. Querying both time-aligned and hierarchical corpora with NXT Search. In *Proceedings of the Forth International Conference on Language Resources and Evaluation (LREC 2004)*, pages 1455–1458, Lisbon.

Roland Hinterhölzl and Svetlana Petrova. 2005. Rhetorical relations and verb placement in early germanic languages. Evidence from the Old High German Tatian translation (9th century). In M. Stede, C. Chiarcos, M. Grabski, and L. Lagerwerf, editors, *Salience in Discourse. Multidisciplinary Approaches to Discourse*, pages 71–79.

Manfred Stede. 2004. The Potsdam Commentary Corpus. In *Proceedings of the ACL Workshop on Discourse Annotation*, pages 96–102, Barcelona.

Andreas Witt, Daniela Goecke, Felix Sasaki, and Harald Lüngen. 2005. Unification of XML documents with concurrent markup. *Literary and Linguistic Computing*, 20(1):103–116.

The NITE XML Toolkit: Demonstration from five corpora

Jonathan Kilgour and **Jean Carletta**
University of Edinburgh
United Kingdom
jonathan@inf.ed.ac.uk

Abstract

The NITE XML Toolkit (NXT) is open source software for working with multimodal, spoken, or text language corpora. It is specifically designed to support the tasks of human annotators and analysts of heavily cross-annotated data sets, and has been used successfully on a range of projects with varying needs. In this text to accompany a demonstration, we describe NXT along with four uses on different corpora that together span its most novel features. The examples involve the AMI and ICSI Meeting Corpora; a study of multimodal reference; a syntactic analysis of Genesis in classical Hebrew; and discourse annotation of Switchboard dialogues.

1 Introduction

Of the software packages that provide support for working with language corpora, the NITE XML Toolkit (NXT) is arguably the most mature, offering to combine multiple audio and video signals with crossing structures of linguistic annotation. It is currently in use on a range of corpora. Current users both create annotations in NXT natively and "up-translate" existing data from other tools into NXT's storage format. Although its biggest strengths are for multimodal language research, some users have found it to be the right solution for work on text and speech corpora without video because of the way it handles annotation and analysis. NXT is open source software, available from Sourceforge and documented at http://www.ltg.ed.ac.uk/NITE. It is written in Java and uses the Java Media Framework (JMF) for its handling of signals.

In this text to accompany a demonstration, we summarize NXT's functionality, comment on its use for four corpora that together showcase its most novel features, and describe funded future development.

2 The NITE XML Toolkit

At its core, NXT consists of three libraries: one for data handling, one for searching data, and one for building GUIs for working with data. The data handling libraries include support for loading, serialization using a stand-off XML format, navigation around loaded data, and changes to the data in line with a specific data model that is intended especially for data sets that contain both timing information and overlapping structural markup. The search facility implements a query language that is designed particularly for the data model and allows the user to find n-tuples of data objects that match a set of conditions based on types, temporal conditions, and structural relationships in the data. The GUI library defines signal players and data displays that update against loaded data and can highlight parts of the display that correspond to current time on the signals or that correspond to matches to a query typed into a standard search interface. This includes support for selection as required for building annotation tools and a specific transcription-oriented display.

NXT also contains a number of end user interfaces and utilities built on top of these libraries. These include a generic display that will work for any NXT format data, configurable GUIs for some common hand-annotation tasks such as markup of named entities, dialogue acts, and a tool for segmenting and labelling a signal as it plays. They also include command line utilities for common search tasks such as counting query results and

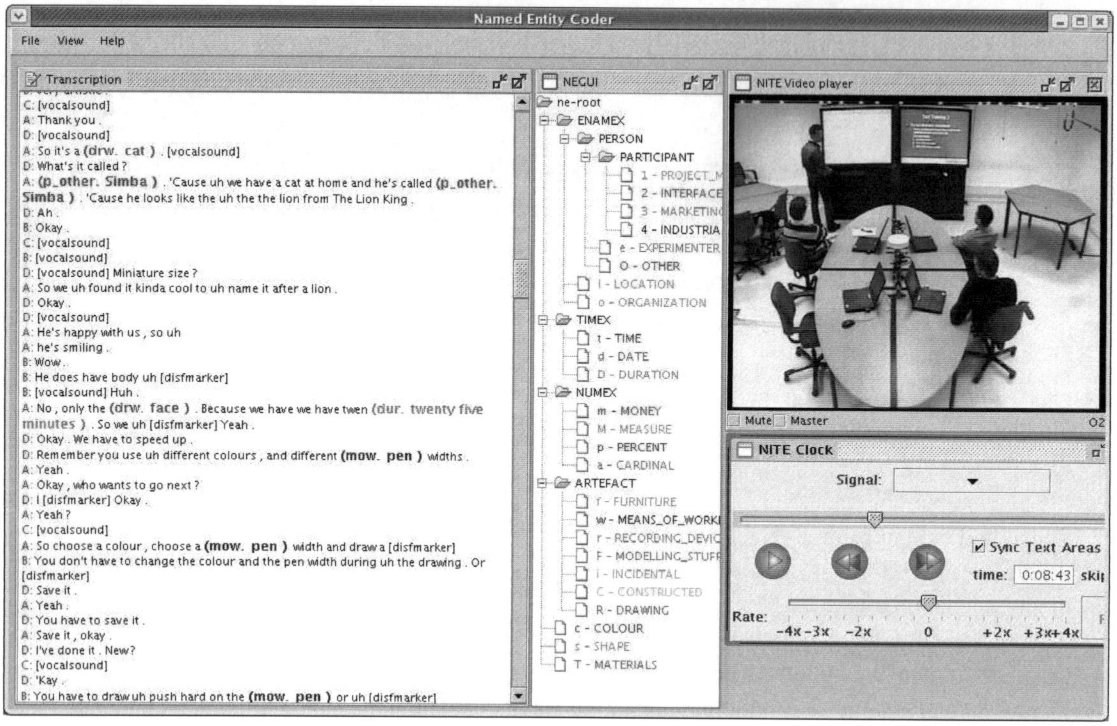

Figure 1: Named entity coding on the AMI corpus

some utilities for transforming data into, for instance, tab-delimited tables.

Finally, a number of projects have contributed sample data and annotation tools as well as mechanisms for transforming data to and from other formats. Writing and testing a new up-translation typically takes someone who understands NXT's format between one and three days. The actual time depends on the complexity of the structure represented in the input data and whether a parser for the data format must be written from scratch. Badly documented formats and ill-formed data take longer to transform.

3 Examples

Example 1: The AMI and ICSI Meeting Corpora

The AMI Project (http://www.amiproject.org) is currently NXT's biggest user, and is also its largest provider of financial support. AMI, which is collecting and transcribing 100 hours of meeting data (Carletta et al., 2005) and annotating part or all of it for a dozen different phenomena, is using NXT's data storage for its reference format, with data being generated natively using NXT GUIs as well as up-translated from other sources. The project uses ChannelTrans (ICSI, nd) for orthographic transcription and Event Editor (Sumec, nd) for straightforward timestamped labelling of video; although NXT comes with an interface for the latter, Event Editor, which is Windows-only and not based on JMF, has better video control and was already familiar to some of the annotators. For annotation, AMI is using the configurable dialogue act and named entity tools as well as tailored GUIs for topic segmentation and extractive summarization that links extracted dialogue acts to the sentences of an abstractive summary they support. Figure 1 shows the named entity annotation tool as configured for the AMI project. Aside from the sheer scale of the exercise, the AMI effort is unique in requiring simultaneous annotation of different levels at different sites. NXT does not support data management, but its stand-off XML data format has made it relatively easy to manage the process using a combination of a CVS repository for version control, web forms for data upload, and wikis for work assignment and progress reports.

The AMI Project piloted many of their techniques on the ICSI Meeting Corpus (Janin et al., 2003), which shares some characteristics with the AMI corpus but is audio-only. More information about this closely related use of NXT can be found in (Carletta and Kilgour, 2005).

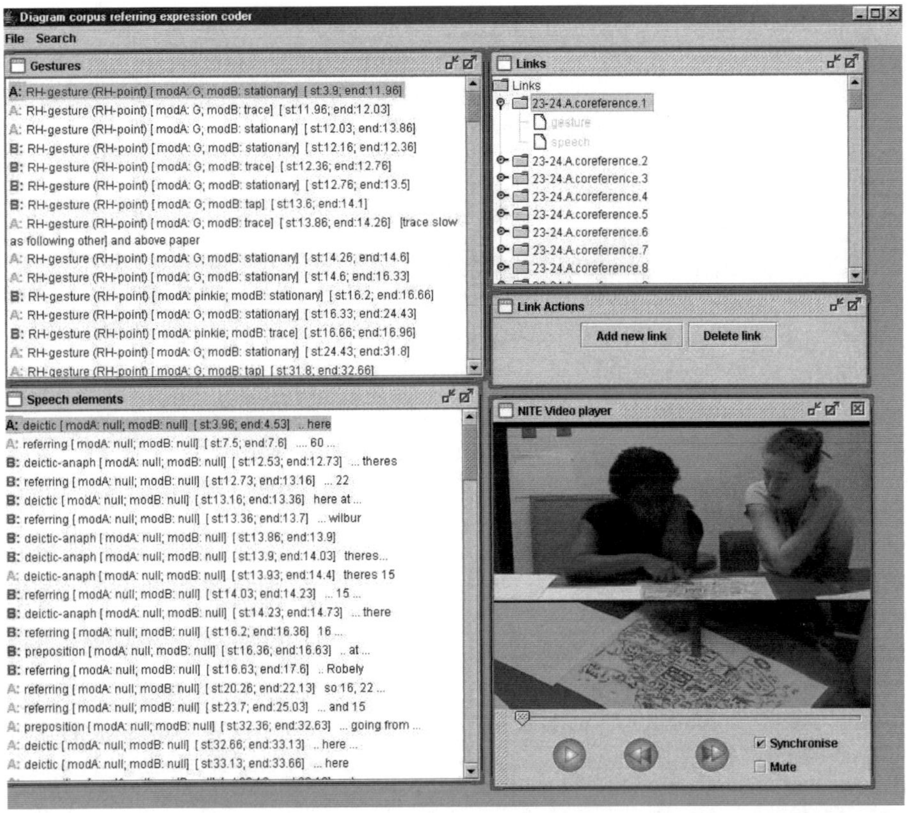

Figure 2: DIAGRAMS corpus: linking gesture and dialogue acts.

Example 2: Multimodal reference

This example is a small project that is looking at the relationship between referring expressions and the hand gestures used to point at a map. Although the transcription, referring expression, and gesture annotations were done in other tools and then up-translated, NXT gave the best support for linking referring expressions with gestures and analysing the results. Figure 2 shows the linking tool. One interesting aspect of this project was that the analysis was performed by a postgraduate psychologist. Analysts with no computational experience find it more difficult to learn how to use the query language, but several have done so. With this kind of data set, simply the ability to play the signals and annotations together and highlight query results provides insights into behaviours that are difficult to reach otherwise.

Example 3: Syntax in Genesis

This example is an annotation of Genesis in classical Hebrew that shows its structural division into books, chapters, verses, and half-verses. The data itself, which is purely textual, was originally stored in an MS Access relational database, but overlapping hierarchies in the structure made it difficult to query in this format. After finding NXT on the web and consulting us about the best way to represent the data using the NXT data model, the user successfully up-translated his data, searched it using NQL, and exported counts to SPSS to create corpus statistics.

Example 4: The Switchboard Corpus

The Switchboard Dialogue Corpus (Godfrey et al., 1992) has been popular for computational discourse research. (Carletta et al., 2004) describes an effort which up-translated its Penn Treebank syntactic analysis to NXT format, added annotations of "markables" for animacy, information structure, and coreference, and used this information all together. This project made heavy use of NXT's query language, including the ability to index query results in the data storage format itself for easy access. The work is now being extended to align an improved version of the transcriptions that includes word timestamps derived by forced alignment with the transcriptions used for the syntactic and discourse annotation, and to add annotations for phonology and syllable structure, all within the same corpus structure.

4 Discussion

It should not be supposed from our list of examples that NXT has been used only for these applications. Particularly novel NXT uses include simultaneous display of annotation with a re-enactment of a human-computer tutorial dialogue driven by the dialogue system itself; hand-annotation of head orientation from video using a flock-of-birds motion sensor mounted on a coffee mug; and annotation of the critiques expressed in conversations about movies. However, most NXT users are applying some kind of discourse annotation. They choose NXT because they need to combine signal labellings with annotations that give structure over the top of orthography, because they want to combine annotations from different sources and so find the stand-off format attractive, or because they need the GUI library in order to develop novel interfaces. Academic software is often inadequately documented, and therefore only usable with the help of its developers. It is inevitable given the size of the target user community that most of them are at least "friends of friends". Enough users have worked independently of the developers that we are confident that all but the newest parts of NXT are understandable from the documentation.

Although NXT is mature enough for use, several projects are investing in further development. The largest current efforts are to create an annotation and analysis tool with a time-aligned "tiered" data display and a query processor with better performance (Mayo et al., 2006). Another priority is better packaging, particularly of the configurable interfaces and of the existing translations from the formats used in transcription and other annotation tools. Finally, contributing projects plan work that will improve interoperability between NXT and other tools, including eyetrackers, NLP applications such as part-of-speech taggers, and machine learning software.

Acknowledgments

NXT prototyping and development has been supported primarily by the European Commission (MATE, LE4-8370; NITE, IST-2000-2609; and AMI, FP6-506811) and Scottish Enterprise via the Edinburgh-Stanford Link. The examples shown are by kind permission of Scottish Enterprise, the AMI Project, and Dr. Matthew Anstey of Charles Sturt University.

References

[Carletta and Kilgour2005] J.C. Carletta and J. Kilgour. 2005. The NITE XML Toolkit meets the ICSI Meeting Corpus: Import, annotation, and browsing. In S. Bengio and H. Bourlard, editors, *Machine Learning for Multimodal Interaction: First International Workshop, MLMI 2004, Martigny, Switzerland, June 21-23, 2004, Revised Selected Papers*, Lecture Notes in Computer Science 3361, pages 111–121. Springer-Verlag, Berlin.

[Carletta et al.2004] Jean Carletta, Shipra Dingare, Malvina Nissim, and Tatiana Nikitina. 2004. Using the NITE XML Toolkit on the switchboard corpus to study syntactic choice: a case study. In *Fourth Language Resources and Evaluation Conference*, Lisbon, Portugal.

[Carletta et al.2005] J. Carletta, Simone Ashby, Sebastien Bourban, Mike Flynn, Mael Guillemot, Thomas Hain, Jaroslav Kadlec, Vasilis Karaiskos, Wessel Kraaij, Melissa Kronenthal, Guillaume Lathoud, Mike Lincoln, Agnes Lisowska, Iain McCowan, Wilfried M. Post, Dennis Reidsma, and Pierre Wellner. 2005. The AMI Meeting Corpus: A pre-announcement. In S. Renals and S. Bengio, editors, *2nd Joint Workshop on Multimodal Interaction and Related Machine Learning Algorithms*, Edinburgh.

[Godfrey et al.1992] J. Godfrey, E. Holliman, and J. McDaniel. 1992. Switchboard: Telephone speech corpus for research development. In *International Conference on Acoustics, Speech, and Signal Processing*, pages 517–520, San Francisco, CA, USA.

[ICSInd] ICSI. n.d. Extensions to Transcriber for meeting recorder transcription. http://www.icsi.berkeley.edu/Speech/mr/channeltrans.html; accessed 14 Oct 05.

[Janin et al.2003] A. Janin, D. Baron, J. Edwards, D. Ellis, D. Gelbart, N. Morgan, B. Peskin, T. Pfau, E. Shriberg, A. Stolcke, and C. Wooters. 2003. The ICSI Meeting Corpus. In *IEEE International Conference on Acoustics, Speech and Signal Processing*, Hong Kong.

[Mayo et al.2006] Neil Mayo, Jonathan Kilgour, and Jean Carletta. 2006. Towards an alternative implementation of NXT's query language via XQuery. In *EACL Workshop on Multi-dimensional Markup in Natural Language Processing (NLPXML)*, Trento, Italy.

[Sumecnd] Stanislav Sumec. n.d. Event Editor. http://www.fit.vutbr.cz/research/grants/m4/editor/; accessed 14 Oct 05.

The SAMMIE Multimodal Dialogue Corpus Meets the Nite XML Toolkit

Ivana Kruijff-Korbayová, Verena Rieser, Ciprian Gerstenberger
Saarland University, Saarbrücken, Germany
vrieser@coli.uni-sb.de

Jan Schehl, Tilman Becker
DFKI, Saarbrücken, Germany
jan.schehl@dfki.de

Abstract

We demonstrate work in progress[1] using the Nite XML Toolkit on a corpus of multimodal dialogues with an MP3 player collected in a Wizard-of-Oz (WOZ) experiments and annotated with a rich feature set at several layers. We designed an NXT data model, converted experiment log file data and manual transcriptions into NXT, and are building annotation tools using NXT libraries.

1 Introduction

In the TALK project[2] we are developing a multimodal dialogue system for an MP3 application for in-car and in-home use. The system should support natural, flexible interaction and collaborative behavior. To achieve this, it needs to provide advanced adaptive multimodal output.

To determine the interaction strategies and range of linguistic behavior naturally occurring in this scenario, we conducted two WOZ experiments: SAMMIE-1 involved only spoken interaction, SAMMIE-2 was multimodal, with speech and screen input and output.[3]

We have been annotating the corpus on several layers, representing linguistic, multimodal and context information. The annotated corpus will be used (i) to investigate various aspects of multimodal presentation and interaction strategies both within and across the annotation layers; (ii) to design an initial policy for reinforcement learning of multimodal clarifications.[4] We use the Nite XML Toolkit (NXT) (Carletta et al., 2003) to represent and browse the data and to develop annotation tools.

Below we briefly describe our experiment setup, the collected data and the annotation layers; we comment on methods and tools for data representation and annotation, and then present our NXT data model.

2 Experiment Setup

24 subjects in SAMMIE-1 and 35 in SAMMIE-2 performed several tasks with an MP3 player application simulated by a wizard. For SAMMIE-1 we had two, for SAMMIE-2 six wizards. The tasks involved searching for titles and building playlists satisfying various constraints. Each session was 30 minutes long. Both users and wizards could speak freely. The interactions were in German (although most of the titles and artist names in the database were English).

SAMMIE-2 had a more complex setup. The tasks the subjects had to fulfill were divided in two classes: with vs. without operating a driving simulator. When presenting the search results, the wizards were free to produce mono- or multimodal output as they saw fit; they could speak freely and/or select one of four automatically generated screen outputs, which contained tables and lists of found songs/albums. The users also had free choice between unconstrained

[1] Our demonstration results from the efforts of a larger team including also N. Blaylock, B. Fromkorth, M. Grác, M. Kaißer, A. Moos, P. Poller and M. Wirth.

[2] TALK (Talk and Look: Tools for Ambient Linguistic Knowledge; http://www.talk-project.org), funded by the EU 6th Framework Program, project No. IST-507802.

[3] SAMMIE stands for Saarbrücken Multimodal MP3 Player Interaction Experiment.

[4] See (Kruijff-Korbayová et al., 2006) for more details about the annotation goals and further usage of the corpus.

natural language and/or selecting items on the screen. Both wizard and user utterances were immediately transcribed. The wizard's utterances were presented to the user via a speech synthesizer. To simulate acoustic understanding problems, the wizard sometimes received only part of the transcribed user's utterance, to elicit CRs. (See (Kruijff-Korbayová et al., 2005) for details.)

3 Collected Data

The SAMMIE-2 data for each session consists of a video and audio recording and a log file.[5] The gathered logging information per session consists of Open Agent Architecture (Martin et al., 1999) (OAA) messages in chronological order, each marked by a timestamp. The log files contain various information, e.g., the transcriptions of the spoken utterances, the wizard's database query and the number of results, the screen option chosen by the wizard, classification of clarification requests (CRs), etc.

4 Annotation Methods and Tools

The rich set of features we are interested in naturally gives rise to a multi-layered view of the corpus, where each layer is to be annotated independently, but subsequent investigations involve exploration and automatic processing of the integrated data across layers.

There are two crucial technical requirements that must be satisfied to make this possible: (i) stand-off annotation at each layer and (ii) alignment of base data across layers. Without the former, we could not keep the layers separate, without the latter we would not be able to align the separate layers. An additional equally important requirement is that elements at different layers of annotation should be allowed to have overlapping spans; this is crucial because, e.g., prosodic units and syntactic phrases need not coincide.

Among the existing toolkits that support multi-layer annotation, it was decided to use NXT (Carletta et al., 2003)[6] in the TALK project. The NXT-based SAMMIE-2 corpus we are demonstrating has been created in several steps: **(1)** The speech data was manually transcribed using the Transcriber tool.[7] **(2)** We automatically extracted features at various annotation layers by parsing the OAA messages in the log files. **(3)** We automatically converted the transcriptions and the information from the log files into our NXT-based data representation format; features annotated in the transcriptions and features automatically extracted from the log files were assigned to elements at the appropriate layers of representation in this step.

Manual annotation: We use tools specifically designed to support the particular annotation tasks. We describe them below.

As already mentioned, we used Transcriber for the manual transcriptions. We also performed certain relatively simple annotations directly on the transcriptions and coded them in-line by using special notation. This includes the identification of self-speech, the identification of expressions referring to domain objects (e.g., songs, artists and albums) and the identification of utterances that convey the results of database queries.

For other manual annotation tasks (the annotation of CRs, task segmentation and completion, referring expressions and the relations between them) we have been building specialized tools based on the NXT library of routines for building displays and interfaces based on Java Swing (Carletta et al., 2003). Although NXT comes with a number of example applications, these are tightly coupled with the architecture of the corpora they were built for. We therefore developed a core basic tool for our own corpus; we modify this tool to suite each annotation task. To facilitate tool development, NXT provides GUI elements linked directly to corpora elements and support for handling complex multi-layer corpora. This proved very helpful.

Figure 4 shows a screenshot of our CR annotation tool. It allows one to select an utterance in the left-hand side of the display by clicking on it, and then choose the attribute values from the pop-down lists on the right-hand side. Cre-

[5]For 19 sessions the full set of data files exists.

[6]`http://www.ltg.ed.ac.uk/NITE/`

[7]`http://trans.sourceforge.net/`

ating relations between elements and creating elements on top of other elements (e.g., words or utterances) are extensions we are currently implementing (and will complete by the time of the workshop). First experiences using the tool to identify CRs are promising.[8] When demonstrating the system we will report the reliability of other manual annotation tasks.

Automatic annotation using indexing: NXT also provides a facility for automatic annotation based on NiteQL query matches (Carletta et al., 2003). Some of our features, e.g., the dialogue history ones, can be easily derived via queries.

5 The SAMMIE NXT Data Model

NXT uses a stand-off XML data format that consist of several XML files that point to each other. The NXT data model is a multi-rooted tree with arbitrary graph structure. Each node has one set of children, and can have multiple parents.

Our corpus consists of the following layers. Two base layers: words and graphical output events; both are time-aligned. On top of these, structural layers correspond to one session per subject, divided into task sections, which consist of turns, and these consist of individual utterances, containing words. Graphical output events will be linked to turns at a featural layer.

Further structural layers are defined for CRs and dialogue acts (units are utterances), domain objects and discourse entities (units are expressions consisting of words). We keep independent layers of annotation separate, even when they can in principle be merged into a single hierarchy.

Figure 2 shows a screenshot made with Amigram (Lauer et al., 2005), a generic tool for browsing and searching NXT data. On the left-hand side one can see the dependencies between the layers. The elements at the respective layers are displayed on the right-hand side.

Below we indicate the features per layer:

- **Words:** Time-stamped words and other sounds; we mark self-speech, pronunciation, deletion status, lemma and POS.

[8]Inter-annotator agreement of 0.788 (κ corrected for prevalence).

- **Graphical output:** The type and amount of information displayed, the option selected by the wizard, and the user's choices.
- **Utterances:** Error rates due to word deletion, and various features describing the syntactic structure, e.g., mood, polarity, diathesis, complexity and taxis, the presence of marked syntactic constructions such as ellipsis, fronting, extraposition, cleft, etc.
- **Turns:** Time delay, dialogue duration so far, and other dialogue history features, i.e. values which accumulate over time.
- **Domain objects and discourse entities:** Properties of referring expressions reflecting the type and information status of discourse entities, and coreference/bridging links between them.
- **Dialogue acts:** DAs based on an agent-based approach to dialogue as collaborative problem-solving (Blaylock et al., 2003), e.g., determining joint objectives, finding and instantiating recipes to accomplish them, executing recipes and monitoring for success. We also annotate propositional content and the database queries.
- **CRs:** Additional features including the source and degree of uncertainty, and characteristics of the CRs strategy.
- **Tasks:** A set of features for estimating user satisfaction online for reinforcement learning (Rieser et al., 2005).
- **Session:** Subject and wizard information, user questionnaire aswers, and accumulating attribute values from other layers.

6 Summary

We described a multi-layered corpus of multimodal dialogues represented and annotated using NXT-based tools. Our data model relates linguistic and graphical realization to a rich set of context features and represents structural, hierarchical interactions between different annotation layers. We combined different annotation methods to construct the corpus. Manual annotation and annotation evaluation is on-going. The corpus will be used (i) investigate multimodal presentation and interaction strategies with respect

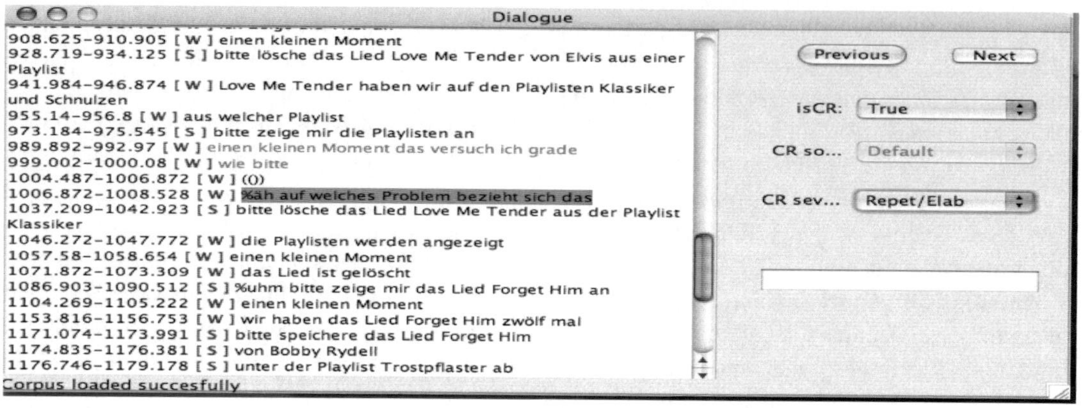

Figure 1: NXT-based tool for annotating CRs

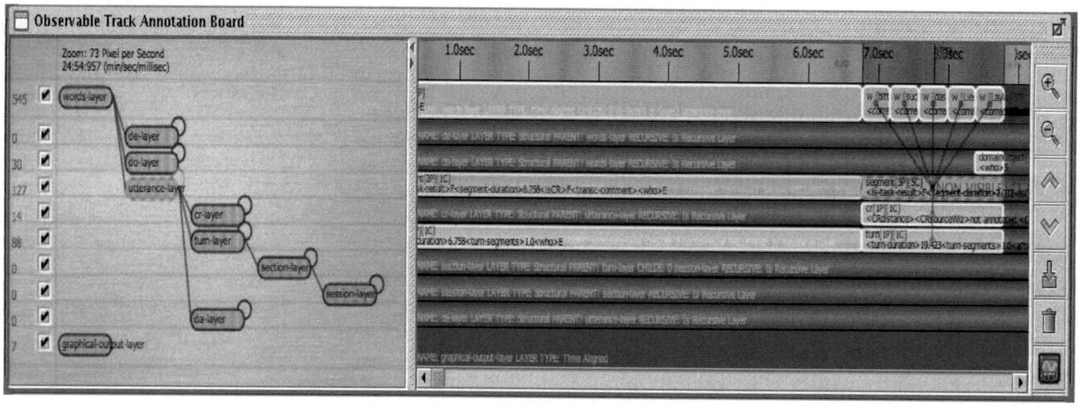

Figure 2: SAMMIE-2 corpus displayed in Amigram

to dialogue context and (ii) to design an initial policy for reinforcement learning of multimodal clarification strategies.

References

[Blaylock et al.2003] N. Blaylock, J. Allen, and G. Ferguson. 2003. Managing communicative intentions with collaborative problem solving. In *Current and New Directions in Discourse and Dialogue*, pages 63–84. Kluwer, Dordrecht.

[Carletta et al.2003] J. Carletta, S. Evert, U. Heid, J. Kilgour, J. Robertson, and H. Voormann. 2003. The NITE XML Toolkit: flexible annotation for multi-modal language data. *Behavior Research Methods, Instruments, and Computers, special issue on Measuring Behavior*. Submitted.

[Kruijff-Korbayová et al.2005] I. Kruijff-Korbayová, T. Becker, N. Blaylock, C. Gerstenberger, M. Kaißer, P. Poller, J. Schehl, and V. Rieser. 2005. An experiment setup for collecting data for adaptive output planning in a multimodal dialogue system. In *Proc. of ENLG*.

[Kruijff-Korbayová et al.2006] I. Kruijff-Korbayová, T. Becker, N. Blaylock, C. Gerstenberger, M. Kaißer, P. Poller, V. Rieser, and J. Schehl. 2006. The SAMMIE corpus of multimodal dialogues with an mp3 player. In *Proc. of LREC (to appear)*.

[Lauer et al.2005] C. Lauer, J. Frey, B. Lang, T. Becker, T. Kleinbauer, and J. Alexandersson. 2005. Amigram - a general-purpose tool for multimodal corpus annotation. In *Proc. of MLMI*.

[Martin et al.1999] D. L. Martin, A. J. Cheyer, and D. B. Moran. 1999. The open agent architecture: A framework for building distributed software systems. *Applied Artificial Intelligence: An International Journal*, 13(1–2):91–128, Jan–Mar.

[Rieser et al.2005] V. Rieser, I. Kruijff-Korbayová, and O. Lemon. 2005. A corpus collection and annotation framework for learning multimodal clarification strategies. In *Proc. of SIGdial*.

Representing and Accessing Multi-Level Annotations in MMAX2

Christoph Müller
EML Research gGmbH
Villa Bosch
Schloß-Wolfsbrunnenweg 33
69118 Heidelberg, Germany
christoph.mueller@eml-research.de

1 Introduction

MMAX2[1] is a versatile, XML-based annotation tool which has already been used in a variety of annotation projects. It is also the tool of choice in the ongoing project DIANA-Summ, which deals with anaphora resolution and its application to spoken dialog summarization. The project uses the ICSI Meeting Corpus (Janin et al., 2003), a corpus of multi-party dialogs which contains a considerable amount of simultaneous speech. It features a semi-automatically generated segmentation in which the corpus developers tried to track the flow of the dialog by inserting segment starts approximately whenever a person started talking. As a result, the corpus has some interesting structural properties, most notably overlap, that are challenging for an XML-based representation format. The following brief overview of MMAX2 focuses on this aspect, using examples from the ICSI Meeting Corpus.

2 The MMAX2 Data Model

Like most current annotation tools, MMAX2 makes use of *stand-off* annotation. The base data is represented as a sequence of `<word>` elements with exactly one PCDATA child each. Normally, these PCDATA children represent orthographical words, but larger or smaller units (e.g. characters) are also possible, depending on the required granularity of the representation.[2]

```
<?xml version="1.0" encoding="US-ASCII"?>
<!DOCTYPE words SYSTEM "words.dtd">
 <words>
  ...
  <word id="word_3710">That</word>
  <word id="word_3711">'s</word>
  <word id="word_3712">just</word>
  <word id="word_3713">a</word>
  <word id="word_3714" meta="true">Pause</word>
  <word id="word_3715">specification</word>
  <word id="word_3716">for</word>
  <word id="word_3717">the</word>
  <word id="word_3718">X_M_L</word>
  <word id="word_3719">Yep</word>
  <word id="word_3720">.</word>
  <word id="word_3721">format</word>
  <word id="word_3722">.</word>
  ...
 </words>
```

The order of the elements in the base data file is determined by the order of the segments that they belong to.

Annotations are represented in the form of `<markable>` elements which reference one or more base data elements by means of a `span` attribute. Each markable is associated with exactly one *markable level* which has a unique, descriptive name and which groups markables that belong to the same category or *annotation dimension*. Each markable level is stored in a separate XML file which bears the level name as an XML name space. The ID of a markable must be unique for the level that it belongs to. Markables can carry arbitrarily many features in the common `attribute=value` format. It is by means of these features that the actual annotation information is represented. For each markable level, admissible attributes and possible values are defined in an *annotation scheme* XML file (not shown). These annotation schemes are much more powerful for expressing attribute-related constraints than e.g. DTDs. The following first example shows the result of the segmentation of the sample base data. The `participant` attribute contains the identifier of the speaker that is associated with the respective segment.

```
<?xml version="1.0" encoding="US-ASCII"?>
<!DOCTYPE markables SYSTEM "markables.dtd">
 <markables xmlns="www.eml.org/NameSpaces/segment">
  ...
  <markable id="markable_468"
            span="word_3710..word_3714"
            participant="me012"/>
  <markable id="markable_469"
            span="word_3715..word_3718"
            participant="me012"/>
  <markable id="markable_470"
            span="word_3719..word_3720"
            participant="mn015"/>
  <markable id="markable_471"
            span="word_3721..word_3722"
            participant="me012"/>
  ...
 </markables>
```

[1] http://mmax.eml-research.de

[2] The `meta` attribute in the example serves to distinguish meta information from actual spoken words.

The next example contains markables representing the nominal and verbal chunks in the sample base data.

```
<?xml version="1.0" encoding="US-ASCII"?>
<!DOCTYPE markables SYSTEM "markables.dtd">
 <markables xmlns="www.eml.org/NameSpaces/chunks">
  ...
  <markable id="markable_7834"
            span="word_3710"
            type="demonstrative"/>
  <markable id="markable_7835"
            span="word_3711"
            type="copula"/>
  <markable id="markable_7836"
            span="word_3713..word_3715"
            type="nn"/>
  <markable id="markable_7837"
            span="word_3711..word_3715"
            type="predication"
            subject="markable_7834"/>
  <markable id="markable_7838"
            span="word_3717..word_3718,word_3721"
            type="nn"/>
  ...
 </markables>
```

The following basic facts about markables in MMAX2 are worth noting:

1. Every markable is defined with reference to the base data. Markables on the same or different levels are independent and ignorant of each other, and only related *indirectly*, i.e. by means of base data elements that they have in common.[3] Structural relations like embedding (*[['s] just [a specification]]*) can only be determined with recourse to the base data elements that each markable spans. This **lazy** representation makes it simple and straightforward to add markables and entire markable levels to existing annotations. It is also a natural way to represent non-hierarchical relations like **overlap** between markables. For example, a segment break runs through the nominal chunk represented by markable `markable_7836` (*[a specification]*) in the example above. If the segment markables were defined in terms of the markables contained in them, this would be a problem because the nominal chunk crosses a segment boundary. The downside of this lazy representation is that more processing is required for e.g. querying, when the structural relations between markables have to be determined.

2. Markables can be *discontinuous*. A markable normally spans a sequence of base data elements. Each *connected* subsequence of these is called a markable *fragment*. A discontinuous markable is one that contains more than one fragment, like markable `markable_7838` (*[the XML format]*) above. Actually, this markable exemplifies what could be called **discontinuous overlap** because it does not only cross a segment boundary, but it also has to omit elements from an intervening segment by another speaker.

[3]Note that this merely means that markables are not *defined* in terms of other markables, while they can indeed *reference* each other: In the above example, markable `markable_7837` (*['s just a specification]*) uses an associative relation (in this case named `subject`) to represent a reference to markable `markable_7834` (*[That]*) on the same level. References to markables on other levels can be represented by prefixing the markable ID with the level name.

3 Accessing Data From Within MMAX2

3.1 Visualization

When a MMAX2 document is currently loaded, the main display contains the base data text plus annotation-related information. This information can comprise

- line breaks (e.g. one after each segment),
- markable feature's values (e.g. the `participant` value at the beginning of each segment),
- literal text (e.g. a tab character after the `participant` value),
- markable customizations, and
- markable handles.

The so-called *markable customizations* are in charge of displaying text in different colors, fonts, font styles, or font sizes depending on a markable's features. The order in which they are applied to the text is determined by the order of the currently available markable levels. Markable customizations are processed bottom-up, so markable levels should be ordered in such a way that levels containing *smaller* elements (e.g. POS tags) should be on top of those levels containing *larger* elements (chunks, segments etc.). This way, smaller elements will not be hidden by larger ones.

When it comes to visualizing several, potentially embedded or overlapping markables, the so-called *markable handles* are of particular importance. In their most simple form, markable handles are pairs of short strings (most often pairs of brackets) that are displayed directly before and after each fragment of a markable. When two or more markables from different levels start at the same base data element, the *nesting order* of the markables (and their handles) is determined on the basis of the order of the currently available markable levels. The color of markable handles can also be customized depending on a markable's features. Figure 1 gives an idea of what the

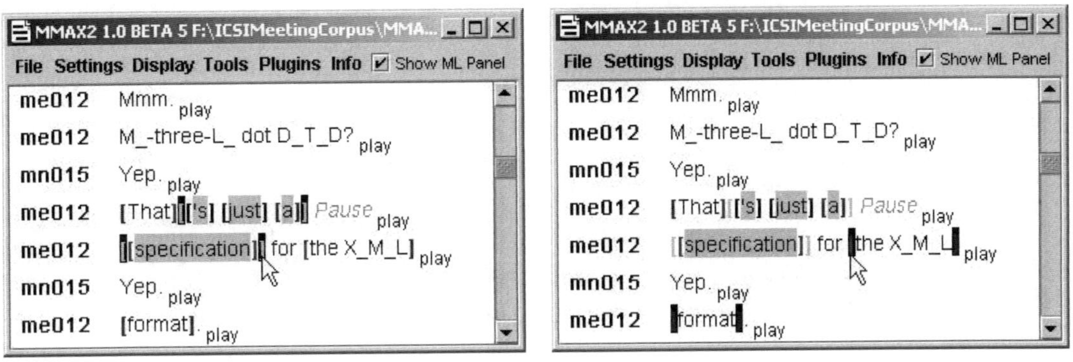

Figure 1: Highlighted markable handles on a discontinuous (left) and an overlapping (right) markable.

MMAX2 main window can look like. Both handles and text background for `chunk` markables with `type=predication` are rendered in light gray. Other handles are rendered in a darker color. Markable handles are sensitive to mouse events: resting the mouse pointer over a markable handle will highlight all handles of the pertaining markable. Reasonable use of markable customizations and handles allows for convenient visualization of even rather complex annotations.

3.2 Querying

MMAX2 includes a query console which can be used to formulate simple queries using a special multi-level query language called *MMAXQL*. A query in MMAXQL consists of a sequence of *query tokens* which describe elements (i.e. either base data elements or markables) to be matched, and *relation operators* which specify which relation should hold between the elements matched by two adjacent query tokens. A single markable query token has the form

```
string/conditions
```

where `string` is an optional regular expression and `conditions` specifies which features(s) the markable should match. The most simple condition is just the name of a markable level, which will match all markables on that level. If a regular expression is also supplied, the query will return only the matching markables. The query

```
[Aa]n?\s.+/chunks
```

will return all markables from the `chunks` level that begin with the indefinite article[4]. Markables with particular features can be queried by specifying the desired attribute-value combinations. The following query e.g. will return all markables from the `chunks` level with a `type` value of either `nn` or `demonstrative`:

```
/chunks.type={nn,demonstrative}
```

If a particular value is defined for *exactly* one attribute on *exactly* one markable level only, both the level and the attribute name can be left out in a query, rendering queries very concise (cf. the access to the `meta` level below).

Relation operators can be used to connect two query tokens to form a complex query. The set of supported sequential and hierarchical relation operators[5] includes `meets` (default), `starts`, `starts_with`, `in`, `dom`, `equals`, `ends`, `ends_with`, `overlaps_right`, and `overlaps_left`. Whether two markables stand in a certain relation is determined with respect to the base data elements that they span. In the current early implementation, for all markables (including discontinuous ones), only the first and last base data element is considered. The result of a query can directly be used as the input to another query. The following example gives an idea of what a more complex query can look like. The query combines the `segment` level, the `meta` level (which contains markables representing e.g. pauses, emphases, or sounds like breathing or mike noise), and the base data level to retrieve those instances of *you know* from the ICSI Meeting corpus that occur in segments spoken by female speakers[6] which also contain a pause or an emphasis (represented on the `meta` level):

```
'[Yy]ou know' in (/participant={f.*} dom /{pause,emphasis})
```

The next query shows how overlap can be han-

[4]The space character in the regular expression must be masked as `\s` because otherwise it will be interpreted as a query token separator.

[5]Associative relations are not discussed here, (Müller, 2005).

[6]The first letter of the `participant` value encodes the speaker's gender.

dled. It retrieves all `chunk` markables along with their pertaining segments by getting two partial lists and merging them using the operator `or`.

```
(/chunks in /segment) or (/chunks overlaps_right /segment)
```

4 Accessing Data by Means of XSL

MMAX2 has a built-in XSL style sheet processor[7] that can be used from the console to read a MMAX2 document and process it with a user-defined XSL style sheet. The XSL processor provides some special extensions for handling stand-off annotation as it is realized in MMAX2. In the current *beta* implementation, only some basic extensions exist. The style sheet processor can be called from the console like this:

```
org.eml.MMAX2.Process -in INFILE.mmax -style STYLEFILE.xsl
```

The root element of each MMAX2 document is the `words` element, i.e. the root of the base data file, which will be matched by the supplied XSL style sheet's default template. The actual processing starts in the XSL template for the `word` elements, i.e. the root element's children. A minimal template looks like this:

```
<xsl:template match="word">
 <xsl:text> </xsl:text>
  <xsl:apply-templates
        select="mmax:getStartedMarkables(@id)"
        mode="opening"/>
   <xsl:value-of select="text()"/>
  <xsl:apply-templates
        select="mmax:getEndedMarkables(@id)"
        mode="closing"/>
</xsl:template>
```

The above template inserts a white space before the current word and then calls an extension function that returns a NodeList containing all markables starting at the word. The template then inserts the word's text and calls another extension function that returns a NodeList of markables ending at the word. The markables returned by the two extension function calls are themselves matched by XSL templates. A minimal template pair for matching starting and ending markables from the `chunks` level and enclosing them in bold brackets (using HTML) looks like this:

```
<xsl:template match="chunks:markable" mode="opening">
 <b>[</b>
</xsl:template>
<xsl:template match="chunks:markable" mode="closing">
 <b>]</b>
</xsl:template>
```

Note how the markable level name (here: `chunks`) is used as a markable name space to control which markables the above templates should match. The following templates wrap a pair of <p> tags around each markable from the `segment` level and adds the value of the `participant` attribute to the beginning of each.

```
<xsl:template match="segment:markable" mode="opening">
 <xsl:text disable-output-escaping="yes">&lt;p&gt;</xsl:text>
 <b>
  <xsl:value-of select="@participant"/>
 </b>
</xsl:template>
<xsl:template match="segment:markable" mode="closing">
 <xsl:text disable-output-escaping="yes">&lt;/p&gt;</xsl:text>
</xsl:template>
```

Creating HTML in this way can be useful for converting a MMAX2 document with multiple levels of annotation to a *lean* version for distribution and (online) viewing.

5 Conclusion

MMAX2 is a practically usable tool for multi-level annotation. Its main field of application is the manual creation of annotated corpora, which is supported by flexible and powerful means of visualizing both simple and complex (incl. overlapping) annotations. MMAX2 also features a simple query language and a way of accessing annotated corpora by means of XSL style sheets. While these two data access methods are somewhat limited in scope, they are still useful in practice. If a query or processing task is beyond the scope of what MMAX2 can do, its simple and open XML data format allows for easy conversion into other XML-based formats, incl. those of other annotation and query tools.

Acknowledgements

This work has partly been funded by the Klaus Tschira Foundation (KTF), Heidelberg, Germany, and by the Deutsche Forschungsgemeinschaft (DFG) in the context of the project DIANA-Summ (STR 545/2-1).

References

Janin, A., D. Baron, J. Edwards, D. Ellis, D. Gelbart, N. Morgan, B. Peskin, T. Pfau, E. Shriberg, A. Stolcke & C. Wooters (2003). The ICSI Meeting Corpus. In *Proceedings of the IEEE International Conference on Acoustics, Speech and Signal Processing,* Hong Kong, pp. 364–367.

Müller, C. (2005). A flexible stand-off data model with query language for multi-level annotation. In *Proceedings of the Interactive Posters/Demonstrations session at the 43rd Annual Meeting of the Association for Computational Linguistics,* Ann Arbor, Mi., 25-30 June 2005, pp. pp. 109–112.

[7]Based on Apache's Xalan

Representing and Accessing Multilevel Linguistic Annotation using the MEANING Format

Emanuele Pianta
ITC-irst
38050, Povo
Trento, Italy
pianta@itc.it

Luisa Bentivogli
ITC-irst
38050, Povo
Trento, Italy
bentivo@itc.it

Christian Girardi
ITC-irst
38050, Povo
Trento, Italy
cgirardi@itc.it

Bernardo Magnini
ITC-irst
38050, Povo
Trento, Italy
magnini@itc.it

Abstract

We present an XML annotation format (MEANING Annotation Format, MAF) specifically designed to represent and integrate different levels of linguistic annotations and a tool that provides flexible access to them (MEANING Browser). We describe our experience in integrating linguistic annotations coming from different sources, and the solutions we adopted to implement efficient access to corpora annotated with the Meaning Format.

1 Introduction

It is well known that when using XML-based annotation schemes to represent multi layer annotations, it can be difficult to handle partially overlapping annotations. Annotating discontinuous elements may be considered as a variant of the same problem (Pianta and Bentivogli, 2004). Other difficulties can arise from the necessity of integrating manual and automatic annotations, as we will show in this paper.

One of the most effective solutions to the above mentioned problems is the so called *stand-off annotation*, based on the separation between textual data and annotations, and between various types of annotation, possibly pointing to same text. This approach has been systematically adopted in the design of MAF, a multilayer XML format developed for the EU-funded MEANING project, in the context of the creation of the Italian MEANING Corpus (Bentivogli et al., 2003).

In this paper we will describe our experience in the use of MAF, with special emphasis on how we solved issues related to representing annotation levels which come from different sources, and can possibly overlap. We will also give details about the solutions we adopted to allow for efficient access and human browsing of MAF standoff annotations.

The rest of the paper is organized as follows. Section 2 describes MAF and the types of annotations which have been represented with it. Section 3 reports on the integration into MAF of linguistic annotations coming from different sources. Section 4 illustrates the strategies adopted to make the information encoded in MAF quickly accessible. Finally, Section 5 presents the MEANING Browser, a tool for accessing and navigating corpora linguistically annotated with MAF.

2 The MEANING Format

Following the proposals for the ISO/TC 37/SC 4 standard for linguistic resources (Ide and Romary, 2002), the MAF scheme is based on annotation structures and data categories. Each type of *annotation structure* (nestable <struct> elements) corresponds to a specific kind of linguistic object (e.g. tokens, lexical units, multiwords), and each instance of a linguistic object is identified by a unique identifier. *Data categories* (<feat> tags) represent attributes of the linguistic objects. Different representation levels are contained in separate documents, or document sections. The XLink and XPointer syntax is used to represent relations between elements in different XML documents, and IDREFs attributes for relations within the same document.

2.1 First version

The first version of the MEANING Format has been used to represent seven kinds of information: orthographic features, the structure of the text, morphosyntactic information, multiwords, syntactic information, named entities, and word senses.

Annotation levels are related to each other following a hierarchy of annotation levels, which reflects a theoretically grounded hierarchy of linguistic objects. The basic (orthographic) annotation level, representing tokens, is implemented with pointers to the character positions in the hub corpus. Then the morphosyntactic level, representing word-related morphological information, contains pointers to the tokens, whereas the multiword level points to the words described at morphosyntactic level.

The following example shows how the morphosyntactic features of the Italian word "andare" (to go) are represented.

```
<struc  type="w-level" id="w_12"
        xlink:href="#xpointer(id('t_10'))">
   <feat type="lemma">andare</feat>
   <feat type="stem">and</feat>
   <feat type="pos">v</feat>
   <feat type="elra-tag">VF</feat>
   <feat type="mood">inf</feat>
   <feat type="tense">pres</feat>
</struc>
```

MAF also specifically addresses the problem of *discontinuous units*, such as for instance non-contiguous multiwords; see "*andarci* veramente *piano*" (*take it* really *easy*). A detailed study of how standoff annotation allows for an elegant treatment of this phenomenon can be found in (Pianta and Bentivogli 2004).

2.2 Second version

The first version of the MEANING Format has recently been extended within the FU-PAT ONTOTEXT project (Magnini et al. 2005).

Within this project, we are creating the Italian Content Annotation Bank (I-CAB), a corpus of Italian news stories annotated with different kinds of semantic information. Annotation is being carried out manually, as we intend I-CAB to become a benchmark for automatic Information Extraction and Ontology Population tasks, including recognition and normalization of various types of entities, temporal expressions, relations between entities, and relations between entities and temporal expressions (e.g. the relation *date-of-birth* connecting a person to a date).

To fulfill I-CAB annotation needs, we extended MAF, by adding a number of new linguistic annotation levels, i.e.:

- temporal expressions
- entities of type person and organization
- mentions (i.e. the textual expressions referring to the entities)

According to the hierarchical approach to representing relations between annotation levels in the first version of the MEANING Format, temporal expressions and entity mentions are represented with pointers to morphosyntactic level entities. Entities, instead, are represented with pointers to entity mentions.

To manually annotate temporal expressions we followed the TIMEX2 markup standard, while to mark entities and mentions we relied on the ACE entity detection task guidelines. To perform the annotation task we used Callisto (http://callisto.mitre.org).

3 Converting linguistic annotations into MAF

The manual annotations produced through Callisto, which is related to novel annotation levels such as temporal expressions and entity mentions, had to be integrated with more traditional annotations which are performed automatically with the TextPro tool, an automatic linguistic analysis Tool Suite developed at ITC-irst.

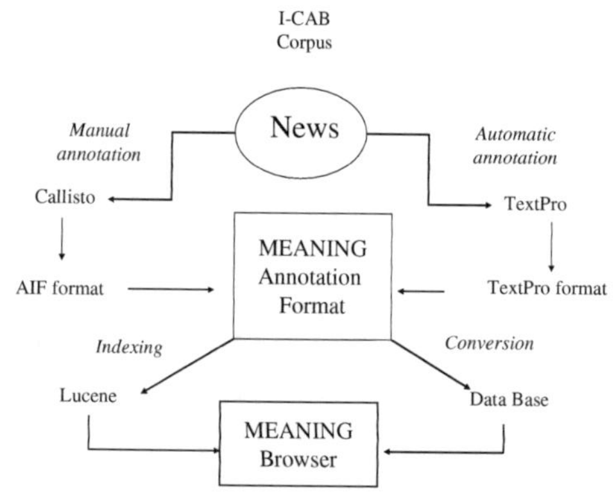

As one can see in the above figure, two different annotation processes (automatic and manual) produce two different formats which must be converted and integrated into MAF in order to be accessed by the MEANING Browser (or any other NLP tool).

3.1 From TextPro format to MEANING Format

TextPro takes a raw text as input and carries out basic processing tasks such as tokenization, morphological analysis, PoS tagging, lemmatization, and multiword recognition. The results of TextPro analyses are represented in a table, where each token is on a row, and columns contain multiple annotation levels. Converting from the TextPro to the MEANING Format requires retrieving the character positions of tokens in the hub corpus, which are not directly available in the TextPro output.

3.2 From AIF format to MEANING format

The Callisto manual annotation tool produces a coding format called AIF (Atlas Interchange Format), which implements a stand-off XML annotation scheme.

When using the Callisto graphical interface, all annotations of temporal expressions and entity mentions are carried out by selecting a sequence of contiguous characters. As a consequence, all AIF annotations make reference to character positions.

However, from Section 2.2 we know that in MAF temporal expressions and entity mentions make reference to morphosyntactic linguistic objects, not characters. This implies that, to go from AIF to the MEANING Format, we need to translate annotations making reference to the position of characters into annotations that point to morphological entities. More precisely, we need to substitute pointers to character positions with pointers to morphosyntactic objects which have been marked automatically by TextPro. Carrying out this step will also achieve the integration of manual and automatic annotations.

The integration step is possible because the MAF hierarchy of annotation levels points, at the lowest level, to character positions. By following the hierarchy of links relating the various annotation levels it is always possible to trace back a linguistic object to some sequence of characters in the raw text, and in the opposite direction, given a string, we know what linguistic objects correspond to it. Summing up, the integration of AIF annotations into MAF requires that, given the character positions contained in the AIF annotation of some string, we substitute the pointers to characters with the pointers to the linguistic objects that cover the same string.

4 Data Access

MAF turned out to be a flexible and expressive means to represent and integrate multiple levels of linguistic annotation. This was achieved mainly thanks to the adoption of the standoff annotation approach. However accessing and retrieving information spread in possibly very large repositories (hundreds of thousands) of XML files may be a challenging task even for Database Management Systems specifically designed to handle XML. To solve this problem we first analyzed existing native XML databases such as eXist, and Apache Xindice, but found that what was available at the time did not suited our needs. For this reason we approached the access problem through a two-fold strategy:

- converting XML data into a relational database
- indexing XML data and accessing them through a search engine (LUCENE)

The conversion of MAF data into a relational database is based on the following strategy. Each annotation level is mapped into a table, where rows represent instances of the relevant linguistic object (e.g. words), and columns represent its attributes (e.g. lemma, PoS, etc). Specific columns contain the object identifiers and the pointers to objects of other types/tables.

Once MAF data are stored in a relational database, they can be accessed quite efficiently. However, when the access to data requires joins of many tables, access times become incompatible with various kinds of applications, such as on-line corpus browsing. For this reason we tried to complement the use of a relational database with the exploitation of the indexing capability of the LUCENE search engine (http://lucene.apache.org/). To this extent we modified the LUCENE analyzer so as to be able to parse XML structures. In this way LUCENE can be configured in order to index any XML structure.

The fast access capabilities of a relational database combined with the extended indexing capabilities of LUCENE enabled us to implement a browser of MAF annotated corpora.

5 The MEANING Browser

The MEANING Browser can be used by humans to navigate any corpus encoded with MAF. The browser is built upon an API which can be used by any automatic system.

In the following, we are going to demonstrate how I-CAB texts and their annotations can be accessed through the MEANING Browser.

The first kind of access to the corpus is word-oriented, and amounts to a concordancer, i.e. a tool able to provide all the occurrences of a certain word in the corpus. The user can alternatively search for all occurrences of a *word form*, or a *lemma*, possibly constraining the search to a certain PoS. Free combinations between these constraints are allowed. The system will return a KWIC-like concordance of all the tokens in the corpus that match the request, within a chosen word window. By clicking on the magnifying glass, one can see the sentence in which the searched word occurs (see Appendix 1).

By clicking on a specific icon a new window is opened where the whole text is displayed and its linguistic annotations are made accessible. A number of graphical widgets allow the user to highlight the desired annotations: e.g. nouns, verbs, multiwords, temporal expressions, mentions of a specific entity.

In Appendix 2 the browser is used to show both nouns (automatically annotated) and entity mentions (from manual annotation). Appendix 3 shows time expressions and discontinuous multiwords; see how the multiword "ha rassegnato … le dimissioni" (*he resigned)* is made discontinuous by the occurrence of a time expression ieri (*yesterday*). The browser will also give morphosyntactic information about single words composing multiwords (governo, *government*). From the same window one can access the XML files encoding multiple annotation levels for the same document.

References

Bentivogli, L., Girardi, C., Pianta, E. 2003. The MEANING Italian Corpus. In *Proceedings of the Corpus Linguistics 2003 conference*, Lancaster, UK.

Ide, N. & Romary, L. 2002. Standards for Language Resources. In *Proceedings of LREC 2002*, Las Palmas, Canary Islands, Spain.

Magnini, B., Negri, M., Pianta, E., Romano, L., Speranza, M., Serafini, L., Girardi, C., Bartalesi, V., Sprugnoli, R. 2005. From Text to Knowledge for the Semantic Web: the ONTOTEXT Project. In *Proceedings of SWAP 2005 Workshop*, Trento, Italy.

Pianta, E. and Bentivogli, L. 2004. Annotating Discontinuous Structures in XML: the Multiword Case. In *Proceedings of the LREC 2004 Satellite Workshop on "XML-based richly annotated corpora"*, Lisbon, Portugal.

Appendix 1

Kwic Concordancer

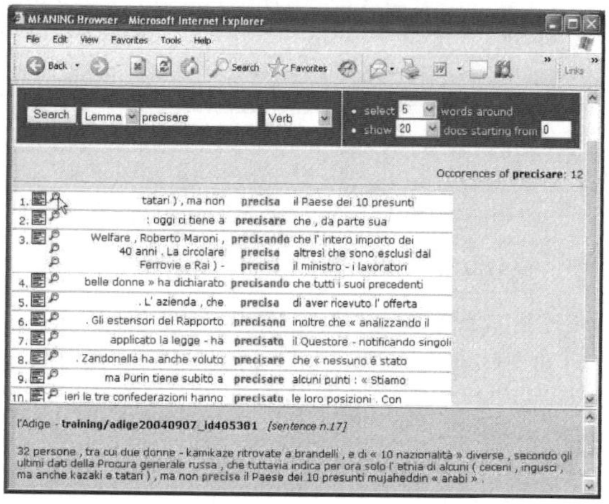

Appendix 2

Browsing nouns (in grey, automatic annotation) and entity mentions (Tony Blair, manual annotation)

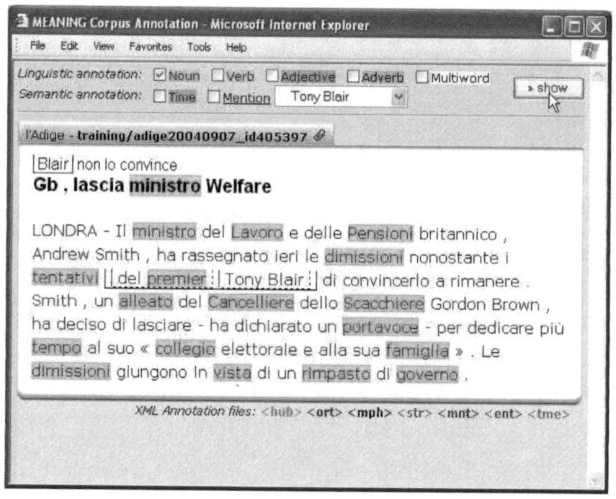

Appendix 3

Browsing discontinuous multiwords (ha rassegnato … le dimissioni, *he resigned*), time expressions (ieri, *yesterday*) and word information (governo)

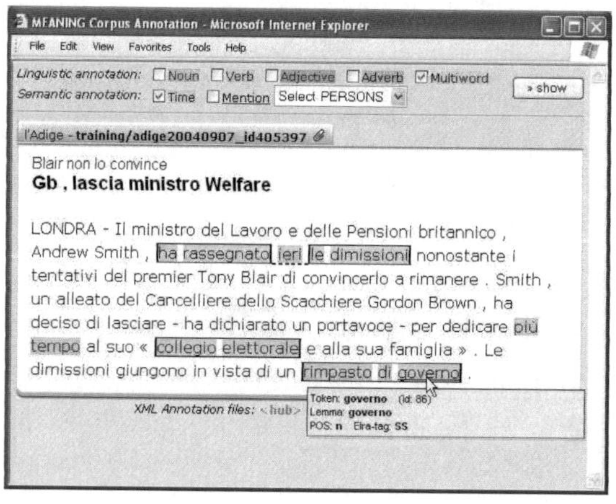

Middleware for Creating and Combining Multi-dimensional NLP Markup

Ulrich Schäfer
German Research Center for Artificial Intelligence (DFKI)
Language Technology Lab
Stuhlsatzenhausweg 3, D-66123 Saarbrücken, Germany
email: `ulrich.schaefer@dfki.de`

Abstract

We present the Heart of Gold middleware by demonstrating three XML-based integration scenarios where multi-dimensional markup produced online by multilingual natural language processing (NLP) components is combined to deliver rich, robust linguistic markup for use in NLP-based applications like information extraction, question answering and semantic web. The scenarios include (1) robust deep-shallow integration, (2) shallow processing cascades, and (3) treebank storage of multi-dimensionally annotated texts.

1 Introduction and Motivation

Heart of Gold is a middleware architecture for creating and combining markup produced by multiple natural language processing components in multilingual environments. It was initially developed for a special sort of multi-dimensional annotation, namely application-oriented, XML- and XSLT-based online integration of various shallow NLP components with a deep HPSG parser for increased robustness in the *hybrid* natural language processing paradigm (Callmeier et al., 2004).

The middleware, however, can also be used for various other online and offline tasks related to multi-dimensional markup creation and integration. These comprise automatic corpus annotation, incorporation of multi-dimensional markup into a single XML representation, and NLP component cascades interleaved with XSL annotation transformation. The middleware provides XML-RPC interfaces for simple, networking-enabled and programming language-independent application and component integration. Heart of Gold is available as one of the DELPH-IN open source tools available from `http://www.delph-in.net`[1].

2 Middleware Architecture

Fig. 1 gives a schematic overview of the middleware server in between applications (above) and external NLP components (below). When a new application session in Heart of Gold is started, it takes a configuration specifying NLP components to start for the session. Each component is started according to its own parameterized configuration. The client can send texts to the middleware and the

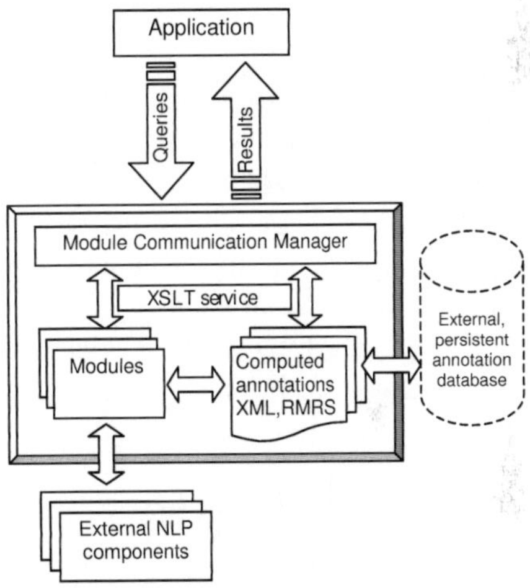

Figure 1: Middleware architecture

NLP components are then queried in a numerically defined processing order ('Depth' in Fig. 4). The shallowest components (e.g. tokenizer) are assigned a low number and are started first etc. The output of each component must be XML markup. Each component gets the output of the previous component as input by default, but can also request (via configuration) other annotations as input. Components may produce multiple output annotations (e.g. in different formats). Thus, the

[1] I would like to thank Robert Barbey, Özgür Demir and Thomas Klöcker for their implementation work, Bernd Kiefer and the co-authors in the cited papers for fruitful cooperation, and the reviewers for valuable comments. This work has been supported by a grant from the German Federal Ministry of Education and Research (FKZ 01IWC02).

component dependency structure in general forms a graph.

2.1 Session and multi-dimensional annotation management

The resulting multi-dimensional annotations are stored in a per-session markup storage (Fig. 2) that groups all annotations for an input query (a sentence or text) in *annotation collections*. The markup storage can also be made persistent by saving it to XML files or to an XML database. Annotations can be accessed uniquely via a URI of

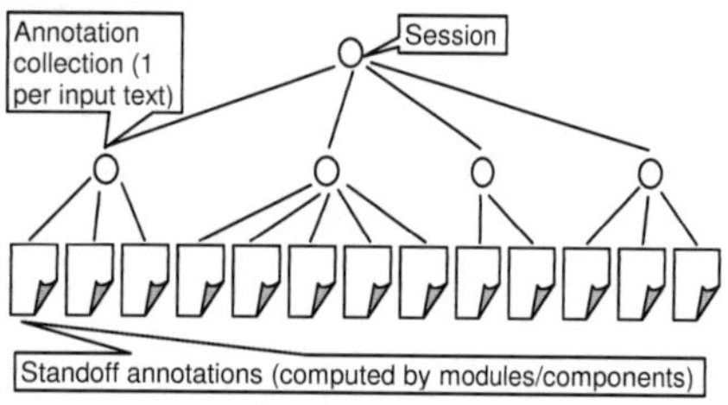

Figure 2: Session and multi-dimensional markup storage

the form `hog://sid/acid/aid` in XPath expressions where `sid` is a session ID, `acid` is an annotation collection ID and `aid` is an annotation identifier typically signifying the name of the producing component. Structured metadata like configuration and processing parameters (e.g. processing time and date, language ID etc.) are always stored within the annotation markup as first root daughter element.

2.2 XML standoff markup as first-class citizen

Unlike other NLP architectures (e.g. GATE (Cunningham et al., 2002) etc.), Heart of Gold treats XML standoff annotations (Thompson and McKelvie, 1997) as first class citizens and natively supports XML (and only XML) markup of any kind. Moreover, Heart of Gold does not prescribe specific DTDs or Schemata for annotations, provided that the markup is well-formed. In this sense, it is a completely open framework that may however be constrained by requirements of the actually configured components. The advantage of this openness is easy integration of new components. Mappings need only be defined for the immediately depending annotations (see next section) which is by far not an n-to-n mapping in practical applications.

However, the fact that a specific DTD or Schema is not imposed by the middleware does not mean that there are no minimal requirements. Linking between different standoff annotations is only possible on the basis of a least common entity, which we propose to be the character spans in the original text[2]. Moreover, we additionally propose the use of the XML ID/IDREF mechanism to facilitate efficient integration and combination of multi-dimensional markup.

Finally, depending on the scenario, specific common, standardized markup formats are appropriate, an example is RMRS (Copestake, 2003) for deep-shallow integration in Section 3 or the XML-encoded typed feature structure markup generated by SProUT (Drożdżyński et al., 2004).

2.3 XSLT as 'glue' and query language

We propose and Heart of Gold heavily relies on the use of XSLT for combining and integrating multi-dimensional XML markup. The general idea has already been presented in (Schäfer, 2003), but the developments and experiences since then have encouraged us to proceed in that direction and Heart of Gold can be considered as a successful, more elaborated proof of concept. The idea is related to the open markup format framework presented above: XSLT can be used to transform XML to other XML formats, or to combine and query annotations. In particular, XSLT stylesheets may resolve conflicts resulting from multi-dimensional markup, choose among alternative readings, follow standoff links, or decide which markup source to give higher preference.

(Carletta et al., 2003), e.g. propose the NXT Search query language that extends XPath by adding query variables, regular expressions, quantification and special support for querying temporal and structural relations. Their main argument against standard XPath is that it is impossible to constrain both structural and temporal relations within a single XPath query. Our argument is that XSLT can complement XPath where XPath alone is not powerful enough, yet providing a standardized language. Further advantages we see in the XSLT approach are portability and efficiency (in contrast to 'proprietary' and slow XPath extensions like NXT), while it has a quite simple syntax in its (currently employed) 1.0 version. XSLT can be conceived as a declarative specification language as long as an XML tree structure

[2] Our experience is that a common tokenization is not realistic—too many existing NLP components have differing concepts of what constitutes a token.

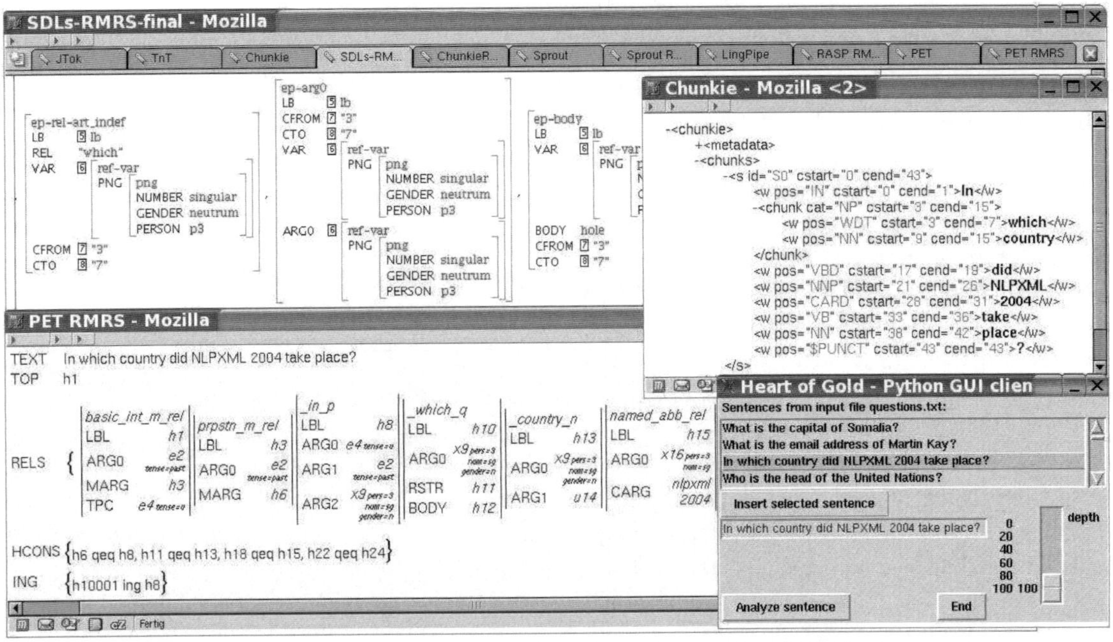

Figure 3: Heart of Gold analysis results in GUI with specialized XML visualizations

is preserved (not necessarily fully isomorphic to the input structure). However, XSLT is Turing-capable and therefore suited to solve in principle any markup integration or query problem. Finally, extensions like the upcoming XSLT/XPath 2.0 version or efficiency gains through XSLTC (translet compilation) can be taken on-the-fly and for free without giving up compatibility. Technically, the built-in Heart of Gold XSLT processor could easily replaced or complemented by an XQuery processor. However, for the combination and transformation of NLP markup, we see no advantage of XQuery over XSLT.

Heart of Gold comes with a built-in XSL transformation service, and module adapters (Section 2.4) can easily implement transformation support by including a few lines of code. Stylesheets can also be generated automatically in Heart of Gold, provided a systematic description of the transformation input format is available. An example is mapping from named entity grammar output type definitions in scenario 1 below. Stylesheets are also employed to visualize the linguistic markup, e.g. by transforming RMRS to HTML (Fig. 3) or LaTeX.

2.4 Integrated NLP components

NLP components are integrated through adapters called modules (either Java-based, subprocesses or via XML-RPC) that are also responsible for generating XML standoff output if this is not supported natively by the components (e.g., TnT, Chunkie). Various shallow and deep NLP components have already been integrated, cf. Fig. 4.

Component	Type	Depth	Languages
JTok	tokenizer	10	de, en, it,...
ChaSen	Jap. tagger	10	ja
TnT	stat. tagger	20	de, en
Chunkie	stat. chunker	30	de, en
ChunkieRmrs	chunk RMRS	35	de, en
LingPipe	stat. NER	40	en, es,...
SDL	subarchitect.		
Sleepy	shallow parser	40	de
SProUT	shallow NLP	40	de, el, en, ja,...
RASP	shallow NLP	50	en
PET	HPSG parser	100	de, el, en, ja,...

Figure 4: Integrated components. References for components and resources not cited are available on http://heartofgold.dfki.de/Publications_Components.html

3 Scenario 1: Deep-Shallow Integration

The idea of hybrid deep-shallow integration is to provide robust linguistic analyses through multi-dimensional NLP markup created by shallow and deep components, e.g. those listed in Fig. 4. Robustness is achieved in two ways: (1) various shallow components perform preprocessing and partial statistical disambiguation (e.g. PoS tagging of unknown words, named entity recognition) that can be used by a deep parser by means of a so-called XML input chart (multi-dimensional markup combined through XSLT in a single XML document in a format convenient for the parser). (2) shallow component's output is transformed through XSLT to partial semantic representations in RMRS syntax (Copestake, 2003) that is potentially more fine-grained and structured than what is digestible by the deep parser as preprocessing input (mainly PoS/NE type and span information via the XML input chart). This allows for (a) a fallback to the shallow representation in case deep parsing fails (e.g. due to ungrammatical input), (b) combination with the RMRS generated by deep parsing or fragments of it in case deep parsing fails.

First application scenarios have been investigated successfully in the DEEPTHOUGHT project (Uszkoreit et al., 2004). A further application (hybrid question analysis) is presented in (Frank et al., 2006). Recently, linking to ontology instances and concepts has been added (Schäfer, 2006).

4 Scenario 2: Shallow Cascades

The second scenario is described in (Frank et al., 2004) in detail. A robust, partial semantics representation is generated from a shallow chunker's output and morphological analysis (English and German) by means of a processing cascade consisting of four SProUT grammar instances with four interleaved XSLT transformations. The cascade is defined using the declarative system description language SDL (Krieger, 2003). An SDL architecture description is compiled into a Java class which is integrated in Heart of Gold as a sub-architecture module (Fig. 5). The scenario is equally a good example for XSLT-based annotation integration. Chunker analysis results are included in the RMRS to be built through an XSLT stylesheet using the XPath expression

```
document($uri)/chunkie/chunks/chunk[
    @cstart=$beginspan and @cend=$endspan]
```

where `$uri` is a variable containing an annotation identifier of the form `hog://sid/acid/aid` as explained in Section 2.1.

5 Scenario 3: Corpus Annotation

Given the powerful online middleware architecture described above, automatic, multi-dimensional corpus annotation can then be regarded as a simple by-product. Heart of Gold supports persistent storage of XML markup either on the file system or to XML databases through the built-in XML:DB interface. Through XSLT, it is possible to combine multi-dimensional markup (that would straightforwardly be stored in multiple XML documents) into a single XML document.

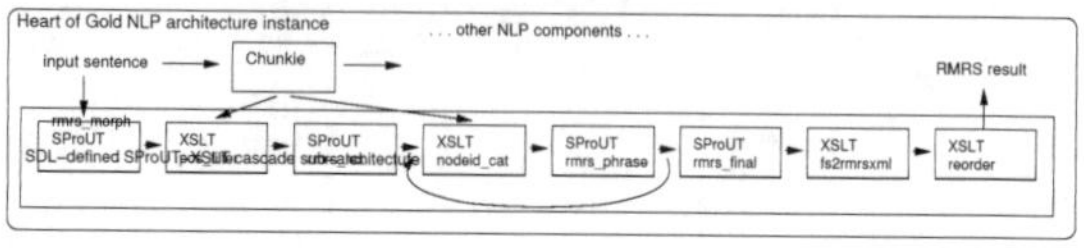

Figure 5: SProUT XSLT cascade in a Heart of Gold architecture instance.

References

U. Callmeier, A. Eisele, U. Schäfer, and M. Siegel. 2004. The DeepThought core architecture framework. In *Proc. of LREC-2004*, pages 1205–1208, Lisbon, Portugal.

J. Carletta, S. Evert, U. Heid, J. Kilgour, J. Robertson, and H. Voormann. 2003. The NITE XML toolkit: flexible annotation for multi-modal language data. *Behavior Research Methods, Instruments, and Computers, special issue on Measuring Behavior*, pages 353–363.

A. Copestake. 2003. Report on the design of RMRS. Technical Report D1.1b, University of Cambridge, UK.

H. Cunningham, D. Maynard, K. Bontcheva, and V. Tablan. 2002. GATE: A framework and graphical development environment for robust NLP tools and applications. In *Proceedings of ACL-2002*.

W. Drożdżyński, H.-U. Krieger, J. Piskorski, U. Schäfer, and F. Xu. 2004. Shallow processing with unification and typed feature structures — foundations and applications. *Künstliche Intelligenz*, 2004(1):17–23.

A. Frank, K. Spreyer, W. Drożdżyński, H.-U. Krieger, and U. Schäfer. 2004. Constraint-based RMRS construction from shallow grammars. In *Proceedings of HPSG-2004*, pages 393–413. CSLI Publications, Stanford.

A. Frank, H.-U. Krieger, F. Xu, H. Uszkoreit, B. Crysmann, and U. Schäfer. 2006. Question answering from structured knowledge sources. *Journal of Applied Logics, Special Issue on Questions and Answers*. To appear.

H.-U. Krieger. 2003. SDL—a description language for building NLP systems. In *Proceedings of the HLT-NAACL Workshop on the Software Engineering and Architecture of Language Technology Systems*, pages 84–91.

U. Schäfer. 2003. WHAT: An XSLT-based infrastructure for the integration of natural language processing components. In *Proceedings of the HLT-NAACL Workshop on the Software Engineering and Architecture of Language Technology Systems*, pages 9–16, Edmonton, Canada.

U. Schäfer. 2006. OntoNERdIE—mapping and linking ontologies to named entity recognition and information extraction resources. In *Proc. of LREC-2006*, Genoa, Italy.

H. S. Thompson and D. McKelvie. 1997. Hyperlink semantics for standoff markup of read-only documents. In *Proceedings of SGML-EU-1997*.

H. Uszkoreit, U. Callmeier, A. Eisele, U. Schäfer, M. Siegel, and J. Uszkoreit. 2004. Hybrid robust deep and shallow semantic processing for creativity support in document production. In *Proc. of KONVENS-2004*, pages 209–216.

Multidimensional markup and heterogeneous linguistic resources

Maik Stührenberg **Andreas Witt** **Daniela Goecke** **Dieter Metzing** **Oliver Schonefeld**
Faculty for Linguistics and Literature
Bielefeld University, Germany
{maik.stuehrenberg|andreas.witt|daniela.goecke|dieter.metzing|oliver.schonefeld}@uni-bielefeld.de

Abstract

The paper discusses two topics: firstly an approach of using multiple layers of annotation is sketched out. Regarding the XML representation this approach is similar to standoff annotation. A second topic is the use of heterogeneous linguistic resources (e.g., XML annotated documents, taggers, lexical nets) as a source for semi-automatic multi-dimensional markup to resolve typical linguistic issues, dealing with anaphora resolution as a case study.[1]

1 Introduction – Why (and how) to use heterogeneous linguistic resources

A large and diverse amount of linguistic resources (audio and video recodings, textual recordings) has been piled up during various projects all over the world. A reasonable subset of these resources consists of machine-readable structured linguistic documents (often XML annotated), dictionaries, grammars or ontologies. Sometimes these are available to the public on the Web, cf. Simons (2004). The availability allows for the sophisticated examination of linguistic questions and the reuse of existing linguistic material. Especially corpora annotated for discourse-related phenomena have become an important source for various linguistic studies. Besides annotated corpora external knowledge bases like lexical nets (e.g., WordNet, GermaNet) and grammars, can be used to support several linguistic processes.

Although XML has recently established itself as the technology and format of choice the before mentioned resources remain heterogeneous in respect of the data format (i.e., the underlying schema) or the functionality provided. A simple approach to make use of different resources is to use them one by one, starting with raw text data (or annotated XML) as input and providing the output of the first process (e.g., a tagger) as input for the next step (e.g., a parser). However, this method may lead to several problems. One possible problem of this method is that the output format of one processing resource can be unemployable as input format for the next. Another potential problem of using XML annotated documents is overlapping annotation. And finally it is sometimes necessary (or desirable) to process only parts of the input document.

The structure of the paper is as follows: In Section 2 our approach of representing multiple annotations is desribed, in Section 3 the use of multi-root trees for the representation of heterogeneous ressources is presented. As a case study, the resolution of anaphoric relations is described in Section 4.

2 Multiple annotations

Representing data corresponding to different levels of annotation is a fundamental problem of text-technological research. Renear et al. (1996) discuss the OHCO-Thesis[2] as one of the basic assumptions about the structure of text and show that this assumption cannot be upheld consistently. Being based on the OHCO-Thesis most markup languages (including SGML and XML) are designed in principle to represent one structure per document. Options to resolve this problem are discussed in Barnard et al. (1995) and several other

[1]The work presented in this paper is part of the project *A2 Sekimo* of the Research Group *Text-technological modelling of information* funded by the German Research Foundation.

[2]The OHCO-Thesis, first presented in DeRose et al. (1990) states "that text is best represented as an ordered hierarchy of content object (OHCO)."

proposals. To avoid drawbacks of the above mentioned approaches Witt (2002; 2004) discusses an XML based solution which is used in our project.

2.1 Representation

We address the issue of overlapping markup by using separate annotations of relevant phenomena (e.g., syntactic information, POS, document structure) according to different document grammars, i.e., the same textual data is encoded several times (in separate files). One advantage of this multiple annotation is that the modeling of information on a level A is not dependent in any way on a level B (in contrast to the standoff annotation model described by Thompson and McKelvie (1997), where a primary modeling level is needed). Additional annotation layers can be added easily without any changes to the layers already established. The primary data (i.e., the text which will be annotated) is separated from the markup and serves as key element for establishing relations between the annotation tiers. Witt et al. (2005) describe a knowledge representation format (in the programming language Prolog[3]) which can be used to draw inferences between separate levels of annotations and in which the parts of text (the `PCDATA` in XML terms) are used as an absolute reference system and as link between the levels of annotation (cf. Bayerl et al. (2003)).

This representation format allows us to use various linguistic resources. A Python script converts the different annotation layers (XML Documents) to the above mentioned Prolog representation which serves as input for the unification process. The elements, attributes and text of all annotation layers are stored as Prolog predicates. As a requirement all files must be identical with respect to their underlying character data, what we call identity of primary data.

2.2 Unification

Figure 1 shows the architecture used for the unification process. Different annotation layers are unified, i.e., merged into one output fact base. A script reconverts the Prolog representation into one well-formed XML document containing the annotations from the layers plus the textual content. In case of overlapping elements (which may be the result of the unification), it converts those elements to milestones or fragments (cf. TEI Guidelines (2004)) according to parameter options. A Java-based GUI is available to ease the use of the above mentioned framework.

3 Multi-rooted trees

Based on the before mentioned architecture we now focus on the usage of heterogeneous linguistic resources (as described in in Section 1) in order to semi-automatically add layers of markup to various XML (or plain text) documents. We prefer the term *multi-rooted trees* in favor of *multiple annotations*, i.e., different layers of annotation are stored in a single representation (based on the above mentioned architecture). The input document is separated into the textual information and the annotation tree (if there is any). Both of these are provided as input for linguistic resources. The output of this process (typically an XML annotated document) is again separated into text and markup and serves as input for another resource. Figure 2 gives an overview over the process.

4 Heterogeneous linguistic resources for anaphora resolution: a case study

We use multi-rooted trees in order to annotate and model coreferential phenomena and anaphoric relations (cf. Sasaki et al (2002)). Base for the resolution of anaphoric relations (both pronominal anaphora and definite description anaphora) is a small test corpus containing German newspaper articles and scientific articles in German and English. Figure 3 shows an excerpt of a German newspaper article taken from "Die Zeit". In this example the first linguistic resource to apply is a parser (in our case Machinese Syntax by Connexor Oy). As a second step an XSLT script uses the input document and the parser output and tags discourse entities (see element `de` in Figure 3) by judging several syntactic criteria provided by the parser. The discourse entities mark the starting point to determine anaphora-antecedent-relations between pairs of discourse entities.

In order to resolve bridging relations (e.g., "door" as a meronym of "room"), WordNet (GermaNet for German texts) is used as a linguistic resource to establish relationships between discourse entities according to the information stored in the synsets[4]. By now, we use an Open Source

[3] An additional representation format integrates the representation of multi-rooted trees developed in the NITE-Project (cf. Carletta et al. (2003)).

[4] A synset represents a concept and consists of a set of one or more synonyms.

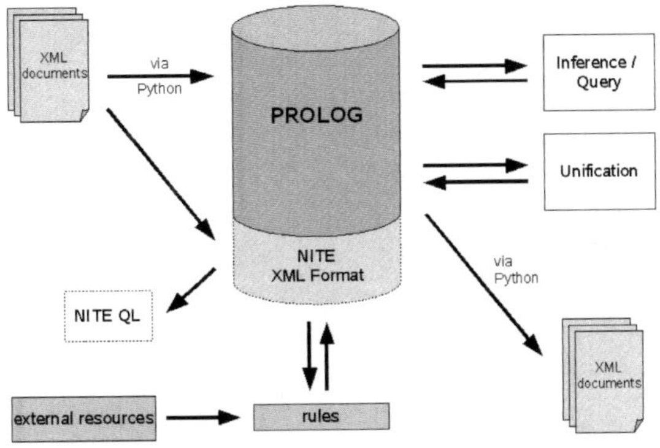

Figure 1: Overview of the architecture

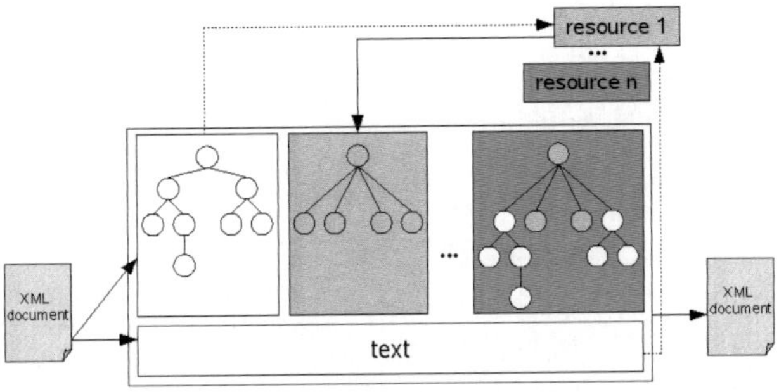

Figure 2: Using heterogeneous linguistic resources

```
<doc_article>
 <doc_sect1>
 <doc_title/>
  <doc_para>
   <chs_sentence id="s22">
    <chs_de deLemma="rolf" deID="de_n_078" deType="nom">Marie Rolfs</chs_de> ist <
     chs_de deLemma="jahr" deID="de_n_079" deType="nom">vier Jahre</chs_de> alt.
   </chs_sentence>
   <chs_sentence id="s23">
    Mit <chs_de deLemma="petra" deID="de_n_080" deType="nom">ihrer
     Zwillingsschwester Petra</chs_de>, <chs_de deLemma="bruder" deID="de_n_081"
     deType="nom">ihrem achtjährigen Bruder</chs_de> und <chs_de deLemma="mutter"
     deID="de_n_082" deType="nom">ihrer Mutter Sabine</chs_de> wohnt <chs_de deLemma
     ="sie" deID="de_n_083" deType="nom">sie</chs_de> in <chs_de deLemma="
     dreizimmerwohnung" deID="de_n_084" deType="nom">einer Dreizimmerwohnung in <
     chs_de deLemma="rahlstedt" deID="de_n_085" deType="nom">Rahlstedt a<chs_de
     deLemma="stadt#rand" deID="de_n_086" deType="nom">m östlichen Hamburger
     Stadtrand</chs_de> </chs_de> </chs_de>.
   </chs_sentence>
   <chs_semRel>
   <chs_cospecLink relType="poss" phorIDRef="de_n_080" antecedentIDRefs="de_n_078"/>
   <chs_cospecLink relType="poss" phorIDRef="de_n_081" antecedentIDRefs="de_n_078"/>
   <chs_cospecLink relType="poss" phorIDRef="de_n_082" antecedentIDRefs="de_n_078"/>
   <chs_cospecLink relType="ident" phorIDRef="de_n_083" antecedentIDRefs="de_n_078"/
    >
   </chs_semRel>
  </doc_para>
 </doc_sect1>
</doc_article>
```

Figure 3: An extract of a German newspaper article marked up by several linguistic resources

native XML database[5] as test tool for querying the GermaNet data[6]. Resolving synonymous or hyperonymous anaphoric relations is done by using XPath or XQuery queries on pairs of discourse entities. Bridging relations are harder to track down and will be focused on in the near future.

Figure 3 shows the shortened and manually revised output of the anaphora resolution. In this example two annotation layers have been merged: the logical document structure (in our case a moddified version of *DocBook*, `doc`) and the level of semantic relations (`chs`). The logical document structure describes the organisation of the text document in terms of chapters, sections, paragraphs, and the like. The level of semantic relations describes discourse entities and relations between them. Corpus investigations give rise to the supposition that the logical text structure influences the search scope of candidates for antecedents. Anaphoric relations are annotated with a `cospecLink` element (lines 12 to 15). The attribute `relType` holds the type of relation between two discourse entities. Line 15 is an example of an identity relation between discourse entity `de_n_078` ("Marie Rolfs", line 6) and discourse entity `de_n_083` ("sie", line 9) whereby the first is marked as antecedent.

5 Conclusion

The architecture shown in this paper provides access to multiple layers of linguistic annotation and allows for the reuse and integration of existing linguistic resources. The resulting additional annotation layers are extremely useful for solving complex linguistic issues like anaphora resolution. It is our goal to enable a semi-automatic anaphora resolution by the end of the project life-span.

References

Barnard, David, Burnard, Lou, Gaspart, Jean-Pierre Gaspart, Price, Lynne A., Spergerg-McQueen, C. M. and Giovanni Battista Varile. 1995. Hierarchical encoding of text: Technical problems and SGML solutions. *Computers and the Humanities*, 29(3):211–231.

Bayerl, Petra Saskia, Lüngen, Harald, Goecke, Daniela, Witt, Andreas and Daniel Naber. 2003. Methods for the semantic analysis of document markup. In *Proceedings of the 2003 ACM symposium on Document engineering*, pages 161–170, New York, NY, USA. ACM Press.

Carletta, Jean Kilgour, Jonathan, O'Donnel, Timothy J., Evert, Stefan and Holger Voormann. 2003. The NITE Object Model Library for Handling Structured Linguistic Annotation on Multimodal Data Sets. In *Proceedings of the EACL Workshop on Language Technology and the Semantic Web (3rd Workshop on NLP and XML (NLPXML-2003))*, Budapest, Hungary.

DeRose, Steven J., Durand, David G., Mylonas, Elli and Allen H. Renear. 1990. What is text, really? *Journal of Computing in Higher Education*, 1(2):3–26.

Renear, Allen, Mylonas, Elli and David Durand. 1996. Refining our notion of what text really is: The problem of overlapping hierarchies. *Research in Humanities Computing. Selected Papers from the ALLC/ACH Conference, Christ Church, Oxford, April 1992*, 4:263–280.

Sasaki, Felix, Wegener, Claudia, Metzing, Dieter Metzing and Jens Pönninghaus. 2002. Co-reference annotation and resources: A multilingual corpus of typologically diverse languages. In *Proceedings of the 3nd International Conference on Language Resources and Evaluation (LREC 2002)*, pages 1225–1230, Las Palmas.

Simons, Gary, Lewis, William, Farrar, Scott, Langendoen, Terence, Fitzsimons, Brian and Hector Gonzalez. 2004. The Semantics of Markup: Mapping Legacy Markup Schemas to a Common Semantics. In Graham Wilcock, Nancy Ide and Laurent Romary, editor, *Proceedings of the 4th Workshop on NLP and XML (NLPXML-2004)*, pages 25–32, Barcelona, Spain, July. Association for Computational Linguistics.

Sperberg-McQueen, C. M. and Lou Burnard, editor. 2004. *Guidelines for Text Encoding and Interchange*. published for the TEI Consortium by Humanities Computing Unit, University of Oxford.

Thompson, Henry S. and David McKelvie. 1997. Hyperlink semantics for standoff markup of read-only documents. In *Proceedings of SGML Europe '97: The next decade – Pushing the Envelope*, pages 227–229, Barcelona.

Witt, Andreas, Goecke, Daniela, Sasaki, Felix and Harald Lüngen. 2005. Unification of XML Documents with Concurrent Markup. *Literary and Lingustic Computing*, 20(1):103–116.

Witt, Andreas. 2002. Meaning and interpretation of concurrent markup. In *ALLCACH2002, Joint Conference of the ALLC and ACH*, Tübingen.

Witt, Andreas. 2004. Multiple hierarchies: new aspects of an old solution. In *Proceedings of Extreme Markup Languages*.

[5]eXist (`http://www.exist-db.org`)

[6]GermaNet is available as an XML representation which can be stored (and queried) in the above mentioned (and additional) native XML database.

Layering and Merging Linguistic Annotations

Keith Suderman
Department of Computer Science
Vassar College
Poughkeepsie, NY USA
suderman@cs.vassar.edu

Nancy Ide
Department of Computer Science
Vassar College
Poughkeepsie, NY USA
ide@cs.vassar.edu

Abstract

The American National Corpus and its annotations are represented in a stand-off XML format compliant with the specifications of ISO TC37 SC4 WG1's Linguistic Annotation Framework. Because few systems that enable search and access of the corpus currently support stand-off markup, the project has developed a SAX *like* parser that generates ANC data with annotations in-line, in a variety of output formats.

1 Introduction

The American National Corpus (ANC) project[1] recently released its 2nd release consisting of approximately 22 million words of data, representing a variety of genres of both written and spoken data. The corpus is annotated with several layers of automatically produced linguistic information, including sentence and token boundaries, part of speech using two different POS tagsets (a version of the Penn tagset[2] and the Biber tagset[3]), and noun chunks and verb chunks.

ANC primary documents are plain text (UTF-16) documents and are treated as "read only" resources. All annotations are represented in stand-off XML documents referencing spans in the primary data or other annotation documents, using the XCES[4] implementation of the specifications of ISO TC37 SC4's Linguistic Annotation Framework (LAF) (Ide and Romary, 2004). Because few systems that enable search and access of the corpus currently support stand-off markup, the project has developed a parser that generates ANC data with annotations in-line, in a variety of output formats.

This demonstration will show the "life-cycle" of an ANC document, from acquisition of a document in any of a variety of formats (MS Word, PDF, HTML, etc.) through annotation and final representation in the stand-off format. The ANC tool for merging annotations of the user's choice with the primary data to produce a single document with in-line annotations will also be demonstrated.

2 ANC Document Life-Cycle

Documents to be included in the ANC are acquired in many different formats, including MS Word, PDF, HTML, Quark Express, etc. Processing involves a series of steps, which are outlined below.

2.1 Conversion from original format to "rudimentary" XML

The ANC receives documents in a variety of different formats. The first step in processing is to convert the input documents into XCES XML with basic structural annotations included. The most common types of file formats encountered are:

- **Microsoft Word.** The release of OpenOffice 2 has greatly simplified the processing of MS Word documents. OpenOffice uses XSL and XSLT stylesheets to export files to XML and ships with stylesheets to generate DocBook and TEI-compliant formats. We modified the TEI stylesheet to create XCES XML. OpenOffice's Java API enables us to automate and integrate OpenOffice with later processing steps.
- **XML/SGML/HTML**. processing of XML files typically involves using XSLT to map element names to XCES. SGML and HTML files typically require preprocessing to render them into valid XML, followed by the application of an XSLT stylesheet to convert them to XCES.

[1] http:// americannationalcorpus.org
[2] http://americannationalcorpus.org/FirstRelease/gatetags.txt
[3] http://americannationalcorpus.org/FirstRelease/Biber-tags.txt
[4] http://www.xces.org

- **Quark Express.** Several publishers provided documents prepared for publication using Quark Express. Quark documents can be exported in XML, but doing so is worthwhile only if the creator of the document takes advantage of Quark's style-definition facilities (which was not the case for any of the contributed Quark documents). We therefore exported the documents in RTF; however, many fonts and special characters are improperly rendered, and fairly extensive manual editing was therefore required to render the files into a format that could be used. Once edited, the same procedures for MS Word documents are used to generate XCES.
- **PDF.** Bitmap PDF files are unusable for our purposes. Adobe Acrobat can generate plain text from PDF, although this process loses much of the formatting information that would be desirable to retain to facilitate later processing. In some cases, ligatures and other special characters are improperly represented in the text version, and it is not always possible to automatically detect and convert them to conform to the original. PDF documents with two or more columns cannot, to our knowledge, be extracted without some misordering of the text in the results.
- **Other formats.** Other formats in which the ANC has acquired documents include plain text and plain text that employed a variety of proprietary markup languages. These documents are processed on a case by case basis, using specialized scripts.

2.2 GATE processing and annotation

We use the University of Sheffield's GATE system[5] for the bulk of ANC document processing and annotation, currently including tokenization, sentence splitting, part of speech tagging, noun chunking, and verb chunking. Most annotations are produced using GATE's built-in ANNIE components; we have, however, modified the ANNIE sentence splitter and created several Java plug-ins for use in GATE that perform basic bookkeeping, renaming of annotations/features, moving of annotations between annotation sets etc. We have also developed a scripting language (XORO[6]) for use with GATE to enable easy bulk processing and re-processing of the entire corpus, or to apply selected annotation steps without having to load the files into a GATE corpus or data store. This eases iterative development as documents are added and tools are refined.

2.3 Creation of standoff annotation documents

We have developed several custom processing resources that plug into GATE to generate standoff annotations in the XCES implementation of the LAF format. The last step in our GATE pipeline is to create the primary text document and generate all the required standoff annotation files.

3 Standoff Format

The ANC standoff format for annotations is a simple graph representation, consisting of one node set and one, or more, edge sets. The node set is represented by the text itself, with an implied node between each character. Each edge set is represented by an XML document and may contain one or more annotation types: logical structure, sentence boundaries, tokens, etc.

An ANC header file for each document is used to associate the source text with the standoff annotation documents; for example:

```
<cesHeader>
  ...
  <annotations>
    <annotation type="content"
       ann.loc="en_4065.txt">
       Text content</annotation>
    <annotation type="logical"
       ann.loc="en_4065-logical.xml">
       Logical structure</annotation>
    <annotation type="s"
       ann.loc="en_4065-s.xml">
       Sentence boundaries</annotation>
    <annotation type="hepple"
       ann.loc="en_4065-hepple.xml">
       Hepple POS tags</annotation>
    <annotation type="biber"
       ann.loc="en_4065-biber.xml">
       Biber POS tags</annotation>
    <annotation type="vp"
       ann.loc="en_4065-vp.xml">
       Verb chunks</annotation>
    <annotation type="np"
       ann.loc="en_4065-np.xml">
       Noun chunks</annotation>
  </annotations>
    ...
</cesHeader>
```

ANC annotation documents are marked up with the XCES representation of the nodes and edge sets of the annotation graph. The following shows a segment of the document containing part of speech annotation:

[5] http://gate.ac.uk
[6] http:// americannationalcorpus.org/xoro.html

```
<cesAna
   xmlns="http://www.xces.org/schema/2003"
   version="1.0.4">
   <struct type="tok" from="4" to="6">
      <feat name="base" value="in"/>
      <feat name="msd" value="IN"/>
   </struct>
   <struct type="tok" from="7" to="11">
      <feat name="msd" value="DT"/>
      <feat name="base" value="this"/>
   </struct>
   <struct type="tok" from="12" to="19">
      <feat name="base" value="chapter"/>
      <feat name="msd" value="NN"/>
   </struct>
   ...
</cesAna>
```

Each `<struct>` element represents an edge in the graph; values of the *from* and *to* attributes denote the nodes (between characters in the primary text document) over which the edge spans.

3.1 Annotating discontiguous spans

Presently, the ANC includes standoff annotations that reference contiguous spans of data in the original (primary) document. However, we plan to add a wide variety of automatically-produced annotations for various linguistic phenomena to the ANC data, some of which will reference discontiguous regions of the primary data, or may reference annotations contained in other standoff documents. This is handled as follows: given an annotation graph, *G*, we create an edge graph *G'* whose nodes can themselves be annotated, thereby allowing for edges between the edges of the original annotation graph *G*.

For example, consider the sentence "My dog has fleas." The standoff annotations for the tokens would be:

```
                          1
0 1 2 3 4 5 6 7 8 9 0 1 2 3 4 5 6
|M|y| |d|o|g| |h|a|s| |f|l|e|a|s|

<struct … id="t1" from="0" to="2"/>
<struct … id="t2" from="3" to="6"/>
<struct … id="t3" from="7" to="10"/>
<struct … id="t4" from="11" to="16"/>
```

Now consider the dependency tree generated by Minipar[7] given in Figure 2. The tree can be represented by annotating the token elements in the standoff annotation document as follows:

```
<!-- Define some pseudo nodes -->
<node type="root" id"E0" ref="t3"/>
<node type="clone" id="E2" ref="t2"/>


<!-- Define edges in dependency tree -->
<struct type="subj" id="s1"
        from="t3" to="E2"/>
<struct type="s" id="s2"
        from="t3" to="t2"/>
<struct type="gen" id="gen"
        from="t2" to="t1"/>
<struct type="obj" id="obj"
        from="t3" to="t4"/>
```

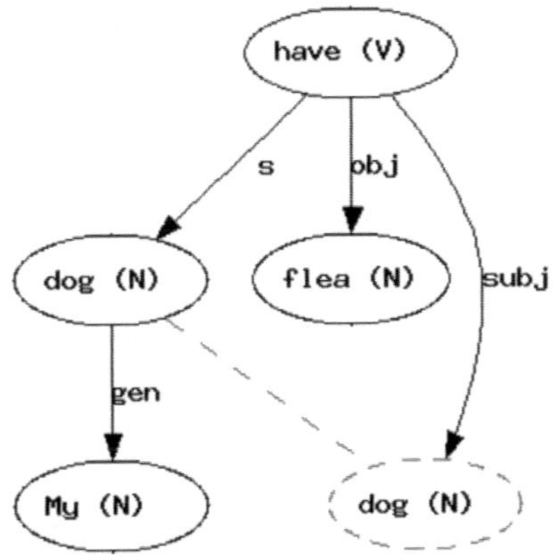

Figure 2. Dependency tree generated by Minipar.[8]

4 Creating In-line Annotation Documents

We have developed an "XCES Parser"[9] that implements the org.xml.sax.XMLReader interface to create ANC documents containing in-line annotations in XML (or any other format).

The XCES parser works as follows: annotations to be loaded are selected with the `org.xml.sax.XMLReader.setProperty()` method. The selected annotation sets are then loaded into a single list in memory and sorted, first by offset and, if the offsets are the same, secondly by annotation type. At present, the ordering of annotation types are hard coded into the parser; work is underway to make the XCES parser "schema aware" so that embedding specifications can be provided by the user. Once the text is loaded and sorted, the appropriate SAX2 events are generated and dispatched to the org.xml.sax.ContentHandler (if one has been registered with the parser) in sequence to simulate the parsing of an XML document. While the parser will allow the programmer to specify an ErrorHandler, DTDHandler, or EntityResolver, at this time no methods from those interfaces will be invoked during parsing.

In the current version of the XCES parser, when overlapping annotations are encountered, they are "truncated". For example:

```
<s>Sentence <em>one.</s><s>Sentence</em>
two.</s>
```

[7] http://www.cs.ualberta.ca/~lindek/minipar.htm

[8] Image generated by http://ai.stanford.edu/~rion/parsing/minipar_viz.html

[9] http://americannationalcorpus.org/tools/index.html#xces-parser

becomes

```
<s>Sentence <em>one.</em></s><s>Sentence
two.</s>
```

Work is underway to provide the option to generate milestones in CLIX/HORSE (DeRose, 2004) format to represent overlapping hierarchies.

4.1 Using the XCES parser

The XCES parser can be used in three ways:

- from the command line. The xces-parser.jar file can be run as a command line program to print XML with inline annotation to standard output.
- as the XML parser used by other applications. For example, Saxon[10] can take the name of the parser to use to parse the source document as a command line parameter. This allows us to apply XSLT stylesheets to ANC documents without having to translate them into XML first.
- as a library for use in other Java applications. For example, The ANC Tool[11] is a graphical front end to the XCES parser.

4.2 The ANC tool

The ANC Tool provides a graphical user interface for the XCES parser and is used to convert ANC documents to other formats. Users specify their choice of annotations to be included. Currently, the ANC Tool can be used to generate the following output formats:

- XML XCES format, suitable for use with the BNC's XAIRA[12] search and access interface;
- Text with part of speech tags appended to each word and separated by an underscore;
- WordSmith/MonoConc Pro format.

The ANC Tool uses multiple implementations of the `org.xml.sax.DocumentHandler` interface, one for each output format, which the XCES parser uses to generate the desired output. Additional output formats can be easily generated by implementing additional interfaces.

Of course, if the target application understands annotation graphs, there is no need to bother with the XCES parser or conversion to XML. For example, we provide several resources for GATE that permit GATE to open and read ANC documents with standoff annotations, or to load standoff annotations into an already loaded document.

[10] http://saxon.sourceforge.net/

[11] http:// americannationalcorpus.org/tools/anctool.html

[12] http://sourceforge.net/projects/xaira

5 Future Work

Currently the XCES parser is a *proof of concept* rather than a production grade tool. The parser is being augmented to invoke all the appropriate methods from the `org.xml.sax.*Handler` interfaces and throw the proper `SAXExceptions` at the appropriate times. We are also providing for some level of SAX conformance, rather than simply "doing what Xerces does".

6 Conclusion

The ANC has implemented an efficient pipeline for the processing of text into a corpus of machine usable documents. For some document types this process is almost completely automated and can be regarded as a *Corpus-Builder-in-a Box*: raw data goes in one end, and a fully annotated corpus with standoff annotations comes out the other.

The use of standoff annotations allows for an accurate representation of the ANC data as provided by the contributors and allows us to easily provide several modular annotation sets that can be included or excluded by the end user as desired. By providing a SAX like parser for ANC documents, we are able to leverage a number of available XML tools without the restrictions imposed by an XML representation of the documents. For users who are not interested in XML or standoff annotations, the plain text version is preserved.

References

DeRose, Steven J. (2004). Markup Overlap: A Review and a Horse. http://www.mulberrytech.com/Extreme/Proceedings/html/2004/DeRose01/EML2004DeRose01.html

Ide, N., Romary, L. (2004). International standard for a linguistic annotation framework. *Journal of Natural Language Engineering*, 10:3-4, 211-225.

XML-based Phrase Alignment in Parallel Treebanks

Martin Volk, Sofia Gustafson-Capková, Joakim Lundborg,
Torsten Marek, Yvonne Samuelsson, Frida Tidström
Stockholm University
Department of Linguistics
106 91 Stockholm, Sweden
volk@ling.su.se

Abstract

This paper describes the usage of XML for representing cross-language phrase alignments in parallel treebanks. We have developed a TreeAligner as a tool for interactively inserting and correcting such alignments as an independent level of treebank annotation.

1 Introduction

The combined research on treebanks and parallel corpora has recently led to parallel treebanks. A parallel treebank consists of syntactically annotated sentences in two or more languages, taken from translated (i.e. parallel) documents. In addition, the syntax trees of two corresponding sentences are aligned on a sub-sentential level. This means word level, phrase level and clause level, but we will refer to it as phrase alignment since it best represents the idea. Parallel treebanks can be used as training or evaluation corpora for word and phrase alignment, as input for example-based machine translation (EBMT), as training corpora for transfer rules, or for translation studies.

We are developing an English-German-Swedish parallel treebank. In this paper we will focus on the representation of the treebank and the alignment. We will briefly explain the steps for building the parallel treebank and describe our new alignment tool. This paper is a follow-up and revision of (Samuelsson and Volk, 2005) based on fresh insights from this tool.

2 Building the treebanks

Our parallel treebank contains the first two chapters of Jostein Gaarder's novel "Sofie's World" with about 500 sentences.[1] In addition it contains 500 sentences from economy texts (a quarterly report by a multinational company as well as part of a bank's annual report).

In creating the parallel treebank, we have first annotated the monolingual treebanks with the ANNOTATE treebank editor.[2] It includes Thorsten Brants' statistical Part-of-Speech Tagger and Chunker. The chunker follows the TIGER annotation guidelines for German (Brants and Hansen, 2002), which gives a flat phrase structure tree. This means, for instance, no unary nodes, no "unnecessary" NPs (noun phrases) within PPs (prepositional phrases) and no finite VPs (verb phrases).

Using a flat tree structure for manual treebank annotation has two advantages for the human annotator: fewer annotation decisions, and a better overview of the trees. This comes at the prize of the trees not being complete from a linguistic point of view. Moreover, flat syntax trees are also problematic for node alignment in a parallel treebank. We prefer to have "deep trees" to be able to draw the alignment on as many levels as possible; in fact, the more detailed the sentence structure is, the more expressive our alignment can become.

As an example, let us look at the work flow for the German-Swedish parallel treebank. We first annotated the German sentences semi-automatically in the flat manner, and we then automatically deepened the flat syntax trees (Samuelsson and Volk, 2004).

[1] A prototype of the parallel treebank was developed by Yvonne Samuelsson and contains the first chapter of the novel in German and Swedish. Later, a French version was added and aligned to the Swedish treebank by (Tidström, 2005). We would like to thank Eckhard Bick, Declan Groves and Jörg Tiedemann for their help.

[2] www.coli.uni-sb.de/sfb378/negra-corpus/annotate.html

We annotated the Swedish sentences by first tagging them with a Part-of-Speech tagger trained on SUC (the Stockholm-Umeå Corpus). Since we did not have a Swedish treebank to train a Swedish chunker, we used a trick to apply the German chunker for Swedish sentences. We mapped the Swedish Part-of-Speech tags in the Swedish sentences to the corresponding German tags. Since the German chunker works on these tags, it then suggested constituents for the Swedish sentences, assuming they were German sentences. These experiments and the resulting time gain were reported in (Volk and Samuelsson, 2004). Upon completion of the Swedish treebank with flat syntax trees, we applied the same deepening method as for German, and we then converted the Part-of-Speech labels back to the Swedish labels.

Finally, we annotated the English sentences according to the Penn Treebank guidelines. We trained the PoS tagger and the chunker on the Penn Treebank and integrated them into ANNOTATE. The English guidelines lead to complete trees so that the deepening step is not needed.

3 XML Representation of the Trees

After finishing the monolingual treebanks with ANNOTATE, the trees were exported from the accompanying SQL database and converted into TIGER-XML. TIGER-XML is a line-based (i.e. not nested and thus database-friendly) representation for graph structures, which includes syntax trees with node labels, edge labels, multiple features on the word level and even crossing edges.[3]

In a TIGER-XML graph each leaf (= token) and each node (= linguistic constituent) has a unique identifier which is prefixed with the sentence number. Leaves are numbered from 1 to 499 and nodes starting from 500 (under the plausible assumption that no sentence will ever have more than 499 tokens). As can be seen in the following example, node 500 in sentence 12 is of the category PP (prepositional phrase). The phrase consists of word number 4, which is the preposition *in*, plus node 502 which in turn is marked as an NP (noun phrase), consisting of the words 5 and 6. It should be noted that the `id` attribute in the token lines serves a dual purpose of identifier and order marker. This makes it possible to represent crossing branches.

```
<s id="s12">
<graph root="s12_501">
<terminals>
 <t id="s12_1" word="Jetzt" pos="ADV" />
 <t id="s12_2" word="bog" pos="VVFIN" />
 <t id="s12_3" word="sie" pos="PPER" />
 <t id="s12_4" word="in" pos="APPR" />
 <t id="s12_5" word="den" pos="ART" />
 <t id="s12_6" word="Kløverveien" pos="NE"/>
 <t id="s12_7" word="ein" pos="PTKVZ" />
 <t id="s12_8" word="." pos="$." />
</terminals>
<nonterminals>
 <nt id="s12_500" cat="PP">
  <edge label="HD" idref="s12_4" />
  <edge label="NK" idref="s12_502" />
 </nt>
<nt id="s12_502" cat="NP">
  <edge label="NK" idref="s12_5" />
  <edge label="HD" idref="s12_6" />
 </nt>
[...]
</nonterminals>
</graph>
</s>
```

[3]See www.ims.uni-stuttgart.de/projekte/TIGER

This means that the token identifiers and constituent identifiers are used as pointers to represent the nested tree structure. This example thus represents the upper tree in figure 1.

One might wonder why tree nesting is not directly mapped into XML nesting. But the requirement that the representation format must support crossing edges rules out this option. TIGER-XML is a powerful representation format and is typically used with constituent symbols on the nodes and functional information on the edge labels. This constitutes a combination of constituent structure and dependency structure information.

4 XML Representation of the Alignment

Phrase alignment can be regarded as an additional layer of information on top of the syntax structure. We use the unique node identifiers for the phrase alignment across parallel trees. We also use an XML representation for storing the alignment. The alignment file first stores the names of the treebank files and assigns identifiers to them. Every single phrase alignment is then stored with the tag `align`. Thus the entry in the following example represents the alignment of node 505 in sentence 13 of language one (German) to the node 506 in sentence 14 of language two (Swedish).

```
<treebanks>
  <tbank file="Sofie_DE.xml" id="De"/>
  <tbank file="Sofie_SV.xml" id="Sv"/>
</treebanks>
<align type="exact">
  <node node_id="s13_505" tbank_id="De"/>
  <node node_id="s14_506" tbank_id="Sv"/>
</align>
```

This representation allows phrase alignments within m:n sentence alignments, which we have used in our project. The XML also allows m:n phrase alignments, which we however have not used for reasons of simplicity and clarity. Two nodes are aligned if the words which they span convey the same meaning and could serve as translation units.

The alignment format allows alignments to be specified between an arbitrary number of nodes, for example nodes from three languages. And it includes an attribute `type` which we currently use to distinguish between exact and approximate alignments.

5 Our Tree Alignment Tool

After finishing the monolingual trees we want to align them on the phrase level. For this purpose we have developed a "TreeAligner". This program is a graphical user interface to insert (or correct) alignments between pairs of syntax trees.[4] The TreeAligner can be seen in the line of tools such as I*Link (Ahrenberg et al., 2002) or Cairo (Smith and Jahr, 2000) but it is especially tailored to visualize and align full syntax trees.

The TreeAligner requires three input files. One TIGER-XML file with the trees from language one, another TIGER-XML file with the trees from language two, plus the alignment file as described above. The alignment file might initially be empty when we want to start manual alignment from scratch, or it might contain automatically computed alignments for correction. The TreeAligner displays tree pairs with the trees in mirror orientation (one top-up and one top-down). See figure 1 for an example. This has the advantage that the alignment lines cross fewer parts of the lower tree. The trees are displayed with node labels and greyed-out edge labels. The PoS labels are omitted in the display since they are not relevant for the task.

Each alignment is displayed as a dotted line between one node (or word) from each tree. Clicking on a node (or a word) in one tree and dragging the mouse pointer to a node (or a word) in the other tree inserts an alignment line. Figure 2 shows an example of a tree pair with alignment lines. Currently the TreeAligner supports two types of alignment lines (displayed in different colors) which are used to indicate exact translation correspondence vs. approximate translation correspondence. However, our experiments indicate that eventually more alignment types will be needed to precisely represent different translation deviations.

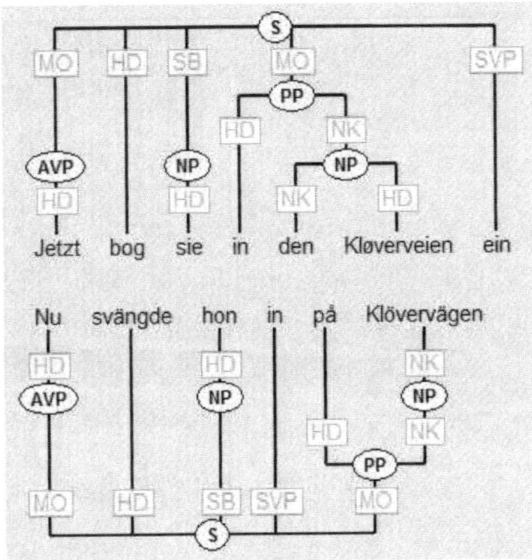

Figure 1: Tree pair German-Swedish in the TreeAligner.

Often one tree needs to be aligned to two trees in the other language. We therefore provide the option to scroll the trees independently. For instance, if we have aligned only a part of tree 20 from language one to tree 18 of language two, we may scroll to tree 19 of language two in order to align the remaining parts of tree 20.[5]

The TreeAligner is designed as a stand-alone tool (i.e. it is not prepared for collaborative annotation). It stores every alignment in an XML file (in the format described above) as soon as the user moves to a new tree pair. It has been tested on parallel treebanks with several hundred trees each.

6 Conclusion

We have shown a straightforward way to tie in XML-based phrase alignment information with syntax trees represented in TIGER-XML. The alignment information is stored independently from the treebank files. This independence allows for a modularization and separation of the annotation but it entails that the synchronization of the

[4] The TreeAligner has been implemented in Python by Joakim Lundborg and is freely available at www.ling.su.se/DaLi/downloads/treealigner/index.htm

[5] The final result of an m:n tree alignment can be visualized with an SVG-based display which we have described in (Samuelsson and Volk, 2005). SVG (Scalable Vector Graphics) describes vector graphics in XML.

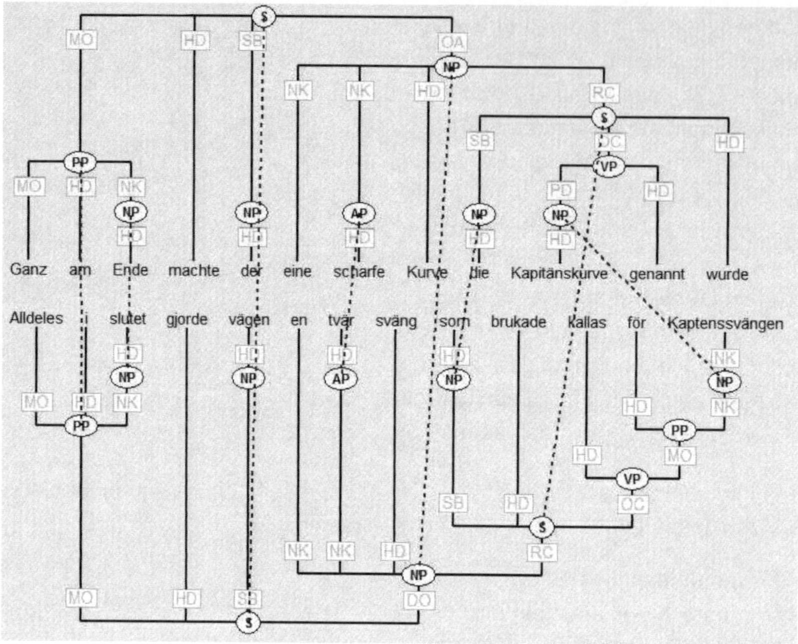

Figure 2: Tree pair German-Swedish with alignment in the TreeAligner.

treebanks with the alignment needs to be guarded separately. If any of the treebanks is modified, the modification of the alignment needs to follow.

We have argued for the use of a graphical TreeAligner to display and interactively modify the alignment between parallel syntax trees. The TreeAligner allows for m:n sentence alignment, word alignment and node alignment. And it supports the distinction between exact and approximate alignments.

As a next step we plan to integrate a component for automatic phrase alignment into the TreeAligner. The user can then select a tree pair and will get automatic phrase alignment predictions. We have already experimented with the projection of automatically computed word alignments to predict phrase alignment. Of course, the automatic phrase alignment has to be manually checked if we want to ensure high quality alignment data.

Another avenue of further research is the inclusion of yet more levels of annotation. For example, we are currently experimenting with the annotation of semantic frames on top of the treebanks. We use the SALSA tool developed at Saarbrücken University (Erk and Pado, 2004) which also assumes TIGER-XML input. So, TIGER-XML has become the lingua franca of treebank annotation which allows for the addition of arbitrary layers.

References

Lars Ahrenberg, Magnus Merkel, and Mikael Andersson. 2002. A system for incremental and interactive word linking. In *Proc. of LREC-2002*, pages 485–490, Las Palmas.

Sabine Brants and Silvia Hansen. 2002. Developments in the TIGER annotation scheme and their realization in the corpus. In *Proc. of LREC-2002*, pages 1643–1649, Las Palmas.

Katrin Erk and Sebastian Pado. 2004. A powerful and versatile XML format for representing role-semantic annotation. In *Proc. of LREC-2004*, Lisbon.

Yvonne Samuelsson and Martin Volk. 2004. Automatic node insertion for treebank deepening. In *Proc. of 3rd Workshop on Treebanks and Linguistic Theories*, Tübingen, December.

Yvonne Samuelsson and Martin Volk. 2005. Presentation and representation of parallel treebanks. In *Proc. of the Treebank-Workshop at Nodalida*, Joensuu, May.

Noah A. Smith and Michael E. Jahr. 2000. Cairo: An alignment visualization tool. In *Proc. of LREC-2000*, Athens.

Frida Tidström. 2005. Extending a parallel treebank with data in French. C-uppsats, Department of Linguistics, Stockholm University, April.

Martin Volk and Yvonne Samuelsson. 2004. Bootstrapping parallel treebanks. In *Proc. of Workshop on Linguistically Interpreted Corpora (LINC) at COLING*, Geneva.

A Standoff Annotation Interface between DELPH-IN Components

Benjamin Waldron and **Ann Copestake**
University of Cambridge Computer Laboratory
JJ Thomson Avenue
Cambridge CB3 0FD, UK
{bmw20,aac10}@cl.cam.ac.uk

Abstract

We present a standoff annotation framework for the integration of NLP components, currently implemented in the context of the DELPH-IN tools[1]. This provides a flexible standoff pointer scheme suitable for various types of data, a lattice encodes structural ambiguity, intra-annotation relationships are encoded, and annotations are decorated with structured content. We provide an XML serialization for intercomponent communication.

1 Background

An NLP system aims to map linguistic data to a description at some suitable level of representation. To achieve this various component processes must perform complex tasks. Increasingly these individual processes are performed by distinct software components in cooperation. The expressiveness of communication between such components hence becomes an issue. For example: we may wish to preserve a linkage from a final semantic analysis to the raw data input; we may wish to pass ambiguity to some later stage where it is more appropriately resolved; we may wish to represent the dependence of certain analyses on other analyses; and we require sufficient expressiveness for the content of individual analyses (henceforth 'annotations'). This work addresses these issues.

Annotations are often associated with a document inline. This provides a convenient and straightforward method of annotating many documents, but suffers from well-known drawbacks. We adopt standoff annotation as an alternative. Here annotations live in a separate standoff annotation document, and are anchored in the raw data via standoff pointers.

2 The DELPH-IN collaboration

DELPH-IN is a loose international collaboration of researchers developing open-source software components for language processing. These components include deep parsers, deep grammars for various natural languages, and tools for shallower processing. The HOG system (Callmeier et al., 2004) for the integration of shallow and deep linguistic processors (using a pipeline making use of XML plus XSLT transformations to pass data between processors) was developed during the Deep Thought project, as was a standard for the integration of semantic analyses produced by diverse components: RMRS (Copestake, 2003) allows underspecification of semantic analyses in such a way that the analysis produced by a shallow component may be considered an underspecification of a fuller semantic analysis produced by a deeper component. Other work (Waldron et al., 2006) has provided a representation of partial analyses at the level of tokenization/morphology – using a modification of MAF (Clement and de la Clergerie, 2005). Current work within the SciBorg project[2] is investigating more fine-grained integration of shallow and deep processors.

3 Standoff Annotation Framework (SAF)

Our standoff annotation framework borrows heavily from the MAF proposal. The key components of our framework are (i) grounding in primary linguistic data via flexible standoff pointers, (ii) dec-

[1] http://wiki.delph-in.net

[2] http://www.sciborg.org.uk/

```
<?xml version='1.0' encoding='UTF8'?>
<!DOCTYPE saf SYSTEM 'saf.dtd'>
<saf addressing='char'>
 <olac:olac xmlns:olac='http://www.language-archives.org/OLAC/1.0/' xml
ns='http://purl.org/dc/elements/1.1/' xmlns:xsi='http://www.w3.org/2001
/XMLSchema-instance' xsi:schemaLocation='http://www.language-archives.o
rg/OLAC/1.0/ http://www.language-archives.org/OLAC/1.0/olac.xsd'>
  <creator>LKB x-preprocessor</creator>
  <created>18:11:31 1/31/2006 (UTC)</created>
 </olac:olac>
 <fsm init='v0' final='v9'>
  <state id='v0'/>...<state id='v9'/>
  <annot type='token' id='t1' from='0' to='6' value='Gutten' source='
v0' target='v1'/>
  ...
  <annot type='token' id='t11' from='30' to='31' value='.' source='v8
' target='v9'/>
 </fsm>
</saf>
```

Figure 1: SAF XML (containing token lattice)

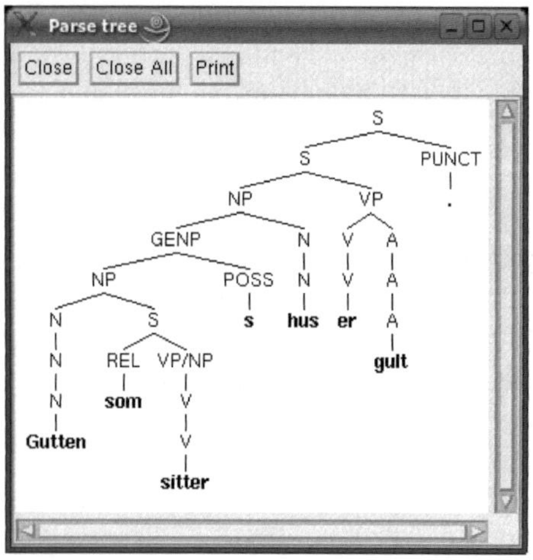

Figure 2: Parse tree (LKB)

```
<saf document='/home/bmw20/b110865
b.xml' addressing='xpoint'>
<annot type='sentence' id='s93' fr
om='/1/3/54.3' to='/1/3/58.89' val
ue='The results of this study are
depicted in Table 2&lt;p/&gt;'/>
</saf>
```

Figure 3: A 'sentence' annotation

oration of individual annotations with structured content, (iii) representation of structural ambiguity via a lattice of annotations and (iv) a structure of intra-annotation dependencies. In each case we have generalized heavily in order to apply the SAF framework to a wide domain. The basic unit of the SAF framework is the annotation. An annotation possesses properties as outlined below.

Each annotation describes a given span in the raw linguistic data. This span is specified by *from* and *to* standoff pointers. In order to cope with different possible data formats (e.g. audio files, XML text, pdf files) we make the pointer scheme a property of each individual SAF object. So annotations with respect to an audio file may use frame offsets, whilst for an XML text file we may use character (or more sophisticated xpoint-based) pointers. When processing XML text files, we have found it easiest to work with a hybrid approach to the standoff pointer scheme. Existing non-XML-aware processing components can often be easily adapted to produce (Unicode) character pointers; for XML-aware components it is easier to work with XML-aware pointing schemes – here we use an extension of the xpoint scheme described in the XPath specification[3]. A mapping between these two sets of points provides interconversion sufficient for our needs.

[3]For example: */1/3.2* specifies the second point in the third element of the first element of the root node, and an extension allows text nodes in non-elements to be referenced also.

```
<fs type="ne-organisation">
  <f name="OrgName">National Aerona
utics and Space Administration</f>
  <f name="OrgType">institution</f>
</fs>
```

Figure 4: Named entity FSR content

Each annotation possesses a *content*, providing a (structured) description of the linguistic data covered by the annotation. E.g. the *content* of an annotation describing a token may be the text of the token itself (see fig. 1); the *content* of an annotation describing a named entity may be a feature structure describing properties of the entity (see fig. 4); the *content* of an annotation describing the semantics of a sentence may be an RMRS description (see fig. 6). In most cases we describe this content via a simple text string, or a feature structure following the TEI/ISO specification[4]. But in some cases other representations are more appropriate (such cases are signalled by the *type* property on annotations). The *content* will generally contain meta-information in addition to the pure content itself. The precise specification for the *content* of different annotation types is a current thrust of development.

Each annotation lives in a global *lattice*. Use of a *lattice* (consisting of a set of nodes – including a special start node and end node – and a set of edges each with a source node and a target node) allows us to handle the ambiguity seen in linguistic analyses of natural languages. E.g. an automatic speech recognition system may output a word lattice, and a lattice representation can be very useful in other contexts where we do not wish to collapse the space of alternative hypotheses too early.

Fig. 2 shows a Norwegian sentence[5] for which the token lattice is very useful. Here the possessive *s* clitic may attach to any word, but unlike in English no apostrophe is used. Hence it not feasible for the tokenizer to resolve this ambiguity in tokenisation. The token lattice (produced by a regex-based SAF-aware preprocessor) provides an elegant solution to this problem: between nodes 2 and 4 (and nodes 4 and 6) the lattice provides alternative paths.[6] The parser is able to resolve the ambiguity with lexical and syntactic knowledge unavailable to the preprocessor component. See fig. 5 for a simple representation of the token lattice, and fig. 1 for the equivalent SAF XML.

```
0-1 [1] Gutten <0 c 6>
1-2 [2] som <7 c 10>
2-3 [3] sitter <11 c 17>
2-4 [5] sitters <11 c 18>
3-4 [4] s <16 c 18>
4-5 [6] hu <19 c 21>
4-6 [8] hus <19 c 22>
5-6 [7] s <20 c 22>
6-7 [9] er <23 c 25>
7-8 [10] gult <26 c 30>
7-9 [12] gult. <26 c 31>
8-9 [11] . <30 c 31>
```

Figure 5: Token lattice with character-point standoff pointers

Each annotation also lives in a hierarchy of annotation dependencies built over the *lattice*. E.g. sentence splitting may be the lowest level; then from each sentence we obtain a set (lattice) of tokens; for individual tokens (or each set of tokens on a partial path through the lattice) we may obtain an analysis from a named-entity component. A parser may build on top of this, producing perhaps a semantic analysis for certain paths in the lattice. Each such level consists of a set of annotations each of which may be said to build on a set of lower annotations. This is encoded by means of a *depends on* property on each annotation. The annotation in fig. 6 exhibits the use of the *depends on* property to mark its dependency on the annotation shown in fig. 3.

A number of well-formedness constrains apply to SAF objects. For example, the ordering of standoff pointers must be consistent with the ordering of annotation elements through all paths in the lattice. Sets of annotations related (directly or indirectly) via the *depends on* property must lie on a single path through the lattice.

4 XML Serialization

Our SAF XML serialization is provided both for inter-component communication and for persistent storage. XML provides a clean standards-based framework in which to serialize our SAF objects. Our serialization was heavily influenced by the MAF XML serialization.

[4]http://www.tei-c.org/release/doc/tei-p5-doc/html/FS.html

[5]Translation: *The boy who is sitting's house is yellow.*

[6]The sentence also exhibits the same phenomena for the final period – it could form part of an abbreviation.

```
<annot type='rmrs' deps='s93'>
 <label vid='1'/>
 <ep cfrom='18476' cto='18526'>
  <gpred>prpstn_m_rel</gpred>
  <label vid='1'/>
  <var sort='e' vid='2'
       tense='present'/>
 </ep>
 ...
 <rarg>
  <rargname>MARG</rargname>
  <label vid='1'/>
  <var sort='h' vid='3'/>
 </rarg>
</annot>
```

Figure 6: An annotation with RMRS content

The SAF XML serialization is contained within the top `saf` XML element. Here the pointer addressing scheme used (e.g. `char` for character point offsets, `xpoint` for our xpoint-based scheme), and the location of the primary data are specified as attributes. This element may contain an optional `olac` element[7] to specify metadata (e.g. creator) and a single `fsm` element holds the rest of the object (as shorthand we also allow a sequence of the `annot` elements defined below in place of the `fsm`). The `fsm` element consists of a number of `state` elements (with attribute `id`) declaring the available lattice nodes, followed by `annot` annotation definitions.

Each annotation (`annot`) element possesses the following attributes: `from` and `to` give standoff pointers into the primary data, encoded according to the scheme specified by the `saf` element's `addressing` attribute; `source` and `target` each give a `state` id (absent if the annotations are listed sequentially outside of an `fsr` element); `deps` is a set of idrefs; `value` is shorthand for a string-valued content; `type` is shorthand for a particular type of annotation content. The annotation content, if not a `value` string, is represented using the TEI/ISO FSR XML format or the appropriate XML format corresponding to the annotation `type`.

5 Summary

We are in the process of SAF-enabling a number of the DELPH-IN processing components. A SAF-aware sentence splitter produces SAF XML describing the span of each sentence, from which a SAF-aware (and XML-aware) preprocessor/tokeniser maps raw sentence text into a SAF XML token lattice (with some additional annotation to describe tokens such as digit sequences). External preprocessor components (such as a morphological analyser for Japanese) may also be manipulated in order to provide SAF input to the parser. SAF is integrated into the parser of the LKB grammar development environment (Copestake, 2002) and can also be used with the PET runtime parser (Callmeier, 2000). The MAF XML format (compatible with SAF) is also integrated into the HOG system, and we hope to generalize this to the full SAF framework.

6 Acknowledgements

The authors wish to thank Bernd Kiefer, Ulrich Schaefer, Dan Flickinger, Stephan Oepen and other colleagues within the DELPH-IN collaboration for many informative discussions. This work was partly funded by a grant from Boeing to Cambridge University, partly by the NorSource Grammar Project[8] at NTNU, and partly by EPSRC project EP/C010035/1.

References

Ulrich Callmeier, Andreas Eisele, Ulrich Schaefer, and Melanie Siegel. 2004. The DeepThought Core Architecture Framework. In *Proceedings of the 4th International Conference on Language Resources and Evaluation, LREC'04*, Lisbon, Portugal.

Ulrich Callmeier. 2000. PET. A Platform for Experimentation with Efficient HPSG Processing Techniques. *Journal of Natural Language Engineering*, 6(1):99–108.

Lionel Clement and Eric Villemonte de la Clergerie. 2005. MAF: a morphosyntactic annotation framework. In *Proceedings of the 2nd Language and Technology Conference*, Poznan, Poland.

Ann Copestake. 2002. *Implementing Typed Feature Structure Grammars*. CSLI Publications, Stanford.

Ann Copestake. 2003. Report on the Design of RMRS. Technical Report D1.1a, University of Cambridge, UK.

Benjamin Waldron, Ann Copestake, Ulrich Schaefer, and Bernd Kiefer. 2006. Preprocessing and Tokenisation Standards in DELPH-IN Tools. In *Proceedings of the 5th International Conference On Language Resources and Evaluation, LREC'06*, Genoa, Italy.

[7] http://www.language-archives.org/OLAC/metadata.html

[8] http://www.ling.hf.ntnu.no/forskning/norsource/